TradeSecrets
BOOK TWO

STEWART • MACDONALD'S
GUITAR SHOP SUPPLY

Stewart MacDonald offers a free 108-page catalog four times each
year. For repair shops all over the country and the world, the Guitar
Shop Supply catalog is the source for tools, materials, and technical
information. Each issue devotes several pages to Dan Erlewine's
"Trade Secrets" newsletter. For your copy, call 1-800-848-2273 or
write us at the address above.

Arranged by volume, not by page number.

TradeSecrets

TradeSecrets

TradeSecrets

This is our tenth year of Trade Secrets, folks — thanks to all of you! *Trade Secrets Book Two* begins where *Book One* ended—wrapping up the first nine years of these popular feature articles that appear regularly in the Stewart-MacDonald catalog. Many of you have sent us ideas and tips, price lists, and shop layouts that we've shared in our pages. This great input inspires all of us to try new things, and gives us a chance to say, "Why didn't I think of that!"

Let's keep it going! We appreciate it when you send drawings or photos to illustrate your story. Of course, a quick sketch can be enough to convey your idea, and we can redraw it for you. Try to include a photo of yourself and your shop, too. Shop layouts are popular, as are "Blue Book" prices that keep repair businesses everywhere up-to-date with the rest of the world.

Don't be afraid to cover subjects that have appeared previously in Trade Secrets articles. Everyone has a little different way of doing things, and it's all good input. So please, take a minute to put your ideas on paper. You'll help make the tenth year of Trade Secrets the best ever!

Dan Erlewine, Editor,
And all the staff at
Stewart-MacDonald's
Guitar Shop Supply

TradeSecrets!

Hot tips & inside scoops. Editor: Dan Erlewine

SHOPPING AROUND... SAN FRANCISCO

HAPPY BIRTHDAY, TRADE SECRETS!

Trade Secrets is five years old. Volume 20 actually marked the end of the fifth year, but instead of publishing it in the catalog we included it as a special "bonus issue" in our new *Trade Secrets Book One*. The new book has all the previous Volumes (1-19) of Trade Secrets bound into one neat package, so now you can throw out all those old catalogs!

TRADE SECRETS HERE THERE & EVERYWHERE!

Starting this issue, two pages of Trade Secrets' usual eight pages have been moved "out in the catalog" in four sections: 1) Tools; 2) Electric Building & Repair; 3) Acoustic Building & Repair; 4) Finishing. Mike Lindskold's "Wiring 101" has a permanent home now too, in the Pickup & Wiring section. Also, this issue starts the first in a series of reports on my recent visit to a dozen repair and building shops in the Bay Area around San Francisco, California.

Dan

In early November 1994, *Guitar Player* magazine brought me out to San Mateo, California, just south of San Francisco. Our mission was to evaluate thirty-six solidbody guitars for the article on "Hardbodies" which ran in GP (February '95). I'd often threatened friends in the Bay Area with visits; this was my

No hardbodies here! Just me and my hosts at Guitar Player: Jas Obrecht, Chris Gill, Dan E. and James Rotondi

chance to make good on those threats. I flew there five days before *Guitar Player* needed me—time enough to visit over a dozen different Bay Area shops, video camera in hand. I couldn't make it to every shop in five days, but I tried, and the resulting video is the best I've been involved with. *Trade Secrets—The Video* takes you into the shops of a dozen established luthiers. Check out their workbenches, shop layouts, and favorite tools, while enjoying some fabulous live Trade Secrets. 👉

Among the list of people and shops visited are: Mark Silber, Eugene Clark, Mario Martello, Santa Cruz Guitar Co., Jeff Traugott, Paul Hostetter, Hideo Kamimoto, Fred Campbell, Gryphon Stringed Instruments (Richard Johnson and Frank Ford), Frank Ford's home shop, Gary Brawer, Dan Ransom, Real Guitars, and Chandler Guitars. We'll be featuring these shop tours here in Trade Secrets for many issues to come—and be sure to check the other four sections of the catalog which now contain Trade Secrets too!

KING OF THE TWO-CAR GARAGE SHOP

That's how Marc Silber refers to Mario Martello (photo, next page), and he's right. You'll never find better use of space, or more work getting done. "Plus, he puts the car in there too sometimes! You can't believe it. And everything is so neat!" says Silber.

Richard Johnson and Frank Ford of Gryphon Stringed Instruments commented, "Mario is one of the most skilled woodworkers we know. We're re-

Continued, next page

Mario becomes animated as he describes the holding power of hide glue!

minded of that every time we look at a friend's B & D Silver Bell No. 3 five-string banjo neck which Mario made in 1962. It's perfect! And his finish work—lacquer or French polish—is the greatest. It's good that folks will get a chance to see him in the new Stew-Mac video!"

As a child in Buenos Aires, Argentina, Mario Martello learned a rich tradition of woodworking from his father, who was a master cabinetmaker. Today Mario lives in a lovely suburban neighborhood set high in the hills overlooking the valleys of Martinez, California. Martello has done contract work for a number of Bay Area music stores and repair shops since the late 1950s, including Jon Lundberg (Jon and Mario are old friends) and Gryphon Stringed Instruments. Although he worked at Satterlee & Chapin Music in San Francisco from 1960 until 1967, for most of his career Mario has preferred to work for himself—picking up and delivering instruments from his home outside the city. At seventy, Mario is in his prime and at the top of his craft.

MARIO'S HOT TIP

A great crack-fixer, Mario uses a 'V' or wedge-shaped tool to final-shape and compress the walls of a crack after the crack has been cleaned and made uniform in shape (some amount of wood may or may not need to be removed, of course, to make

room for the new splint). He then inserts a matching 'V'-shaped splint, which he shapes with a file and sanding blocks on a hardwood block with a ledge rabbeted along one edge (lower drawing below). Mario only uses hot hide glue for gluing splints.

Mario uses a sharp-bladed marking gauge to cut strips of wood (spruce is shown in the photo below) to a uniform width for shaping into splints.

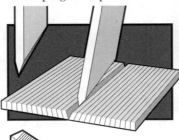

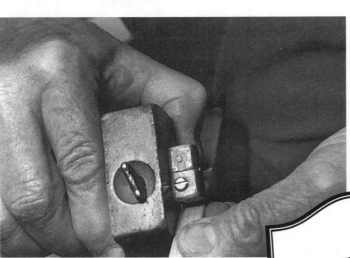

Using the marking gauge to create uniform strips of wood for splints.

SANTA CRUZ GUITAR COMPANY

The Santa Cruz crew's made up of: front row (left–right): Roy McAllister, Darren Webb, Joe Connolly; middle (left–right): Adam Rose, Richard Hoover, Dan Roberts, Tim Rotterman; back (left–right): Steve Weidel, Tobin Shaffer, Bill Hardin, Bill Rushing, Joe Victor. Not pictured: Joe Orlando and TaTa Chook.

Santa Cruz, California, is home to a number of terrific guitar builders and repairmen, and of course the famed Santa Cruz Guitar Company. SCGC builder/owner Richard Hoover gave me a guided tour (see Trade Secrets in the Finishing and Tool sections). Hoover's company has been a training ground for luthiers, and not just locally: "There are SCGC apprentices with established practices in Africa, Germany, and Italy. We hear that there's actually a "Santa Cruz style" of building being carried on; that's the legacy I'll be most proud of."

One local SCGC protégé is Richard's friend Jeff Traugott, who builds and repairs guitars right around the corner: "Jeff was our main neck setter for years, and he still does specialty work for us on occasion. You won't find a better neck resetter anywhere."

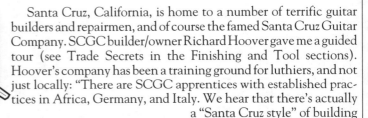

Jeff Traugott pickin' and grinnin' while Richard Hoover frets the chords.

JEFF TRAUGOTT GUITARS

"Richard Hoover taught me most of what I know. As a repairman, he raised repair work—and neck resetting in particular—to new levels in our area. When Richard set a neck you could never tell it had been done," says Jeff of his mentor. Traugott specializes in neck resetting, fret work, nuts, saddles, and bridges. He almost never fixes cracks or does other structural repairs: "That's just not been the direction my business has gone, and I'm not good at making money on those types of repair. But a lot of people shy away from neck resets, and perhaps rightly so on vintage stuff. And I've been able to do enough resets on valuable guitars so as to be comfortable with them. In 1993 I reset 83 necks, and so far this year (November '94) I've done 103." Here are a few of Jeff's repair prices along with some neck resetting "Hot Tips"…

JEFF TRAUGOTT GUITARS
REPAIR PRICE LIST (RETAIL)

Jeff's shop rate is $40 per hour, which translates to these repair charges for his most frequent jobs.

NECK RESET
Flattop (includes refret, bone saddle) $450
Archtop (includes refret and setup) $600
(*add $50 to above for new nut)
REFRET ONLY
Bound fingerboard $200
Unbound fingerboard $175
NEW NUT (bone) $50
FIT NEW SADDLE (bone)
Standard saddle $30
Compensated saddle $40
Fill slot in bridge, recut slot $100
FRET MILL $75
REPLACE BRIDGE $220
(make & install, doesn't include pins or saddle)
TRUSS ROD & ACTION ADJUSTMENT $40

HOT TIP #1 FROM JEFF

When "micro-sanding," or thicknessing nuts, saddles, and especially the wood shims often needed to tighten the dovetail during a neck reset, Jeff uses a "holding table." It's a 12" square piece of tile, marble, or glass (it must be flat) backed with 3/4" plywood for rigidity. Lay a full sheet of 120-grit sandpaper face side up on the "table" and hold it with spring clamps on the four corners to keep it flat and steady. Now lay your wood shim stock, saddle, etc. on the table and the clean sandpaper grit will hold the piece while you sand and thickness it from above with sandpaper and small sanding blocks. "The rubber-dipped clamps do a nice job of keeping the table from moving on the bench," says Jeff.

HOT TIP #2 FROM JEFF

During a neck reset, to lift the fretboard extension or "tongue" (after it's been heated) free from the guitar top, I start with a small palette knife which I made from a clock spring (below, left). This is only to start the corners. Then I follow with the main "lifting" knife, made from a Hyde brand 2"-wide spackling knife. Remove the plastic handles from the knife to give it a low profile (below, right), and bevel one side of the leading edge. The bevel is held down as you work the knife under the fretboard tongue (illustration).

We'll hear more from Jeff on neck resetting next issue!

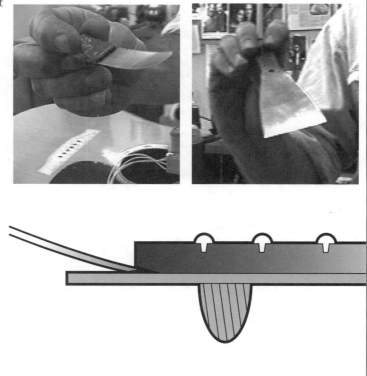

The school/shop at Formentera

FORMENTERA GUITARS: "MADE IN THE SUN"

Formentera Guitars' Guitar Building Institute is in the village of San Fernando, on the island of Formentera, in the Baleares chain of islands in Spain. Owned and operated by two German luthiers, Thomas Stratmann and Ekkehard Hoffmann, the school "graduates enthusiastic youngsters aged 15 to 50 after a two-and-a-half week intensive building course. Each student leaves with a high quality finished instrument, and the work timetable is well adapted to the Spanish *siesta*, leaving plenty of time to spend on the beaches!" Courses run from May through October. Last

summer about 50 people attended—from Germany, Switzerland, Austria, Spain, England, Brazil, and the U.S.A. For details contact:

November –April:
Formentera Guitars
c/o Stratmann Originals
D-30952 Empelde
Hansastrasse 1A
Germany (Tel) 49 511 43 61 40
(FAX: 49 511 434 01 24)
May–October:
Formentera Guitars
C. St. Jaume
San Fernando
Formentera
Baleares—Espana (FAX) 971-328405

Thomas Stratmann (left)
and Ekkehard Hoffmann

Stew-Mac Presents:
The Second Annual Great Northwoods Seminar

Michigan's northern lower peninsula is spectacular in October. See for yourself at this year's Great Northwoods Building & Repair Seminar in Big Rapids, Michigan. Hosted by Brian Galloup and Susan Hutchinson at the Guitar Hospital repair shop and training school, the three-day seminar will feature building and repair experts sharing their knowledge in an informal setting. The Guitar Hospital is a workshop complex which can handle a crowd comfortably, with individual workbenches for twenty students to work simultaneously during hands-on demonstrations.

Don MacRostie demonstrates airbrushing at the 1994 seminar

Attendance is limited to 30 students on a *first come first served* basis, so sign up now! This year's instructors are unsigned as of this writing, but trust our "Dean of Curriculum," Dan Erlewine, to bring in the best experts in the field. The faculty isn't determined, but we hope to bring you some of these well-known luthiers:

Yasuhiko Iwanade, formerly of Fender's Custom Shop, now "Yas" runs Guitarix in Tokyo, Japan. Neck design, shaping, and fretting. Vintage finishing materials & techniques.

Tom Marcell, from John Monteleone's shop in New York City. Master touch-up man and restorationist Marcell makes a return engagement to the seminar!

Jeff Traugott, from Santa Cruz, CA, will appeal to both steel-string builders and repairmen. Learn neck resetting from the best!

Thomas Humphrey, famed classical guitar builder from New York City and inventor of the "Millennium" guitar, will add new dimension to our seminar. He'll lecture on many aspects of acoustic construction, including wood selection, joinery, bridge making and installation, and demonstrate French polishing.

Frank Ford, from Gryphon Stringed Instruments in Palo Alto. Frank's a 25-year veteran with hands-on, inside-out knowledge of vintage instrument repair.

Lindy Fralin and/or **Seymour Duncan**: Learn about pickup winding, rewinding, design, and repair.

The three-day seminar runs Thurs– Sat, October 5–7, 1995. A farewell jam session and barbecue winds things up on a fun note. For details on courses, pricing, and accommodations contact:

The Guitar Hospital
Attn: Northwoods Seminar
10495 Northland Dr.
Big Rapids, MI 49307
Or call (616) 796-5611

TradeSecrets!

Here's a note to "Trade Secrets" readers from Linda Manzer, one of several world-renowned guitar builders from Toronto, Ontario, Canada.

Dear Dan:

It appears that my comments about epoxy fret jobs in Volume 8 of "Trade Secrets" (Spring, 1992) were heard around the world. Let me update and clarify my "fretting method" status. Although I was intrigued by the idea of epoxy fretting for a short while that spring—and did actually fret three instruments that way—I found that it was not the method for me, and quickly returned to a hammer and the traditional method. I see from reading your new "Fretwork" book that we are in agreement!

I don't like the idea of a guitar—especially a new guitar—having its frets held in by epoxy. It simply scares me wondering if the epoxy could one day fail or shift. I also think about down the road when someone in a distant land tries to refret and is forced to re-epoxy, when they're either not willing to, or unfamiliar with the technique. An accident waiting to happen!

The epoxy method may be suitable for some refrets when the slot is too wide to grab the fret any more, and I certainly agree that by filling any air space between the fret tang and an oversized slot with glue you will add to the sustain and eliminate dead notes. But you won't catch me epoxying-in frets on any new guitars that I build. So there!

Best regards,
Linda Manzer

WHY MAKE IT HARD ON YOURSELF?

"When spraying my necks I used to hold the upper fretboard overhang. Occasionally because of the neck's weight and length, and the long stretch needed to reach and spray the top of the peghead, my rubber gloved hand would slip. I'd touch the lacquer, and I'd have to sand and re-spray. That was the "old bad way" (**Fig. 1**) of neck holding.

With the "new improved" method (**Fig. 2**) I have total control, and reaching those difficult spots is easy because I'm holding the neck at its midpoint. The holder is simply a 1" dowel glued, screwed, and centered into a piece of scrap plywood (1/2" x 10" x 1-1/2") that's slightly slimmer than the fretboard. I use a strong double-sided tape and fasten the jig directly to the unfretted fretboard (I usually spray unfretted necks, and my fretboards are almost flat. For fretted necks, or arched fingerboards, the jig can be notched and/or arched accordingly).

Linda Manzer

FITTING TUNERS IN SLOTTED PEGHEADS

Dan Roberts hails from Helena, Montana. Before moving to Santa Cruz in 1992, he worked as Acoustic Guitar Division Plant Manager at Gibson Montana in nearby Bozeman. At SCGC, Dan works in the R&D department, which he loves. Here's his advice for installing tuners in slotted-peghead instruments: "We use a lot of Irving Sloane W48 three-on-a-plate tuners, and also the individual Waverly W-16s. In production, after drilling the 1/4" (.250")

Ed was frustrated... tired... irritable... and no wonder! He was still spraying necks while holding them the BAD OLD WAY!

Fig. 1

Fig. 2

Look at Ed now! He's having fun... getting more out of life! He's discovered the NEW MANZER METHOD!

Part A: plywood
Part B: dowel

ARE YOU DOING THINGS THE HARD WAY?

tuner post holes, we ream them with a .254" six-flute machinists reamer chucked into a hand-held Makita drill. Then after the neck's gone through the finishing department, we ream the holes again —this time with a slightly smaller (.253") hand-held reamer in a T-handle. It removes most, but not all, of the built-up lacquer, and the extra clearance keeps the tuner posts from binding while still maintaining a tight fit."

HOW DOES THIS CHISELER DO IT? WITH MIRRORS!

SCGC's Richard Hoover tells a story of working with a Swedish finish carpenter (could he have meant Swedish/Finnish carpenter?) named Miles, who polished his handsaw until it reflected, like a spitshine, the piece of wood he was cutting: "Common cuts such as 90° or 45° angles showed themselves instantly, with no layout, as soon as the wood grains lined up. I adapted his trick to a chisel for cutting the miter-joints we use for guitar binding and marquetry. In the polished bevel you'll see what the miter will look like when it's completed (see photo, far right)—and you hope that your actual job is as good as that! I sharpen the chisel as usual, and then take it a step beyond by using an old Yugoslavian razor hone, which I found at a flea market, to give it the polish."

SEE-THROUGH TEMPLATES FOR PEARL INLAY

Rolfe Gerhardt of Phoenix Mandolins (photo below) shares some inlay making secrets. He never liked the idea of sticking paper patterns onto abalone, as the paper blocked his view of the shell patterns and sometimes came unstuck. So he made acrylic templates for frequently-used inlays. The acrylic is easy to cut and shape with pearl saw

blades and needle files. The template is made a pen-line larger than the final pattern. Because they're transparent, the templates allow positioning for the best-looking shell patterns and for the most pieces from the shellplate. A thin-line waterproof pen marks the pattern onto the shellplate (top photo, right).

Rolfe uses a furniture repair "stick lacquer" heating iron to put a thin coating of wax on the shellplate (center photo). This is much less bother than dressing the saw blade with lubricant, and holds down dust considerably!

The pieces of the Phoenix peghead inlays are carefully fitted, superglued together, and inlaid as one piece. To achieve this, the design is drawn on a scrap of wood, and then covered with clear self-adhesive plastic. "Slik-strip" and other brands are available in .010" to .030" thickness and up to 3" widths. These plastics are sold to stick to saw fences and other machine tool parts to reduce friction (bottom photo). The high-density plastics are glue-proof, so the inlay parts can be glued together with cyanoacrylate without sticking to the plastic. (Note: Trace your pearl patterns face down on the shell, and the final pieces will be level on their upper, or "face" side. You'll notice backward numbering in these photos.)

Rolfe designed and built Unicorn mandolins in the 1970s until Dave Sinko took over in 1980. Rolfe then started two new designs from scratch in 1989, and is now building the tools and fixtures for them. He plans to display both new models at the 1995 ASIA (Association of Stringed Instrument Artisans) gathering.

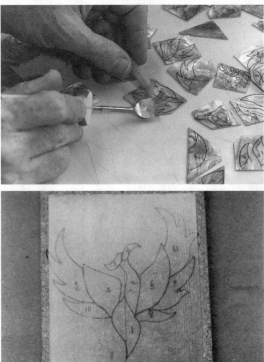

Hot Tips!

SUPPLE SANDING

Paul Hostetter's shop sits on the hillside above his house, deep in the mountains outside Santa Cruz. The road to Paul's winds down, down, down, through dark, shadowy redwood forests, and it's beautiful there! An acclaimed guitarist and musician, as well as a veteran repairman and builder, Paul is at home working on any stringed instrument. For example, he was building a "Cümbüs" for Martin Simpson while I was there—a metal-bodied, 6-string fretless instrument with a side-mounted friction tuning peg similar to the 5th-string peg on a 5-string banjo. Paul's design for the 6th-string hole was practical and elegant, with a slotted opening on the bottom to allow for the string winds of a friction tuning peg. The neck was made of Mango wood, and it was the greatest-looking (and feeling) piece of finished wood I have ever touched!

Paul Hostetter

PAUL'S TRADE SECRET

To sand curves and hard-to-reach places, Paul sticks fiber-reinforced "strapping tape" onto the backside of

Never heard of a Cümbüs? I hadn't either. Evidently, the six strings tune this way: **G G D G C D**

   6th string   Octave
   (drone)

whatever sandpaper he's using. The result? Super-strong, untearable, flexible sanding strips in any type, or grit, of sandpaper he prefers!

TradeSecrets! ▰▰▰▰▰▰▰▰

Hot Tips!

WATCH OUT FOR THIS SCALPER AT THE BALLGAME!

Thought you'd enjoy this photo of a guitar which I recently completed for an Atlanta Braves baseball fan.

Made from maple (it's heavy), and shaped like a tomahawk, it was fun to build. The end result was a satisfied customer.

Jim Spiers,
Rock N' Roll Repair,
Snellville, Georgia

"SIZE XXL PLEASE"

Dear Larry:
Here's a picture (at right) of the extra-large guitar I told you about. We stood it next to my son's guitar for size comparison. It was made for me by Denny Smerdel, here in Indianapolis. My large hands forced me to give up guitar and switch to bass 25 years ago because I couldn't finger the chords. Now I'm playing guitar again thanks to Denny's great idea of using your No.

Larry Anderson,
Stew-Mac Customer Service

1065-R replacement 34" scale bass fingerboard on a larger than normal guitar neck. Here's how we did it…

I experimented by placing my hand on the fingerboard in chord positions, searching for the spot where it felt most comfortable. It was the fourth fret. So Denny cut off the first three fret spaces and used the remaining fingerboard (which originally had 24 frets and a 34" scale.) After our work it was a 28.5" scale, and had 21 frets. Then he added an extra fret into the blank space at the end of the fingerboard to give a total of 22 frets in all. He left the width at 2-1/2" at the body, and only narrowed it to 2-1/8" at the nut.

The body is a custom-made bass body (a ready-made bass body would work). Your No. 577 Schaller roller bridge allowed us to space the strings at the bridge to match the wide fretboard, and Lawrence "blade-style" humbuckers solved any problem due to

strings not lining up with pickup pole pieces. This is a "baritone" guitar, according to its scale length, but I string it with .010" thru .046" strings and tune it to standard. Thanks for your support!

John D. Magee
Indianapolis, Indiana

Hot Tips!

RAIDIN' THE FRIDGE

Ever wish your "door-jamb" spray gun had a quart can? Mario Martello did, so he drilled a hole in a mayonnaise jar lid, inserted the spray-gun siphon down through it, tightened the hex nut, and presto! A quart "cup" you can see through!

SPACEMAN SPRAYS AT SANTA CRUZ?

"Finishing at SCGC is very Hi-Tech!"

Richard Hoover demonstrates the neck holder (right) used at the Santa Cruz Guitar Co. to spray necks (SCGC necks are finished before being assembled to the body). It's simply a stick "handle" mounted to a neck block. A blunt-nosed drywall screw, threaded into an angled hole at the rear of the block (right), puts just enough pressure lightly against the neck's dovetail to hold the neck in the fixture while it's being sprayed.

Mario had repaired a long crack in the side of a 1950s Martin D-28. To fill the small chips, sinks, and holes in the finish along the repaired crackline he used very thick lacquer sealer which he applied with a brush (that's

Mario in the photo below). Mario keeps an open jar of sealer sitting on his bench with a brush suspended across the mouth of the jar and hanging down into the sealer. The unlidded jar allows the solvents to evaporate, keeping the sealer thick. When I seemed surprised at brushing so freely onto the finish of a vintage Martin, he said "No problem. Paint four, maybe five coats, let it dry, and then sand it out in a couple days. I bring back the shine by French polishing."

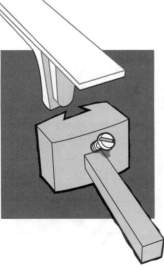

Hot Tips!

FRETTING TIPS FROM A PERFECTIONIST:

Tim Rotterman *is* the fret department at the Santa Cruz Guitar Company. Tim's fret-

ting area is in the final setup room, where he works with Joe Victor (final assembly and setup) and Bill Harding (neck-fitting/bridge gluing). Tim's loaded with trade secrets:

SAFETY-EDGED FILE

"When trimming/beveling the fret ends, it's easy to scar the guitar's top when you're filing on the fretboard extension, or 'tongue,' over the body. For protection we use light masking tape on the finish, covered with a 'bib' made from a laminated-paper office desk guard. But the file drags on the guard, and is constantly digging into it. So I superglued .060" plastic binding strips (it happened to be tortoise shell) onto the thin, sharp, 'dangerous' edges of my file and then smoothly beveled the new plastic edges (photos below).

Now the file glides smoothly and easily, thanks to the plastic. And if I slip while filing, the 'dangerous' edge can't damage the fret tops when it skids across. The plastic edges safeguard against that!"

FACETED FRET ENDS

"An SCGC trademark is our faceted fret end (top photo, below). It was invented by Jeff Traugott. Using a 'cant,' or 'cantsaw' file with the center peak ground smooth (center photo), learn to make one stroke on each side of the fret (bottom) to create three facets. Run extremely straight with the file stroke or the shape no longer looks correct. This look matches the crisp lines of our guitars, doesn't feel sharp, is original, and certainly saves time over rounding the ends in the traditional way. After being final-sanded and steel-wooled, it looks great—like the facets of a diamond!"

YOU'LL FIND EXTRA TRADE SECRETS THROUGHOUT THE CATALOG!

TradeSecrets!
Hot tips & inside scoops. Editor: Dan Erlewine

VOLUME 22

ONE OF FRANK FORD'S *Twisted* IDEAS!

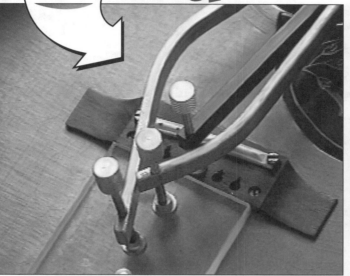

Shoppin' around: inside looks at busy repair shops

LAST CALL FOR THIS FALL!

The 2nd annual Great Northwoods Building & Repair Seminar takes place October 5-7, 1995, at Bryan Galloup's Guitar Hospital in Big Rapids, Michigan. Call (616)-796-5611

for details. We have seven great secret traders: Tom Marcell, Yasuhiko Iwanade, Frank Ford, Thomas Humphrey, Jeff Traugott, Seymour Duncan, Lindy Fralin, and we're hoping for a guest appearance by Mario Martello, the "grand master" of the San Francisco repair scene.

CHECK OUT THESE CLAMPS! They're Frank Ford's clever twist on common steel bridge clamps. With a simple bend, they become right and left-hand "reach around" clamps for in-line clamping of a crack, loose bracing, etc. These, and other *great* Frank Ford tools are on the videotape *Trade Secrets On The Road* (Frank's in Volume Two). Or, meet Frank in person at the Great Northwoods Seminar in October!

Another Frank Ford original: a heavy lead shock absorber with a handgrip. This dead weight reaches through the sound hole and supports a flattop's fretboard extension from inside during fretting. "It's the first tool I ever made," says Frank. "Hold it through the soundhole, and while supporting the top and fret-board extension, you can hammer as hard as you *need* to." [*See page 53 for more from Frank Ford.*]

A LESSON IN NEATNESS...

Interlochen Guitar Repair owner/operator Dan Kelchak is a fine guitar picker! I heard him play at last year's "Great Northwoods Building & Repair Seminar," then drove north to Grawn, Michigan (outside Traverse City), to watch Dan *work* on a couple of guitars. He fixes 'em just like he plays 'em.

Kelchak's basement shop is neatly organized—essential for a full-time repair shop operating in a room measuring 9-1/2 feet wide by 25 feet long! He uses the 16" open space of the trusses for storing all his wood and extra guitars (photo, facing page).

Dan was a travelling performer (he did a solo acoustic act all over the midwest in the early '70s) who was forced to do his own guitar maintenance: "In the afternoons, waiting for the night's gig, I'd set up guitars for

Dan Kelchak and his basement shop

FRETTING—THE KELCHAK METHOD

"My first neck stress-jig was as described by Don Teeter in his second book, and eventually I developed my own version (photo).

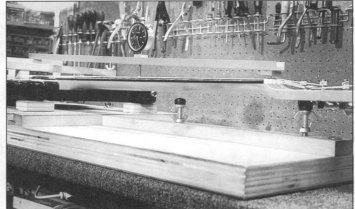

I like the idea of having a measurement to refer to. I can take a guitar out of the clamps if absolutely necessary and still get back to where I was. Here's how my jig works…

1 Tune to pitch with the string gauge of choice and adjust the neck (now I use the notched straight edge—wish they were available in more scale lengths). Figure out where you want the fretboard to be when you do the work.

2 Clamp the body into the jig, check again with a backlight and straightedge, and try to adjust the neck as flat as possible. My backlight is a fluorescent GE "Brite-stick," mounted on two uprights with Velcro so it's height-adjustable. A second backlight

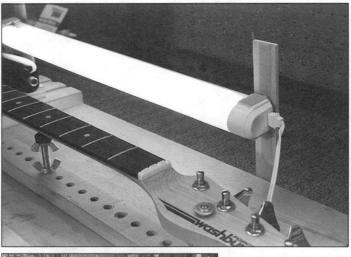

all the musicians that I'd meet—for fun, not money. I wanted the experience of doing lots of set-ups.

"Also in 1975 I was given Don Teeter's *Care & Maintenance of The Acoustic Guitar—Volume One*. For someone to give me Don's book in 1975—the year it came it out—was almost like divine intervention! So I sort of look at my guitar repair history as if I had no choice.

"Then in 1975 I played Traverse City and fell in love with the area. So I moved here as soon as I could—in 1977. I found enough local playing gigs to almost make it (I was single, too, which helped). I began augmenting my playing jobs by doing guitar repair—and finally charging a fee. I hung out my

shingle in 1979. That first year I made $3000 repairing guitars, but I was saying to myself '*I love this!*' Then my income doubled each year for a number of years. It eventually levelled off to what I consider a modest, respectable living that has ranged from $25,000 to $32,000 per year. I could surely make more by re-pairing more, but I'd rather make any supplemental income by playing music. It's important to my well-being, and fortunately I've always made good money in this area playing. Our family has always gotten by, been able to buy the things we need, and we're happy. My wife Renee and I home-school our three chil-dren (Kahla 13, Justin 10, and Nicole 7)—we recognize that raising a family is work enough.

I use is one of those mini-fluorescent bulbs which replace an incan-descent bulb (detailed on page 27).

Continued…

3 Bring up the headstock support until it just touches the back of the peghead. Don T. supports under the nut, but I prefer to go almost 3" back under the peghead—I feel it's more accurate.

4 Lay the long aluminum bar on the fretboard with the dial touching between the 8th & 9th frets, or close to the center of the fretboard. A nail in a small wood block is double-stick taped to the bar, and the nail touches the fretboard right in front of the nut between the D and G strings.

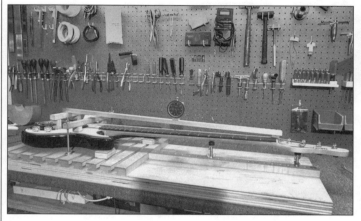

5 In the photo above you'll see the test bar resting on wooden blocks over the bridge and pickups (at that time I hadn't made the test bar long enough for a bass). On guitars, with their shorter scale, my test bar reaches all the way past the bridge and rests on a single block of wood behind the tailpiece. I double-stick tape the block to the test bar. With a longer test bar, basses will be this easy, too.

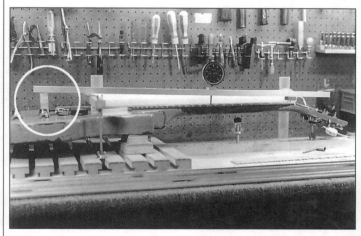

6 When the bar is stable, zero the dial-caliper.

7 Take off the strings and remove the frets. I use a Weller solder-gun with the tip/loop cut—a trick I learned in 'Trade Secrets,' by the way. (Trade Secrets Book One, Volume 3)

At right: From the first Lost Mountain Seminar (1983): Bill Eaton, Richard Schneider, Tom Beltran, Michel Geslain, Steve Thady, Mark Wescott.

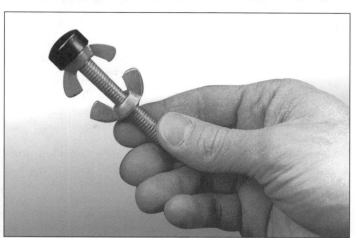

9 Adjust the peghead support until you read zero again. The support is simply a 3/8"-18 threaded machine bolt with two wingnuts (the top wing serves as a handle to raise the support, the bottom wing locks the depth of the bolt in the threaded lower maple block. The support cap is a plastic cap with an oval surface that I found at the hardware store. It just happened to drop over the hex-head perfectly (it's a replaceable tip for a cane, I believe).

10 Go for it. Flatten the board end-to-end. I level in the lie of the strings so all my fret jobs end up slightly compound. You explained this well in Stew-Mac's *Fretwork* book Dan.

11 Once the neck is level, fret with whatever style you like. I use a machinist's screw-clamp to approximate your 'Jaws,' Dan.
   [Dan Kelchak's fretting clamp is detailed on page 6.]

LOST MOUNTAIN SEMINAR AUGUST 5–13

Richard Schneider's Lost Mountain Seminar is moving. This year's course (August 5–13) will be the last on Lost Mountain, and perhaps for several years, due to Richard's commitments for 1996 and 1997. The 9-day seminar on the history and evolution of Kasha design theory includes actual hands-on construction of both classical and steel-string soundboards, using the most recent Kasha-Schneider design. Contact: Charles Merrill, P.O. Box 44, Carlsborg, WA 98324, or call (360) 683-2778.

The GRYPHON formula for success

Frank Ford and his partner Richard Johnston own and operate the renowned Gryphon Stringed Instruments in Palo Alto, California. The Gryphon name is known and respected because, starting in 1969, Frank and Richard earned their stripes the hard way as repairmen and builders of hand-made guitars, mandolins, and banjos. In 1973 they blended retailing with craftsmanship and their recipe worked—they now have a 26-year history of creating happy customers.

These days, Richard minds the store and Frank does the lion's share of the repair work—working in the store shop during the day, and at his home shop evenings and weekends. Richard still does some of the repairs—to keep in shape—but somebody's got to mind the store. Besides, Frank *loves* to repair guitars (luckily he's encouraged in his habit by his wife Joy, who keeps equally busy as a well-known West Coast potter.)

THE WAY FRANK THINKS:

"I used to enjoy making elegant multiple-bound archtop guitar fingerrests. But then I started keeping track of my time at the bench (on a computer). Oy, was I ever losing money on fingerrests! I learned that:

1 *Actual* total working time at the bench was much less than I thought.

2 I spent more time than I expected talking to customers and suppliers, setting up for, and then cleaning up after repairs, schlepping parts, etc.

3 Some fun jobs were real losers, economically.

4 Some structural reconstruction took far less time than I imagined.

5 I could put together a *real* price list and learn to estimate jobs realistically.

6 I was no longer angry about being underpaid once I straightened out my rates.

7 Keeping track of the time isn't really that difficult.

"I now keep my Macintosh turned on all the time in my work room and use the Claris Filemaker Pro program to keep extremely accurate records (1300 jobs). In short, now I can *manage* my repair business.

"The time-log showed me that when repairing full-time (40 hours per week) I only managed about 20 *actual* productive hours at the bench, or about 1000 hours per year. Then I was able to come up with this *simple* formula for making a living doing full-time repairwork…

"I estimated the yearly income I need to make and added my expenses for a year. That number divided by 1000 is the hourly rate I had to charge to make my goal. I wasn't surprised to find that my hourly rate came out to about the same as my local car mechanic or plumber charges. Now I *really* like to make fingerrests again."

Frank Ford
Gryphon Stringed
Instruments
Palo Alto, California

Frank Ford

Richard Johnston

Gryphon Stringed Instruments

Frank in his shop at home.

Frank uses a home-computer database program to keep accurate job records (FileMaker Pro on the Macintosh).

GRYPHON REPAIR PRICE LIST

GUITAR
(Generally Martin or equivalent)

Strap Button

(Install anytime while-U-wait)	$3

Re-string (Labor only)

Steel-string	$5
Classic	$8
12-string	$10
Harp, Autoharp, Zither, Labor Only, PER STRING	$2-10

Install new tuning gears
Labor only, with purchase of gears, not including filling holes or finish

touchup:	6 for $20

Lower action (Minimum charge)	$25
12-string	$40
If bridge needs reshaping, add	$15

Refret
D-18, -28, -35, etc.

(with or without binding)	$260

Refret/reset

D-18, -28, etc. (no binding)	$430
Special finish work, binding, etc. add	$50 – $150

Reglue binding at waist

(D-35) each area	$75

Inlay:
(Replace diamond & square inlay

when refretting) each piece	$30
Dot inlay (edge or face of fretboard) each	$10

Reglue bridge

6-string	$70
12-string	$80
With pickup, add	$20

Replace bridge
(includes price of stock bridge)

6-string	$142
12-string	$162

Carve and set new bridge

-18, 28, -35, etc.	$190
0-16 NY, etc.	$165
12-string (-18, 20, 28, 35)	$230
Pyramid	$330

Bridge overhaul

New saddle slot, saddle, set-up	$80
Fill saddle slot, saddle, set-up	$110

Nut (New bone nut)

6-string	$50
12-string nut	$80

Saddle (New short saddle (blind end)	$30
New long (through-cut)	$60
Fat compensated saddle	$125

Continued…

GRYPHON
PRICES, CONT. FROM PG 18

Pickup Installation:
(with purchase of pickup)
Install Martin Thinline Gold Plus pickup $50
Rout for new deeper saddle
and install Thinline $85
Inlay saddle slot, rout & install Thinline $105
Left-hand Conversion
New nut & saddle, edge dots.
No pickguard $160
Strut job
(Reconfigure top braces
to pre-war specs $150
Pickguard Reglue original guard
(under finish style) $45
Sdd finish, new stock guard
on top of finish $95
Crack repair (Minimum) $35
Finishing
Top only, (includes bridge
removal & reglue) $295
All other finishing by individual quote.

MISCELLANEOUS
New bridge for CHEAP classic $70
Make ebony bridge top only,
L-5, F-5, (archtop guitar/mandolin etc.) $65
Make & install new L-5 fingerrest,
w/b/w binding $350

BANJO
Install plastic head
(modern) labor only $40
Install plastic head on old,
weird, difficult, etc labor only $65
Install skin head labor only $75

CASE REPAIR
Install new handle, latch or hinge
labor each $20.
Install post loops for sling, etc.
labor each $10

Thanks, Frank! See you
in the Fall! —Dan

Charles Fox Is Back In School!

As a teacher, that is! In 1973 Charles Fox (left) started the first lutherie school in North America, The Guitar Research & Design Center in South Strafford, Vermont. After a 12-year absence, Charles—inventor of innumerable lutherie tools & techniques, including the Universal Side-Bender—has returned to guitar building and teaching full-time. His new American School Of Lutherie features a 7-day, 70-hour course that starts beginners off right at the top. It minimizes the learning curve and puts them years ahead in their work. Experienced pros break out of old habits and look at guitar building in a new creative light. The course's compressed nature is good for those unable to be away from their present home and business for an extended time period. I spoke with several of Charles' Spring '95 students while on their fifth day of school.

■ Economist Loren Deck (at left in the center photo) is 27 years old and works for a mutual fund company. "We covered both steel-string and classical construction. This goes beyond the missing pages in all the books I've read. Without hesitation I'll do it again."
■ John Murray (second from left in the photo) is a 31-year old electrician from Boston. He says, "It's fantastic. What sold me on Charles was that *he* had invented the Universal Side Bender (which I'd used previously and loved). In one week he has taught me what I wanted (what I needed). It'd take years of trial and error to figure out what Charles shows you—*if* you even could!"
■ Marilyn Minger (at the center of the photo) is 43 years old and practices corporate law in San Francisco: "I'm new to lutherie. I need to work with my hands, and wanted an end product of my labors that I could feel connected to. Charles is a *very* good teacher. First he says 'This is how I do it,' and then he shows you how other people do it."
■ 48-year old Dennis Scannell works in the renewable-energy field: "This course is perfect for someone on a professional schedule. Perfectly intense! Total immersion! After five days I have nothing but an immense amount of respect for Mr. Fox. He's one of the best teachers of my life!"
■ World-renowned banjo maker Bart Reiter (bottom photo) went from the first Charles Fox school into a successful 9-year career as the head repairman of Elderly Instruments' repair shop in East Lansing Michigan. Now Bart's company, Reiter Banjos in Haslett, Michigan, is one of the most successful banjo manufacturers of our time—having produced over 1200 banjos and nearly 300 reproduction necks. Bart speaks highly of his mentor:
"Charles always said 'There are no trade secrets,' and he saw no reason to hide his most-successful methods! Charles' school was the best experience of my whole life, and it led to my career."

Let us know about your lutherie school! *More lutherie schools will be featured in upcoming issues. Also, we're updating the list of schools for future* Trade Secrets, *and for* The Guitar Player Repair Guide. *If you have a training school or apprenticeship program, let us know about it. We especially need to know more about **international** schools!*

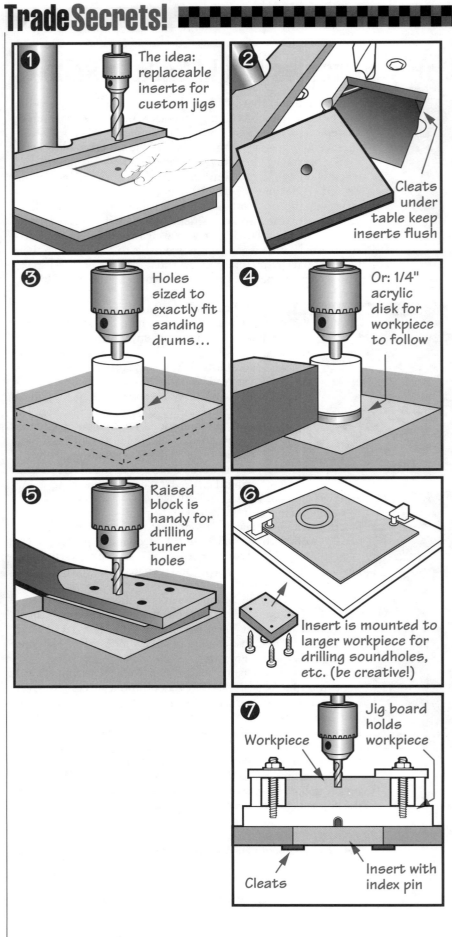

1 The idea: replaceable inserts for custom jigs

2 Cleats under table keep inserts flush

3 Holes sized to exactly fit sanding drums...

4 Or: 1/4" acrylic disk for workpiece to follow

5 Raised block is handy for drilling tuner holes

6 Insert is mounted to larger workpiece for drilling soundholes, etc. (be creative!)

7 Workpiece   Jig board holds workpiece

Cleats   Insert with index pin

Clever Like A Fox!

"One of the most generally useful things around our shop is an auxiliary table mounted on, and set two inches higher than, the drill press table. It serves as a quick-change, replaceable-insert, drill press fixture. Mount the table permanently—you'll never want to remove it.

1 Mount the board—I use "mdf" medium-density fiber board—to your table with the top surface level and square to the quill. Give yourself a good-sized table while you're at it—perhaps 18" x 24"?

2 Locate the quill's exact center on the table and lay out a 5" square around it. Then drill, saber-saw, scrape and file an extremely-square hole. On the table saw, cut square wooden plugs (inserts) of the same table material until they drop *exactly* into the hole. Once you get the right set-up on your table saw, make plenty of blocks (I have dozens) to avoid going through it again soon.

Cleats on the underside corners of the square hole catch the plugs, keeping them flush with the surface, and preventing them from falling through. If you've done your job correctly, the plugs will drop into the square hole and hold firmly (rasp some wells into the table for your fingertips, to allow the blocks to be lifted out).

NOW YOU CAN DO MILLIONS OF THINGS...

3 Have exact-size holes to match sanding drums and support the work. The auxiliary table raises the work 2" above the steel of the drill press table—allowing full use of the sanding drum's surface.

4 A 1/4" acrylic disc screwed flat to a plug becomes a template-follower for flush-sanding parts with a drum.

5 A block mounted a few inches higher than the table supports a peghead for drilling tuner holes.

6 The plug can be mounted on the underside of any larger set-up and simply used to locate it.

7 Use index pins of various sizes for template-following or centered drilling operations.

■ Make drilling fixtures for individual operations (bridge pin/tailblock holes, fingerboard inlays, etc.). Remember that you're always indexed to the quill—the same every time!

■ Have disposable backing boards for everyday drilling.

■ Keep one clean plug with a perfect 1/2" hole for recentering the head or table after it's been swung from side to side. A 1/2" steel test bar in the revolving chuck will center in the drilled hole. Put an arrow or mark on the plug for orientation."

Charles Fox,
American School
Of Lutherie

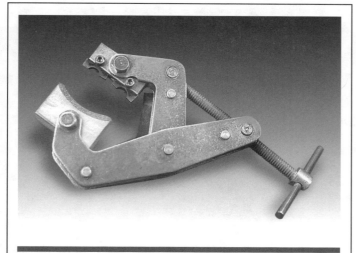

SON OF "JAWS"

Dan Kelchak (see additional story on page 15) modified a 3" Kant-Twist cantilevered machinists' clamp (above) to make his own version of 'Jaws' (see Trade Secrets Book One—Volume 15). The two cauls, or pressure "shoes" in the upper jaw allow the clamp to squeeze frets into any fretboard radius. One pair of shoes fits all! Here Dan describes his technique…

1 Coat the bottom of the fret with superglue accelerator.
2 Install the fret. I like a tight fit—the glue mostly just fills the gaps.
3 Mask off each side with 1/4" masking tape.
4 Run a small bead of superglue along the length of the fret on each side, and watch for the glue to run under, down, and in.
5 Remove the tape, clean off any squeeze-out, and re-clamp before the accelerator kicks off.

Since the accelerator was put on beforehand, it's not quite as strong as a direct wet application, and it sets the glue slowly enough to allow time for this step. The accelerator keeps the superglue from soaking too far into the endgrain of the fretboard, keeping it where it's needed to hold in the fret. Leave the clamp in place for a minute or two while you prepare the next fret.

Dan Kelchak, Interlochen Guitar Repair

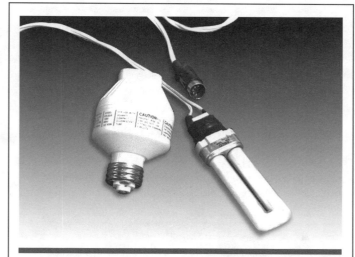

GOOD LIGHTING IS A MUST!

A strong backlight makes reading the fretboard with straight-edges easier and more accurate. Along with the GE "Brite-stick" described in this issue's "Trade Secrets," Dan Kelchak uses this adaptation of a mini-fluorescent made to replace an incandescent bulb. He removed the bulb from the screw-in unit, installed a length of lamp cord directly onto the exposed prongs, and insulated them with heat-shrink tubing (photo above). On the other end, he installed an insulated DIN

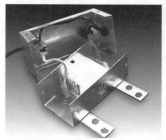

(MIDI) connector. He broke apart the plastic transformer housing, took out the electronics, and mounted them safely in an aluminum box (left). The box has a female DIN receptacle to accept the lamp cord, and an on/off switch. It fastens to the underside of the bench. This is the ideal back-light for zeroing-in on a high or low fret. The bottom photo shows this versatile light in use on Dan's bench.

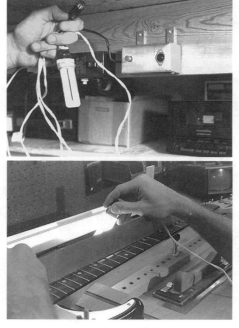

A SPACE-SAVING SETUP FOR SPRAYING

Dan Kelchak (see additional story on page 15) does a minimal amount of finishing. Mostly it's touch-ups on repair work like maple-neck refrets, broken pegheads, structural cracks, punctures, etc. "I only do major refinishing in the warm months, when I can spray outside and then let the instrument hang outdoors long enough for the solvents to evaporate. But I have to do smaller jobs year-round. It's not a good idea to be in the same room with freshly-sprayed finishes until the solvents have evaporated, and the air is replaced by clean air. So I open a window at the back of the basement and run the fan for several minutes, on and off all day, until I can't smell any fumes.

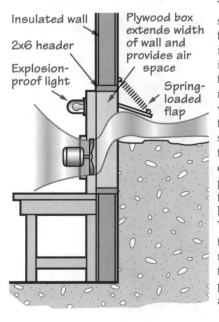

Dan uses a Dayton hazardous-location, explosion-proof, cast aluminum blade venturi fan (shown above), available from the Grainger Company (Model 7F448 in their 1989 catalog). His basement walls are wood with 6" studs on 12" centers. With a section of insulation removed, the fan vents directly into the "duct" between the studs and blows outside.

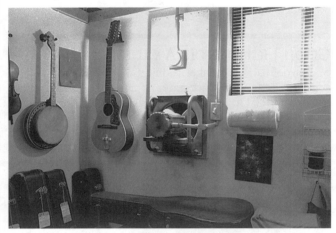

Insulated wall

2x6 header

Explosion-proof light

Plywood box extends width of wall and provides air space

Spring-loaded flap

To increase the duct size, he boxed out from the wall several inches. The duct area is smoothly painted to facilitate overspray removal several times a year. A spring-loaded flap door on the outside can be pulled shut from inside with a cable. The explosion-proof light over the fan is a "Perfect-line" brand Model VC-10 Vaporproof surface fixture w/glass globe, mounted into a "Perfect-line" 4" weatherproof outlet box (from an electrical supply).

SWISS ARMY CLAMP?

Hello Dan,
The Trade Secrets Book One and Shop Talk 4 are great. Congratulations!

Here's the fixture I use to hold instruments, or just parts, in a favorable working position simply by clamping the longer end of the fixture into a vise. It works great for holding acoustic bodies, for example.

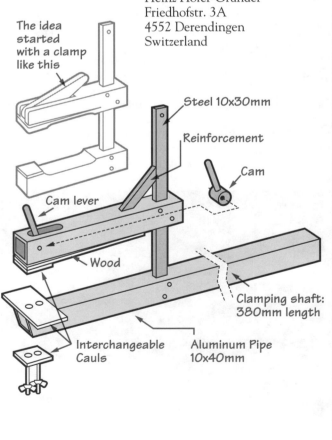

The idea came from the well-known "cam clamp." I made it out of lightweight aluminum channel (wood should be okay, too). Use quick-change cauls to accommodate a variety of clamping needs. It gives me a helpful fixture not only to work on a body, but also on a new top or back, etc.! Enclosed you will find a drawing and basic plans.

Yours sincerely,
Heinz Hofer-Grunder
Friedhofstr. 3A
4552 Derendingen
Switzerland

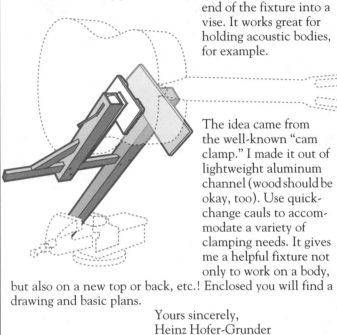

The idea started with a clamp like this

Steel 10x30mm

Reinforcement

Cam

Cam lever

Wood

Interchangeable Cauls

Aluminum Pipe 10x40mm

Clamping shaft: 380mm length

ASIA & GAL:
LUTHERIE CONVENTIONS PROVIDE A DOUBLE WHAMMY!

This year, because of an apparent scheduling mix-up, the GAL (Guild of American Luthiers) held its semi-annual convention in July during their "off" year—only weeks after the ASIA organization's (Association of Stringed Instrument Artisans) June convention, "Symposium." It was difficult to attend two conventions within several weeks of each other, but those of us who did (mostly suppliers) had a great time, and learned plenty.

Both ASIA and GAL have always supported stringed instrument building, and in recent years repair work has gained an almost equal following in their convention schedules. I was pleased to help organize repair panels, lectures, and demonstrations at both conventions.

ASIA-going repairers in Easton, Pennsylvania, enjoyed an afternoon of live demos by: John Calkin, Mark Campellone, Don MacRostie, Frank Ford, Joe Pickarelli, Brian Monty, Bob Benedetto, Rich Starkey, and Tom Humphrey.

GAL convention-goers in Tacoma, Washington, encouraged Frank Ford, Bryan Galloup, and me to demonstrate fretting for more than just the advertised afternoon, so we continued on the following day for another good-sized crowd.

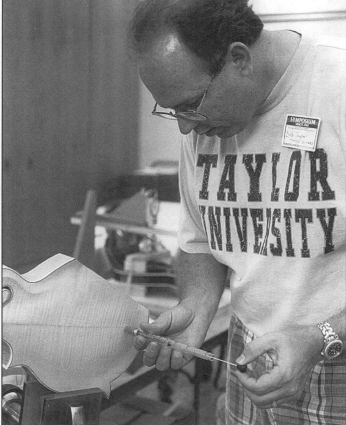

At the ASIA Convention, John Calkin's demonstration of high-tech finishing got the instant admiration of Stew-Mac's Mike Lindskold.

Also at ASIA (top photo): Mark Campellone bends sides for an archtop guitar while Linda Manzer, Evan Davis, and Abe Wechter discuss the pros & cons. Bottom: Bob Taylor is awe-struck by the Hacklinger Gauge at the ASIA convention. This type of tool is right down his alley.

At GAL: Paul Hostetter with France's Maurice Dupont. A brilliant repairman and builder, Maurice (holding guitar) is world-renowned for his Selmer-style "Django" guitars.

Paul Warmoth shows Bryan Galloup (hidden behind Paul) how to clean files. (That's dad back in the corner working on the lathe).

LIKE FATHER, LIKE SON

In Tacoma, a great "Trade Secret" came from nearby Puyallup at the Warmoth Guitar Products factory, where brothers Ken and Paul Warmoth gave us the red carpet tour (see page 42 for more on Warmoth's finishing). Their father, Jim Warmoth, a master machinist, built most of the shop's machinery. At 78 years young, Jim still builds and maintains the tooling everyday. Jim taught Paul this watchmaker's trick for cleaning files, and Paul showed it to us.

"Use a piece of thin (about .030") metal, like the "banding" used on shipping palettes. Break off a 3" or 4" length and rub the flat side of one corner across the file teeth (center photo). Instantly the steel becomes grooved, custom-fit to the file's teeth, and cleans them perfectly all the way to the bottom—especially good for both super glue and aluminum build-up!

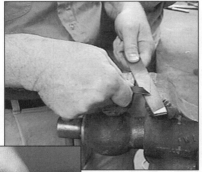

SADDLE SEATER

Like most of the C.F. Martin & Co. luthiers, Rich Starkey is always coming up with clever tools. He created this tool, made of ebony, which fits over the strings and "re-seats" the saddle after the strings are at tension. It's especially helpful to create a good fit and balance between the saddle and a piezo transducer strip pickup. Tap the saddle on both the treble and bass sides to remove its tendency to lean.

DOC VISITS THE SPECIALIST

Billy Gee, the "Guitar Specialist," lives in Moravian Falls, North Carolina, with his wife Brenda, a first-grade teacher. Three days a week he works at North Wilkesboro Music Center in Wilkesboro, North Carolina, both as a salesman and a minor repair/service center. Billy also services two other area stores, working a half-day at each on Wednesday when the Music Center is closed.

"The Music Center is my main job, and I do minor repair and set-up work there as part of my salary. They encourage me to take the big jobs home, do the work, and keep all the money. I do the same for the two "satellite" stores (minor work for the "rent" and major work for myself). The Music Center is a warranty repair center for Fender, Taylor, Martin, Ovation, and Takamine—and we're an in-store service center for Gibson—so it can get pretty busy; but I usually have two or three days free each week to repair at my home shop (*top photo at right*)."

A professional guitarist and bass player, Gee's skills as a player came in handy a couple of years ago, when he set up and balanced a Fishman Thinline saddle pickup, and installed the Corian saddle recommended by Fishman, on a new Gallagher "Doc Watson" model for Doc himself! More recently, Billy installed a Fishman Acoustic Matrix saddle-transducer in Doc's Martin D-28, the guitar with a neck made by Wayne Henderson. Billy recorded the set-up measurements on the Gallagher when it came in, because Doc liked the way it played.

"Doc still plays the Gallagher guitar today, although he replaced the Thinline with another Matrix. The measurements below are the most important ones, but I have more (neck width, saddle height, string spacing, etc.) if anyone wants them. I hope this information helps somebody play even a tenth as good as Doc!

Billy Gee,
"Guitar Specialist"

MEASUREMENTS FROM DOC WATSON'S GUITAR:

Scale length: 25-1/4"
Strings: John Pearse #300M (.013", .017", .026" w, .035"w, .045"w, .056"w.)
Action (at 12th fret): 6/64" on the treble side, 7/64" on the bass
Relief: .005" at 5th & 6th frets
Frets: (.110" X .035")
Fretboard Radius: 10"
String clearance at 1st fret: treble: .018, bass: .025"

Fishman's Rick Turner commented that "Billy Gee is the reason that Doc plays our pickup. After the installation, Doc called and said it was the best pickup he'd heard so far. Today, Doc's a Fishman endorser and uses the Matrix Natural, in the 1/8" format, mounted in a number of guitars. But the Gallagher cutaway and the Martin D-28 are his main guitars."

Doc Watson checks out the Fishman saddle pickup installed by Billy Gee.

THE GUITAR SPECIALIST'S HOT TIP

Transferring finish materials from gallon cans be messy and wasteful. Use the siphon pump designed for "Kero Sun" 5-gallon kerosene cans. It makes a neat convenient way of getting thinner (or lacquer, etc.) where you want it. You can pump as much or as little as you want, and with a little practice you won't spill a drop!

Billy Gee

WHOOPS! DEPT.

The last Trade Secrets featured Charles Fox, and his American School of Lutherie, without printing the address! Interested persons may contact Charles at :
The American School of Lutherie,
420 Moore Lane,
Healdsburg, California 95448
(707) 433-7384

ADJUSTING OLDER RICKENBACKER TRUSS RODS

Yasuhiko ("Yas") Iwanade introduced me to his longtime friend Naoki Ogane at the '95 NAMM show in Anaheim, California. "Naoki and I go way back," said Yas. "We spent many years together repairing and restoring guitars. His particular interest has always been Rickenbacker, and he knows them inside and out. He even wrote a book about them! Now he's excited to share what he has with others."

That evening Naoki showed me his photo album of repairs. He's great! Experienced in all forms of repair, and a highly-skilled woodworker, Naoki truly *is* a Rickenbacker specialist. His book *Rickenbacker, Pioneer of the Electric Guitar*, has not yet been translated from Japanese into English—but we hope that it will be.

Here's an excerpt from Naoki's book (copyright 1995 Rittor Music, Inc., and reprinted with permission from *Rickenbacker—Pioneer of the Electric Guitar*). The book is filled with all the information you could ever need on Rickenbacker guitars, and it also contains an excellent "Maintenance Guide" chapter. Here's an excerpt from that chapter…

Yasuhiko Iwanade and Naoki Ogane

Adjusting a Rick neck made before 1984 can be tricky. Due to improper adjustment, we see some Rickenbackers with the fingerboard separating at the nut. To avoid that, follow this method—it's the best way. And don't try this unless you have previous experience with guitar repair!

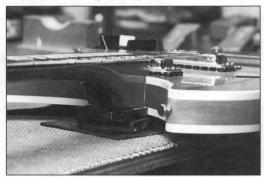

1 Unscrew and remove the nameplate/truss rod cover. Be careful not to chip off the paint.

2 To prevent the de-lamination of the fingerboard, place a clamp by the nut. Note the neck support.

3 I support the heel too, with these rubber clamp pads (they'll be used later).

4 Clamp the end of the body to secure it to the bench. The heel support and neck rest support the weight.

5 Carefully loosen both truss rod nuts with a 1/4" box wrench.

6 Remove the aluminum block with small pliers.

7 Remove the front pickup and wrap it with something to avoid scratches on the body.

8 To avoid a scratch when pulling out a truss rod, protect the headstock with thin metallic plate.

9 Push out both truss rods by inserting and pushing a steel rod from the neck end hole.

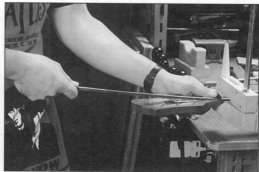

10 When the tip of the truss rod comes out of the neck, pull it out slowly and carefully.

11 The truss rods have a concave bow once out of the neck (top photo). Give them a back bow by bending them carefully by hand (lower photo).

12 Place the support where the neck has warped most. Make sure that the spacer at the neck joint is touching only the heel (and not the body) and then clamp the heel firmly. Place another clamp at the nut end to create an appropriate amount of back bow.

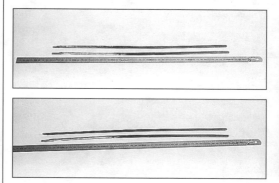

13 Insert reshaped truss rods from the head end. If there is too much resistance, do not force it. Pull it out and take care of the problem and try again.

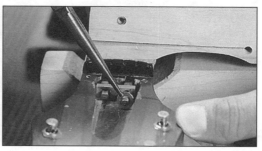
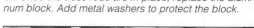

14 Once the truss rods are in place, replace the aluminum block. Add metal washers to protect the block.

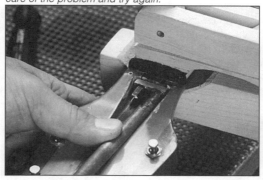

15 Replace the truss rod nuts. Tighten them while paying attention to balance the pressure on each of the two rods.

16 Remove the clamp at the head end.
17 Remove the clamp that was used to prevent fingerboard delamination.
18 Restring and fine-tune the truss rods. Replace the nameplate/truss rod cover. The work is done.

OUT OF THE CLOSET...

Roger Sadowsky sends us this: "I credit John Montelone for one of the best tips I've ever gotten. We had an archtop with a rim (side) sprung to the point that we could not clamp it flush with the back. John said 'Get a plastic wardrobe (a portable closet) and hang the guitar in there with a pan of water for a couple of weeks. It'll re-hydrate, and the pieces will go together as they did when the guitar was built.' It worked, and we've since set up a permanent wardrobe big enough to hang three or four guitars. We use it for all dryness-related problems before attempting to repair or set them up.

"Every day we remove our pan of water (a 9"x9"x2" Rubbermaid container with an inch of water) and get it hot enough in the microwave so that it's steaming before we replace it. We keep a hygrometer in there and the relative-humidity in the 80 to 90 percent range. The wardrobe is sealed on all sides, and we hang the instrument on the clothes-hanger bar with a strap across the headstock tied from key to key. You can find a wardrobe many places, and they're in the 'Hold Everything' catalog (1-800-421-2264) for sure."

Roger Sadowsky (left) and Ken Fallon.

Roberto-Venn
School of Luthiery

ROBERTO-VENN STUDENT CLEANS UP!

Kiyoshi Nishigai (right) of Tokyo graduated from the Roberto-Venn School of Luthiery in August, 1995. The 46-year-old luthier previously worked in Japan's record-production industry (recording Rita Coolidge, among others), but he decided to trade his hobby for his job and enrolled at Roberto-Venn to perfect his skills. Also a student of Trade Secrets, Kiyoshi shares one with us...

"I enjoy reading Trade Secrets, so it's nice to be able to pass one on. It's a very simple tool and easy to make. First make an extra-thick (3/4") Dremel Moto-Tool base (I used clear acrylic). Drill, then install two 3/8" diameter brass pipes in it, and connect them to a vacuum cleaner with silicon tubes (photo and drawing at right).

"It works very well. I can see the drawn lines of inlay patterns, etc. clearly and keep my working area clean. I hope you'll tell your readers about Roberto-Venn!"

Sincerely,
Kiyoshi Hishigai,
Tokyo, Japan

Thank you Kiyoshi, what a clever tool! And you're right, we *should* tell folks about Roberto-Venn. So here goes...

"The school was started in 1975 by John Roberts and Robert (Bob) Venn," says School Director William Eaton. "John Roberts still owns the school, though he's retired now, and Bob died in 1991. Those two guys were quite a team, and we're proud to carry on their dream.

"An accredited school with a curriculum geared toward industry training, our objective is to see that graduates are prepared for occupation at the entry level. Having learned the basic funda-

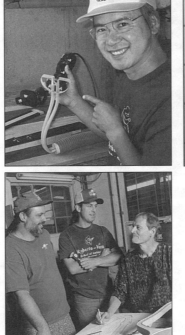

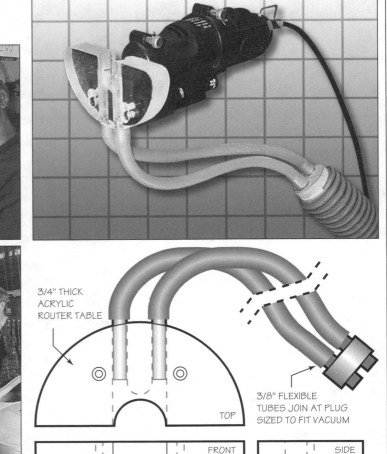

3/4" THICK ACRYLIC ROUTER TABLE

TOP

3/8" FLEXIBLE TUBES JOIN AT PLUG SIZED TO FIT VACUUM

FRONT

SIDE

RADIUSED BOTTOM EDGE

Left to right: John Reuter, Director of Training; Joe Vallee, Electric Instructor; and Bill Eaton

mentals needed to get started in the field, students leave here with an aptitude and affinity to excel (and nice-quality acoustic and electric guitars which they build during the course). We have graduates working at Gibson, Taylor, Santa Cruz, and Fender, for example."

Santa Cruz Guitar Company's Richard Hoover says, "The school's head instructor John Reuter is good at screening people who want to be guitar makers. He zeros-in on their aptitude, attitude, and work ethic, and tells it like it is. He sent us two of our valued employees: Addam Stark and Darren Webb."

The tuition is $4350 for the basic four-month builder's course, and $5550 for the new five-month course (which includes four weeks of repair training). Enrollment is usually 20 to 25 in a class, and the next course starts on February 5th, 1996. To learn more (about student housing, transportation, etc.), speak with Kim Shannon, Director of Student Activities."

Roberto-Venn
School Of Luthiery
4011 S. 16 Street
Phoenix, AZ 85040
(602) 243-1179

Roberto-Venn Class of 1994

TradeSecrets!

Please Pass The Can of Worms...

A letter from Roger Sadowsky to Stew-Mac's Dan Erlewine on glue-in fret jobs:

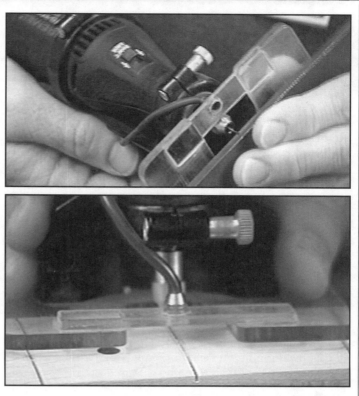

Note the blow-hose attached to the extra plate on Ken Fallon's Dremel-Tool router base. The hose, attached to an air line, blows the slot free as he routs.

Dan: Beginning with the '93 ASIA Symposium in Amherst, you started a valuable discussion which enabled all of us to review the way we approach fretting and refretting, especially with regard to issues like glue/no glue and how much compression to use. This discussion has continued to the present day and I feel that those of us who continue to do "glue-in, reduced-compression" fret jobs have gotten some bad press.

As an example, I cite the comments by Linda Manzer in a recent Trade Secrets in which she states "I don't like the idea of a guitar... especially a new guitar... having its frets held in by epoxy. It simply scares me wondering if the epoxy could one day fail or shift." I have only the highest regard for my dear friend Linda (it was I who taught her how to do a glue-style fret job) and respect her preference for staying with a traditional hammer-in method. However, I found her comments disparaging of a glue-in approach, and I would like some equal time!

I think that what came out of all the fretting talk is that we all want to see a fret slot which is the right size for a given fret. In the '70s, some of us did, perhaps, widen the slot a bit more than necessary, and we have moved towards a tighter fit, even when using glue. At Sadowsky Guitars we feel that:

■ Epoxy is as thermoplastic as any other glue and it would be naive to say that it has any more probability of "failing or shifting" than any other glue. I would also like to point out that the end grain of a raw fret slot might even have a greater probability of "failing or shifting" than epoxy!

■ An instrument builder is less likely to need glue (or glue-in methods as opposed to a ham-

mer only) than a repairperson, as a builder has greater control over the fret slot in relation to the fret wire. A repairperson is dealing with a wide variety of fingerboard materials of various condition, and a wide variety of fretwires.

■ Some of us prefer to use glue on *any* job, believing that it results in a superior fret job with better tone.

■ Our fret slots are tight enough to touch the tang, but not be wedged open by it. Yet the fret is not loose within the slot. It is only the barb which we are seating into the wood.

■ We are still strong advocates of a reduced-compression approach to fretting. My reasoning, and the reason I got into the glue-in fret job to begin with, is that I am unwilling to have all my fretboard preparation undone by a high-compression fret job that may back-bow the neck in an uncontrollable manner. We have labeled the use of a hammer-tap to engage the *barbs only* into the wood "reduced-compression" fretting.

I described our fret process in detail at "Symposium 1985" and you can read about it in *American Lutherie #6*. You can also watch Ken Fallon demonstrate aspects of an unbound fret job in the ASIA video "Masters of Repair," available from Stew-Mac. But in brief, our fret jobs go something like this:

■ We spend an hour just prepping the fretboard, whereas some shops will do the entire fret job in that time. That's OK, but we string to tension, check and mark-out the board, unstring and sand, restring and check. We repeat this process as many times as necessary to achieve a perfect fingerboard when under string tension.

■ Next we choose the right-sized cutter (dental burr) so we

can achieve a light hammer-tap to seat each fret. We start with our smallest cutter and work upwards until we find the right cutter for the particular fret job. We use S.S. White and Midwest American #56 FG (Friction-Grip) burrs which are available from dental supply houses. The SS White cuts a tighter slot than the Midwest American. In addition to these two cutters, we keep about four cutters of each brand, ranging from oldest to newest. The older ones cut a tighter slot than the newer cutters. This gives us a good range of cutters and enables us to achieve a perfect fit. If necessary, we will also pull our fret wire through files clamped in a vise to reduce the width of the tang a bit. All of this work is to achieve the best possible fret wire/fret slot match.

■ We test the fret/slot fit with a piece of fretwire, radiused to match the curve of the board.

■ We secure our frets with super glue on unbound boards

(wicked in from the fret overhang) and 24-hour epoxy on bound fingerboards. Either way, we clamp our frets after they have been hammer-tapped in.

■ The rest is your basic fret leveling and crowning, etc.

CONCLUSION

My primary points are:

■ Nobody wants an excessively-wide slot.

■ We use super glue for unbound boards, 24-hour epoxy for bound boards.

■ We are strong advocates of reduced-compression fretting to maintain the integrity of our fingerboard truing process.

■ We don't agree that fretting in this way detracts from the tone, or makes it harder to refret in the future.

Roger Sadowsky,
Sadowsky Guitars

Thanks, Roger! Our fretting styles are very similar, and I add my two cent's worth on page 42!

Your pal, Dan

The Sandman Meets Buck Rogers...

Thanks to Tom Anderson, the Warmoth factory no longer "wet-sands" the final finish coat before buffing. Tom introduced them to 3M's 256L Production Resin Bond Fre-Cut Film paper. "We no longer have problems with the finish lifting around holes since we started dry-sanding" says Paul Warmoth. "We use 1000-grit, and then go right to buffing. Sometimes we'll also use 800- and 1200-grits. We sand with an air-powered dual-action sander because it's fast, and leaves no scratches. Ours is a 'Dynabrade' model."

Another Warmoth sander, powered by the human hand, is this quick-change, padded, low-tech block sander made by Red Devil. It fits in the palm of your hand , and breaks apart in seconds for instant paper-changing (two photos above).

Paul Warmoth demonstrates the new "Buck Rogers Model" UV finish-curing chamber (above) that dries a finish in **12 seconds** using ultraviolet light! The Warmoths teamed up with Bob Taylor and Tom Anderson, to design and build three automated chambers (and to defray the cost of the very-expensive equipment by over $15,000).

While we watched, Paul's son Chris used a gravity-feed HVLP spray gun to coat a sample board with finish. The sprayed piece emerged from the UV-curing chamber after 12 seconds—dry!

Dan Erlewine On Fretting: To Glue or Not To Glue?

On page 6 is a letter from Roger Sadowsky of Sadowsky Guitars. The subject is the glue-in fret job—a topic that's drawing out a lot of opinion. Here's Dan's point of view:

Roger: Thanks for your input! Our Trade Secrets pages are open to a fretting discussion any time someone starts one up. I've been a little hesitant lately because I don't want to hog the show or bore people with too much fretting. Our fretting styles are quite similar in that I am in support of epoxy glue, glue-in fret jobs, a well-matched fret-to-slot, and "reduced-compression" fretting.

Here, briefly, are my current thoughts on fretting:

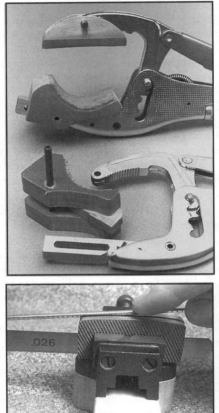

■ I use a "reduced-compression" fretting style with a tight fit, but glue is necessary to hold the frets in. I select from hide glue, Titebond, super glue, and epoxies.

■ Generally, I clamp my frets with "Jaws" or another clamping device (*photo, right*). A light hammer tap wouldn't *always* seat frets in the slots as I prepare them—but it would depend on the wood and my treatment (or non-treatment) of the barbs.

■ Like you Roger, I want full contact between the fret tang and fret slot walls. Since I haven't perfect control of what the barbs might do to my prep work (and like you, don't want to see backbow), I remove some or all of the barb, within certain guidelines, by drawing the fretwire between two pieces of metal file (*shown at right*). (This is well covered in our new book *Fretwork*.)

■ I sometimes fret without glue and use the hammer-in, high-compression method on vintage work that requires it.

■ I almost always use my neck-jig, to which has been added a peghead-tensioning device that allows me to fret with the truss rod under full tension.

TradeSecrets!

Hot tips & inside scoops. Editor: Dan Erlewine

Great Northwoods Building & Repair Seminar 1995

The 2nd Great Northwoods Building and Repair Seminar a great success!

I've just returned from The Great Northwoods Building & Repair Seminar, and I've got Trade Secrets on my mind. This year's event saw a great turnout at Brian Galloup's building/repair school in Michigan. (Next year's Seminar is scheduled for August or September, and those who sign up early can help choose the date. This year we were full, so keep in mind it's on first call basis.) It's gonna take more than one issue of Trade Secrets to cover all the hot tips from this seminar. Let's start with some tips on Fender finishes…

Dan

FINISHING DEPARTMENT

Returning to the Northwoods Seminar for the second straight year, Yasuhiko Iwanade (*below*) was a major contributor to its

success. "Yas" demonstrated a "three-tone" sunburst on alder, using two different Fender spraying methods: a Pre-Mid '60s style, and a Post-Mid '60s style.

Yasuhiko is 41 years old and has been playing, building, and repairing guitars since he was 14. He worked in the Fender Custom Shop (a dream come

true) in early-'90, '91, and until mid-'93, when he returned to Tokyo. Two of Yas's years spent at Fender overlapped with his good friend Michael Stevens, who co-founded the Custom Shop along with John Page.

"I was the only one in our school who went to see the Beatles in '66," says Yas, "and in high school, our band's drummer was the son of the founder of the Guyatone Guitar Company (the chief competitor of the Teisco company), so I was around lots of guitars, and came to love them. After high school I went to London for college with the half-excuse 'to study English' (which I did.) But I really wanted to get outside of Japan, to England especially, so I could see lots of live bands like the Rolling Stone, Humble Pie, etc.. And though I was a student there for two years, I was out regularly jamming with every band I could find.

"I returned to Tokyo in '77, and though I still wanted to be a professional musician, my destiny changed when I got a job in a retail store and began learning guitar from the non-playing end. My focus was 90% on American guitars, and I started writing around 1979 in order to introduce American guitar culture to Japan. I was always fascinated by American guitars (still am!)—the sound, the way they were made, and people who create them."

[A regular columnist in a leading Japanese guitar magazine during the '80s, Yas just started to write magazine articles again for Guitar Magazine and Bass Magazine, both published by Rittor Music. Rittor is the publisher of Yasuhiko's book The Fender Stratocaster—an excellent book for details, and detail-photos, on the Strat. Even though it isn't yet translated into English, it's still my favorite book on the subject! —Dan]

"After a few years in retail I went on my own and started 'Guitarix, Inc.' (I was around 25). I became more involved with vintage guitars, which by necessity caused me to learn more complex work than the setups, pickup switching, and minor jobs I'd been doing since high school. I learned restoration-grade fretting and finishing, and soon got into building—starting by myself in '83, and growing into a larger 'factory' of three workers two years later. I say 'Factory,' not because of the size, but because of the kind of machinery I had there (big industrial-grade machines). I was deeply into it, following an intense desire to learn the trade in an industrial way. The experience of having to make it on my own as a maker, plus my love for Fender guitars, eventually led to my getting the 'dream job' at the Fender Custom Shop in 1990. Then in 1993 I returned to Tokyo, re-opened Guitarix on a small scale, and went to work for Yamano Music."

Today Yasuhiko lives with his wife Miyoko (a copyright and trademark attorney) in Tokyo, Japan. Yas spends most of his time working for Yamano Music Co. (the sole distributors of both Fender and Gibson in Japan), the balance of his time he devotes to Guitarix. He travels almost monthly between the US and Japan, as a Marketing/International-Relations/Artist-relations Coordinator. This is a task he is well-suited for because he knows the guitars and the industry so well. Yasuhiko loves his job at Yamano, but at times he does miss working with his hands, and the shop atmosphere in general.

Yasuhiko Iwanade demonstrates the bleaching steps used prior to finishing at Fender in the early 1960s.

At the Great Northwoods Seminar, Yasuhiko taught us things about sunburst Strat-finishing that were a revelation:
1 Bleaching an alder body before applying a yellow stain base-coat;
2 The "pre-mid '60s" spraying method for bodies, and the "unique" drying stand it employs;
3 A version of the revolving spray carousel used by Fender;
4 The "post-mid '60s" spraying method still in use today.
Here's Yas…

BLEACHING AN ALDER BODY BEFORE APPLYING A YELLOW STAIN BASE-COAT

"Because alder varies so much in color from piece to piece, Fender bleached their alder bodies, starting when they switched from ash to alder in '56. Glued-up bodies would thus have a uniform color to receive the water-based, yellow pigment stain which was sprayed onto the bare wood as a background for the sunburst. I discovered the bleaching techinque only after doing a number of restorations which required the finish to be completely stripped. After stripping, and while sanding a body, I noticed that the wood got darker as I sanded into bare wood—this told me that the surface might have been bleached.

"I was finally convinced when I realized that what I'd thought was rubbing compound slopped into many of the body routs during buffing (and I'd seen it often), was actually bleached sawdust! The bleach ran into the cavities and bleached the lumps of sawdust clinging to the cavity walls. The bleach turned the sawdust into a paste that clung even better as it dried, and they finished right over it. I should have known all along because the sawdust was *under* the finish (rubbing compound wouldn't have been under the finish)."

"In very late '63 or very early '64, because production was up, Fender dropped the time-consuming bleaching step in favor of a semi-transparent whitish-yellow *lacquer-based* 'shader' sprayed on top of a clear sealer coat to *simulate* the effect of bleaching the wood a uniform color. Like the earlier yellow, the '64 shader was also a pigmented color.

"The '64 sunburst looks different because the yellow-pigmented coat has white in it too, producing a slightly milky-yellow look. White pigment was mixed-in because of its hiding power (yellow alone can't always take care of the strong color contrast between two different pieces of unbleached alder.) With the pre-'64 finish, the yellow water-stain was sprayed *on the bare wood*, and any whiteness comes from the bleached wood, since the stain had no white, it doesn't hide the wood grain nearly as much the later '64 yellow shader coat does. The '64 shader coat hides the grain because it's *transluscent*—not *transparent*. You can see through it, but not clearly (somewhat like a dusty window).

"So depending on the year, the yellow was either under, or over, a sealer coat of 'Fullerplast,' a catalyzed-finish that hardens chemically and uses very little thinner (5—10% vs. lacquer's 50%). I'm guessing Fender used 'Fullerplast' as a sealer to prevent the finish from going too deeply into the wood. Alder really sucks up lacquer—you can spray lacquer sealer on it all day

and it keeps disappearing. That's no problem if you have plenty of time (days, sometimes) for the solvents to escape from the wood—then lacquer sealer will do a great job. But since lacquer dries faster on the surface than at the bottom of the film, it's easy to trap solvents under the finish, creating poor adhesion, discoloration, poor drying, and other problems, especially in a production situation. With 'Fullerplast,' since it cures chemically and is unaffected by solvents after it's cured, the subsequent lacquer coats dry better on it.

"Fullerplast soaks in on the first coat only. I keep the first coat fairly thin for it to go into the wood to get good adhesion. I usually lay on a few more full-strength coats of Fullerplast to ensure a relatively-flat surface for the Sunburst to land safely-on. If you shoot within 2 to 3 hour intervals, you don't need to "scuff-sand" between coats because you will get enough chemical bond between coats. If you wait longer than 4 hours, scuff-sand the finish with 220-grit to give the finish something for the next coat to cling to). I always level, and scuff-sand the final sealer coat, and then spray a wash coat of lacquer just before the color, for better adhesion—an added insurance.

"The disadvantage of Fullerplast, and other finishes like it, are that it will dry and set-up in the gun, it's more expensive, and it requires constant

cleanup. But used with care in a proper spray environment, it definitely does the job! Certainly Fender had fewer worries with Fullerplast than with conventional lacquer.

"I don't use any dye-stains (transparent) on either a two-tone or a three-tone Fender sunburst—I use only pigment-stains. I believe that even the yellow was a pigment, because if you use bleach you can't use dye since any un-neutralized bleach residue could easily cause a dye to fade or discolor (especially yellow)—even after a guitar had left the factory.

"Two other big reasons for using pigment are: 1) it won't fade or discolor over the years as much as dyes will; 2) it's light-reflecting characteristics (especially yellow), cause the light to come back up through the finish so the sunburst glows. But the pigments I use are of the finely-ground type, and the effect is subtle. A 'coarse' pigment-grind could block out the wood color and make it look somewhat artificial.

"Both the red and brown of the sunburst are also pigment colors. In my case, the brown is made from concentrated pigment paste (two parts red to one part black) which is cut with lots of thinner. There's a *little* clear lacquer added in to help the color stick to the surface it's sprayed on, and the consistency is like any washcoat; because the pigment is strong, there's very little color buildup during the sunbursting, and the finish remains thin.

"Fender used two shades of brown, weaker 'Salem maple,' and stronger 'Salem maple,' for the sunburst. The darker one was used on the edge, or 'rim,' because it covered quickly with

little finish build-up. It was too strong to create a nice, delicate sunburst, however, so they thinned it to a lighter shade for the top and back sunburst graduation. They let the brown 'flash-off,' then when it's dry, brush off any dry overspray of brown using a soft clean brush or lint-free rag, working from the center towards the edge. This was an important step to achieve clean sunbursts (see Step #9 below).

"My red is made the same way as the brown—red pigment paste, mixed with clear lacquer and lots of thinner, and shot very thin. I can't tell you *what* color red it is because it has no name. There are many reds of course, so you'll have to use what you can find (or like). It's important to shoot the red *after* the dark brown to enhance the transition area from brown to yellow, and give the brown that beautiful chocolate look!

"When I study most original 'three-tone' sunburst finishes, I see *two* layers of red. The first is a 1" to 1-1/2" band of red *inside* the brown transition area, achieved by shooting outwards (aiming the spray gun from center towards the edge of body). The second is a weaker, more 'over-sprayed,' wider pattern which subtly graduates the red area into the center, and covers almost the entire yellow center area including the area under the pickguard. (This latter effect can only be achieved by spraying inwards, and also from farther away. In other words, you shoot the red twice: once to smooth out and sweeten the brown transition area, and the second time to smooth out its own (the red) transition area!"

To accommodate Yas's spray techniques, Bryan Galloup built a "spray-table" which has a circular plywood turntable resting on it. The turntable has three wheels, and is center-pinned to the table so it can be revolved without running off onto the floor. This is Yas's version of the spray turntable used at Fender. The circular shape lets the operator turn the table easily with a free hand without needing to look away from the work while spraying. We do not know when Fender started using a turntable, but we'd guess it would have been in the '50s.

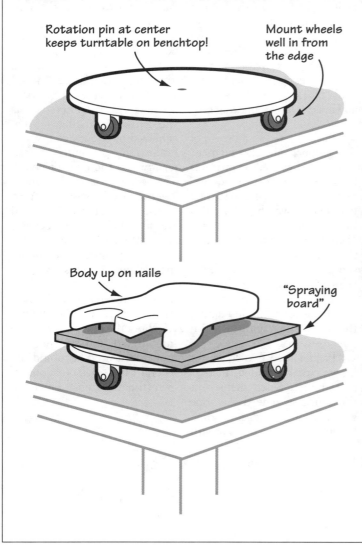

Rotation pin at center keeps turntable on benchtop!

Mount wheels well in from the edge

Body up on nails

"Spraying board"

THE "PRE-MID '60S SPRAYING METHOD":

"Up until sometime in '64 (and I've never seen a '65 body with this), Fender drove nails into the face of the guitar as a 'stand' to support the wet body

after it was turned over onto its face for spraying the back side. For years I'd heard that the marks made by the nails were 'tooling' marks, but if production methods had required indexing, the marks would've been in the *exact* same spot each time—but they weren't! Finally, I saw an old factory picture in which the guitar seemed to be 'floating' off the surface of the table. Then I knew! It was very exciting, and soon I talked with a couple of old-timers who verified my suspicions.

"They drove a nail at a 60-degree angle in the jack cup hole, one under the pickguard near the bass side, front edge of the bridge, and another between the neck pocket and front pickup hole. In earlier days, there was even a fourth hole in the lower horn. If you look at a Tele you'll see a similar mark—either right by the screw hole, or else on the wall of the control cavity, which is probably a better place for it."

"The bodies were sprayed while resting on a board, hitting the face first, and then flipping it over, onto the nails, to spray the back. I don't know, but I would guess they were using a turntable. They probably set the board on the turntable for spraying, and then lifted the board—body and all—to set it somewhere to dry."

THE "POST-MID '60S" SPRAYING METHOD:

In addition to the spray table Yas also made a right-angle stand for spraying the bodies—also inspired by one used by Fender. "We don't know exactly when Fender began using the stand for spraying," says Yas, "but we do know that in '62 Fender began bolting a handle into the neck pocket (because that's when a shadow of it started showing up in the paint).

"Initially, the handle was used just to store the bodies for drying—otherwise they wouldn't have continued to use the nails. The handle allowed the bodies to be 'hung' (stored almost horizontally, actually) on the 'branches' of what Fender calls a 'tree' for drying bodies. The tree holds 44 bodies on one stand, and can be rolled about on wheels. Both the handle-shadow, and the nail-hole marks, overlapped for three years (from '62—'64'), so it must have been very early in '65 that someone looked at the hollow-tube handles, and thought of using them on a stand, over the turntable, for holding bodies while spraying."

The stand Yas uses is made from two pieces of 3/4" plumbing pipe, an elbow, and a flange to mount it to the edge of the carousel table. The body holder is a 1" electrical conduit pipe flattened on one end, with holes drilled through the flat area for screwing it to the body cavity. The "handle" fastens into the two neck-mounting holes on the bass side of the neck pocket with two sheet metal screws. Only enough of the sharp sheet metal screw thread cuts into the wood to hold it, and no sign is left when it's removed. The tube slides* onto the stand and becomes a "no fatigue" rotating handle for spraying (the diameters of the plumbing pipe and electrical tubing differ, allowing one to slide over the other). Combined with the revolving turntable, it allows the finisher complete mastery over the work.

Yas took the "handle" trick one step further by using it for necks, too. He took a Fender truss rod nut, ground off the screwdriver slots, and welded it to a truss rod. Then he welded the truss rod to a piece of the 1"

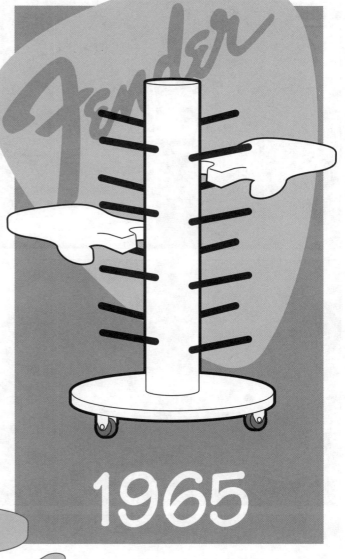

1965

1" electrical conduit flattened on end (sheet metal screws fasten to neck mount holes)

Old truss rod with conduit welded on

Grind the "X" slots from a truss rod nut and weld to this end

conduit and bent one end into a hook. This is his "neck holder" for spraying necks. It slides onto the stand, like the bodies, and it can be hung from the hook for storage once it's dry. (You could do the same thing with a piece of 3/8" steel rod by tapping a thread into the end.) "It offers especially good control for tinting necks a vintage color, or for spraying," he says, " and the hook lets you hang the neck out of the way for drying. If I'm spraying clear I'll leave the neck on the hanger so it remains level while the finish sets up. The lacquer flows out level and without sagging. Turning it once or twice avoids any sags."

FENDER'S EARLY '60S "3-TONE SUNBURST" FINISH SCHEDULE

Here's the finishing procedure Yas used at the Northwoods Seminar to get the vintage look:

1 PREP SAND BODY

2 BLEACH:

Apply between half to full strength of two-part (A,B) bleach with sponge. Cover top and back, sides not necessary

3 NEUTRALIZE

To stop the bleaching action, neutralize it with a 3 % solution of acetic acid (white vinegar can also be used), following the instructions with the bleach kit you are using. Unneutralized bleach attracts moisture, which is another reason for neutralizing it (self-neutralizing bleach does not need this step.) Sand off any 'fir,' or raised fibers when the wood is dry.

4 YELLOW STAIN:

Dilute yellow pigment stain with water, and spray on. Let dry at least six hours.

5 WASH COAT:

Use Fullerplast (dilute 1 part thinner : 2 parts Fullerplast). Let dry 2 hour.

6 SEALER COAT:

Shoot 2 to 4 'double' coats of full-strength Fullerplast, and dry 2 hours between each coat. You want the sealer coat as thin as possible, but thick enough to sand somewhat flat. Let dry overnight in warm place.

7 SAND FLAT & SCUFF:

Do not try to sand perfectly flat (70% to 80% is fine). You don't want to go through the finish, but you do want to dull the surface and eliminate the shiny spots because the finish can't cling to them. For this levelling, a Porter Cable Speed Bloc sander and #220-grit Fre-Cut sandpaper does a good job, or use a felt-block.

8 WASH COAT LACQUER:

To help color stick to the Fullerplast, apply one mist coat of thinned lacquer. When dry, get rid of any grime or dust that may have been trapped—it will cause unwanted 'shadows' if left on. Knock down these 'high-spots' by lightly sanding with #600-grit.

9 SHOOT SUNBURST

Shoot outside brown first, beginning with the sides. Try to avoid overspray by shooting outward. When the sides are dark enough, begin shooting the edges of the top and back where they meet the side. Shoot outward to avoid overspray on main body.

NOTE: At this point, switch to the lighter brown and finish the sunburst from the center out to where the lighter brown meets the darker brown as it wraps over the corner. Don't forget to brush off any overspray as mentioned earlier!!

10 SPRAY RED

Red is shot slightly further away from the surface. You can raise the pressure if necessary and/or thin down the paint. Shoot outward first, to establish the 'band' mentioned earlier, then shoot inward with the gun held even further away. The paint needs to be well-thinned, especially when you hold the spray gun far away, because the finish has more time to dry and create overspray buildup. NOTE: You cannot use the brush on the red because it is too delicate, and being the final color coat, you will ruin the look if you mess with it.

11 LET DRY, WASHCOAT

After drying, washcoat with thin lacquer to stabilize the color.

12 TOP COAT:

Apply 1 single coat, then follow with 3 to 4 'double' coats. Sand between every 2 coats if possible.

Thanks, Yas, from all of us!

HAND-CUT SOUNDHOLE PURFLING! AND CHECK OUT THIS TWIST ON A CLASSICAL BRIDGE

Abel Garcia's rosette (soundhole purfling) is made entirely from hand-cut pieces of wood using the techniques he demonstrated at the Northwoods Seminar. Beautiful work, Abel!

The bridge on Abel's guitar, is unusual, too: it differs from many classical guitar bridges that you'll see. Instead of having only one hole for each string in the tie-block, there are two. This gives a greater string angle to the saddle, and less wear on the string since it doesn't have to wrap around itself as in the normal classical string tie. This stringing method has been around for a number of years, but I'd never seen it before. Any comment, Trade Secrets readers?

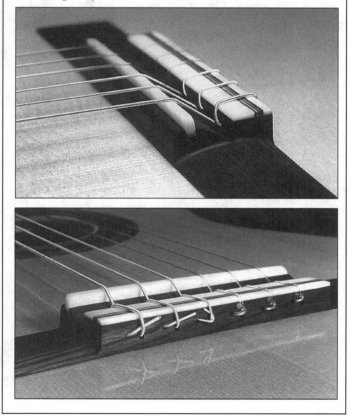

HERRINGBONE THE EASY WAY

Abel Garcia's method of making herringbone allows you to suit your needs. Glue your wood strips together on edge (alternate the colors), and clamp them to dry on a sheet of waxed paper. If you stagger the strip ends on a 45-degree slant, you'll have less waste on the first cut.

Next, trim the rough ends at 45-degrees, and then start slicing angled pieces. Place the pieces together in a long row, glue them together, and then glue a thin strip on one, or both edges depending upon the design. The edge strip keeps the pieces aligned while gluing and drying, and adds

With Martha Humphrey assisting, Abel Garcia gave a slide show on "Guitar Making in Paracho, Mexico" at the Great Northwoods Seminar. Afterward, Abel described how to make and sharpen the cuchillo (guitarmaker's knife), how to cut inlay strips, and finally, how to make herringbone purfling . . .

decorative trim. When dry, stand the strip on edge and slice it in half along the center. Open the two pieces in a bookmatch and you have herringbone!

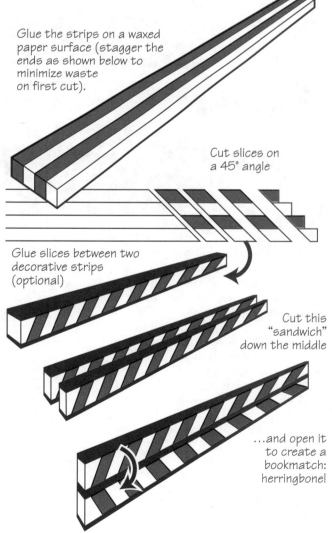

Glue the strips on a waxed paper surface (stagger the ends as shown below to minimize waste on first cut).

Cut slices on a 45° angle

Glue slices between two decorative strips (optional)

Cut this "sandwich" down the middle

...and open it to create a bookmatch: herringbone!

ABEL GARCIA CUTS UP IN CLASS

Abel Garcia, from the famous guitar-making town of Paracho in the mountains of Michoacan, Mexico, demonstrated the famous *cuchillo*, (guitarmaker's knife) at the Great Northwoods Seminar this year. The *cuchillo* is an all-purpose tool used for cutting tops to shape, cutting wood braces, purfling grooves, and binding from stock—even delicate inlay strips. To our amazement, Abel cut the entire outline of a cedar top, freehand, with his cuchillo! (*Photos, right.*)

The *cuchillo* is similar to the traditional violinmaker's

Abel Garcia

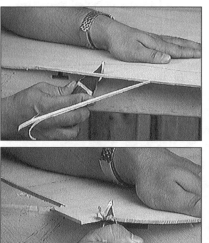

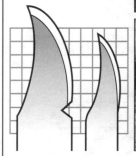

knife, but it has a curved cutting edge. The edge is beveled on both sides (a V-shape), and the top edge is relieved to keep it from contacting and marring the wood when carving curved surfaces like the neck's heel. The notch in the large knife blade gives the relief necessary so that the entire cutting edge can be sharpened on the stone. The smaller knife doesn't have this notch (Abel is only concerned with keeping its tip sharp).

Abel uses the small knife for slicing inlay strips and spruce braces from flat stock. To do this, the knife is held vertically and used on a pull stroke, with the point protruding through a hardwood "stripping block" with slits in it at measured intervals. Glued to the underside is a wood shim the same thickness as the wood to be stripped—creating an edge guide and raising the stripping block to the height of the piece to be cut.

Here's A Hot Tip!

John Reuter, Director of Training at the Roberto-Venn Guitar Repair School, repaired an old Gibson LG1 flattop with this clever trick …

"It was a very common patch job with an added twist. There was a 3/8" hole drilled through the face of the guitar for a volume control. The spruce top was heavily 'washboarded' from years of heavy strumming, and the customer wanted the control removed and the hole to 'disappear.' I explained that no matter how well done, the patch would show (but in the end it almost didn't).

"I cut the hole into a uniform shape for fitting a patch (top photo), and found a couple of spruce scraps that match in color and grain structure. The twist was to match the washboard look of the top. I charred the surface of the spruce patching wood with a lighter, then removed the blackened softwood from between the hard grain lines with a wire brush.

"The rest was pretty straightforward patching: I cut and fit the patch to match the grain lines and glued a backing piece of cross-grained, slightly oversized spruce to the inside of the top to reinforce the hole. After gluing in the patch, I rubbed my dirty hands over the patch to match the color and weathering of the raw spruce where the finish was missing."

John Reuter,
Director of Training,
Roberto-Venn School of Luthiery

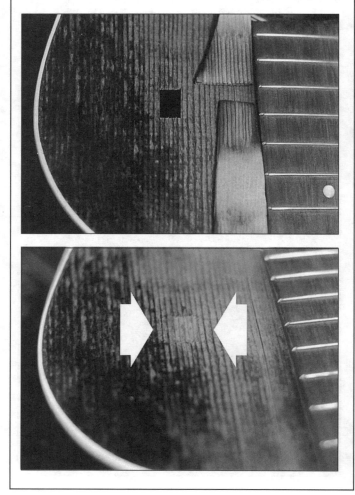

YOU'LL FIND EXTRA TRADE SECRETS THROUGHOUT THE CATALOG!

TradeSecrets!
Hot tips & inside scoops. Editor: Dan Erlewine

VOLUME 25

TRADE SECRETS INTERNATIONAL
Great Tip from Great Britain!

Dear Sir:

I have just acquired your book Trade Secrets, *and would like to have your catalog. Enclosed are details of my binding/veneer thick-nesser for the Trade Secrets section of the catalog.*

Regards,
Peter L. Giolitto
Guitar Maker
26 Delaporte Close
Epsom Surrey
KT174AF England

P.S. I enclose a photo of my oak version [above] which has a brass anvil and a slotted blade held between blocks with a bolt and wing nut. You can't see the stop, but it's there.

Dear Peter:

My crude attempt at a binding thicknesser was shown in Vol. 18 of Trade Secrets Book One, *but yours is much better! Coincidentally, your letter arrived right when I was about to thickness some binding for a 1958 Gibson L-5 guitar. When your letter arrived, I recognized a good thing and made a version of your tool that weekend.*

As you can see in the photos at right, I changed your idea a little by making the stop adjustable and using throwaway razor blades for the cutting edge. I intend to make one like yours because it looks so nice, and I think it will be more rugged and take thicker binding down faster.

—Dan

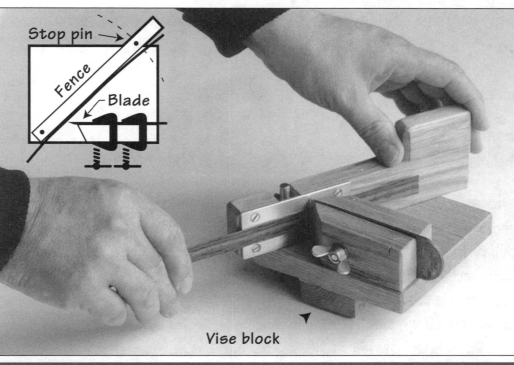

HOW TO MAKE THE GIOLITTO BINDING SCRAPER

1 A 6" square of thick plywood has a clamping block on the underside for clamping it into a bench vise.
2 A fence from 2" x 1" hardwood is pivoted on one corner on a wood screw with the head removed.
3 The other end of the fence also has a wood screw minus the head on the underside—which creates a stop.
4 A blade clamping block is glued in the position shown.

HOW TO USE THE SCRAPER

1 Make sure the fence stop is touching the base.
2 Sharpen a small plane blade with a burr and clamp to the block, setting the required thickness with a feeler gauge.
3 Move the fence slightly and insert the material to be thicknessed, leave half protruding (to hold onto while pulling)
4 Gently hold the fence against the material with one hand and pull with the other to remove material.
5 Reverse material and repeat.
6 Continue this process until the stop touches the base and the blade ceases to cut. The material will then be the desired

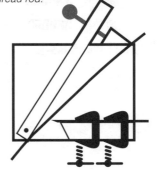

In this adaptation, the stop is lower than the table, and it adjusts with all-thread rod.

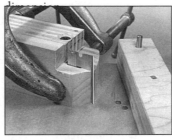

In Dan's version, the top of the blade is exposed so you can get hold of it.

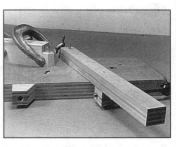

Patience Is The Secret To Tom Blackshear's Success

Tom Blackshear is recognized as one of today's foremost classical guitar makers. Tom lives and works in San Antonio, Texas. "I'm a family man," says Blackshear, "my wife Dottie, and sons Sam (16) and Josh (9) are the most important persons in my life, and at 54 years old, after building since 1958, I'm just getting to the level of building which I've always worked toward. Perhaps this will give hope and a proper perspective to those just starting out. It hasn't come easy." Here's Tom:

We have another business which helps pay the bills, a 20-year old carpet cleaning and chemical supply, under the name Blackshear & Sons, Inc. About three years ago, I decided to improve the business end of my guitar building by acquiring more precise equipment, attending guitar building conferences and classes, and promoting my guitars throughout the U.S. In the 30-plus years I'd been building I never put much effort into any kind of marketing or advertising—selling mostly to those who came to my shop. To expand the business, I need to reach out to those who can't sit here in the shop and watch as I fine-tune a guitar for them.

To this end, thanks to the support of Tim Miklaucic, who owns the Guitar Salon International in Santa Monica, California, I have started building more guitars, and shipping them around the country. Tim has sold a number of my guitars, and we both appreciate a certain sound quality in a guitar, but it's one which I could never *quite* get. This is a sound character that some of the great makers like Santos Hernandez, Marcello Barbero, and Miguel Rodriguez produced in their guitars—a very deep, bell-like quality, a haunting sound with overtones, and a slight echo.

I finally found it this fall after a 37-year search. In November, I got my hands on a wonderful guitar built in 1962 by Miguel Rodriguez, of Cordoba, Spain (Raphael Rodriguez actually, under his brother Miguel's label). When I studied the top graduation, all of the things I'd been working toward for years became crystal clear to me.

I was ready for what I found, but if I'd examined that guitar even five years ago, I probably wouldn't have understood it. Everything finally came together for me in this great guitar built by a master.

I had the guitar long enough to patiently measure it with the Hacklinger gauge. I had known for many years that thinning a top toward the middle produces a lower pitch and a bolder note, and that thinning toward the outside results in a higher pitch and a thinner edge to the note. The top graduation of the

Rodriguez, however, was far more defined than I would have thought. I used this information to graduate the top of a guitar that I was just completing.

Since the new top was already braced and on the guitar, it was a little tough to measure as I graduated it—but the Hacklinger gauge made that possible, since the magnet placed inside the guitar follows the measuring tool—even over braces (photos). With the gauge, we can more clearly define how to graduate the top, and avoid an inconsistent sound.

My discovery, "reverse graduation" is what I'll call it, dramatically improved my guitar in two ways: 1) It refined an already-good sound character until it's almost right on to that of the Spanish makers—really, I'm that close to it; 2) The volume was strengthened considerably, which in turn resulted in improved action (since the increase in the top thickness under the bridge stiffens the top, the strings can be closer to the fingerboard without buzzing, and you don't have to play as hard to get the same volume because of the higher pitch of the notes.) I've got my bass strings set at 1/8" over the 12th fret on the bass side, and a little less on the treble; that's *low* for a classic!

My new top graduation starts, and ends, with a thicker top than I previously used, and is exactly the opposite in its extremes. There are three basic ways to build a top:

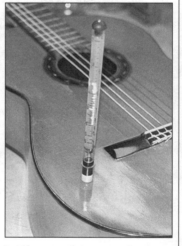

1 The simplest is to leave it ungraduated, or level (one thickness, as it comes from the thickness sander).
2 The "old" way I did it, in which you *thin* it around the bridge area, generally from the front of the bridge to 1-1/2" in back of the bridge, and all the way across the top.
3 The "new," or "reverse" graduation leaves the top *thicker* under the bridge (thicknesses across the top are illustrated

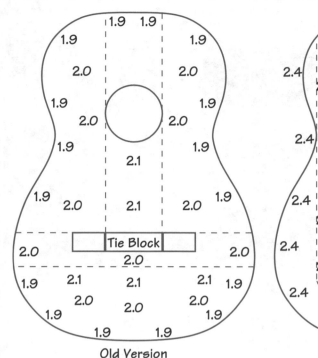

Old Version

Most Recent

EASY GLUE REMOVAL

Like many experienced professionals, Tom Blackshear could fill a whole book with "hot tips." Here are two quickies that I thought you'd like…

I always glue the bridge on "in the white" (no finish) and then final-tune the guitar. Then I remove the bridge and finish the instrument. I tape off the bridge area and French-polish the top, although I lacquer the back and sides. About a week goes by between taking the bridge off, finishing the guitar, and regluing the bridge.

To remove the bridge, I mask off the top with cardboard and aluminum foil, heat the bridge with a 150-watt "soft-white" bulb, and use a thin spatula about 10-12" long to work the bridge off once the glue has become soft. You need to worry about the heat factor, so apply the heat from each side of the bridge (not directly over the center seam of the top, which you don't want to come unglued.)

Then, to remove glue from the spruce top I use paper towels saturated with 190-proof grain alcohol (Everclear) to dampen the glue. It softens like jelly, and can be removed with a scraper. Be careful to stay off that center seam! Using this technique, I have removed and replaced bridges as many as five times without trouble. After the top is French-polished, I use a white polyvinyl glue to reapply the bridge. If you want easier bridge removal the first time, you may want to try hide glue.

above), and tapers out to the edges. I've known this for some time, but have never been able to define it as clearly until I found the Hacklinger gauge.

My old version of top graduating—thinner under the bridge—has produced a wonderful full-noted sound for me for many years. And it produces something in the treble that really helps a player get color. The new way loses some of the color in the treble, but it picks up a sweetness in the treble that *wasn't* there—so there is a tradeoff. And as I already mentioned, the notes in both the bass and treble gained a sharper edge which increased the volume (or at least gave the sensation of increased volume.)

Here's a description of my most recent top graduation and a drawing with the measurements if anyone would like to try them. I included a drawing with the old measurements too.
1 Sand the top uniformly to 2.7mm (I use a Performax double-drum 37"-wide belt sander with 120-grit on the front, and 150-grit on the back). The

GSI's Tim Miklaucic says: "Tom Blackshear builds a very, very strong guitar with a kind of breathy, deep tone. Fast like a flamenco, with surprising sustain, and elegant workmanship and detailing, his guitars sound as though they were made in southern Spain."

top remains exactly 2.7mm in the center section, under the fretboard, and from the soundhole to 1-1/2" behind the bridge.
2 Use a block plane to define the graduations and the edges of the outside, and finish with a scraper and fine sandpaper. The 2.7mm thins to 2.6mm in line with the tie block ends (dotted line), becomes 2.5 at the bridge ends, and about 1" to 1-1/2" out from that the top becomes a uniform 2.4mm everywhere.

3 Notice that the 2.6, 2.5, and 2.4mm graduations sort of squeeze together in tighter curves as they wrap around the bridge in the lower bout.

I was a professional flamenco player in the '50s, and I'm still devoted to the music, but the musician's *lifestyle* (living on the road) wasn't for me. I've always approached building from a serious player's point of view. So when I finally got the sound I've been after I thought Oh my gosh, what will I do—go back to playing!?" Actually, I won't, I'm too much of a family man, but I know in my gut that this new graduation is going to make a great flamenco guitar—and because of this I'm really excited!

My flamenco guitars are sturdy-sounding, but I wanted to get a sharper edge on the sound of the strings. To do that I had thinned the struts rather than thinning the top on the outside edges. Reverse graduation will work as well for the flamenco guitar as it does for my concert classical guitars; I'm inclined to believe it would work for any guitar with nylon strings.

TIE BLOCK DRILL-JIG

Dan, you asked for comment on Abel Garcia's use of two string holes in the tie block of a classical guitar. This is an interesting way of approaching the string-tie if the tie-block is thick enough, but it won't work for those of us who build with a bridge which is 5/16" thick—there's simply not enough wood to risk drilling twice as many holes through this area. By the way: when I drill the tie-block holes I use a steel drilling jig which a machine shop made for me to guide the drill bit accurately and at the correct angle.

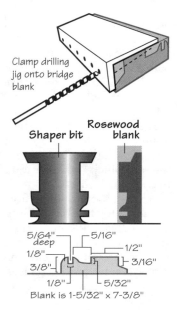

Clamp drilling jig onto bridge blank

Shaper bit   Rosewood blank

5/64" deep — 5/16"
1/8"   1/2"
3/8"   3/16"
1/8"   5/32"
Blank is 1-5/32" x 7-3/8"

I recently had a shaper cutter made that allows me to cut the profile of my bridge in one pass, and into a rosewood blank long enough for three or four bridges. I'm gearing up to make some guitars this year! Bye for now...

— *Tom Blackshear*

GREAT NORTHWOODS BUILDING & REPAIR SEMINAR 1996

For the third consecutive year, Bryan Galloup will host this three-day seminar at the "Guitar Hospital Building & Repair School" facility. Sponsored by Stewart-MacDonald, the event features intensive workshops on a variety of subjects. There's room for 30 people, and we sign 'em up early on a first-come basis.

We'll be in Michigan when the weather is perfect (September 12–14). This year's guest instructors are still undecided as of this writing, but by the time you read this, we'll have the info you need. You can contact Bryan or Susan Galloup at:

The Guitar Hospital
10495 Northland Drive
Big Rapids, Michigan 49307
(616) 796-5611

LEEDS GUITARMAKERS' SCHOOL

William Cumpiano, who along with John Natelson co-authored *Guitarmaking: Tradition and Technology*, has teamed with Ivon Schmukler to found the Leeds Guitarmakers' School. The school offers a variety of primary and master courses in classic, steel-string flattop, carved-top, and solidbody electric guitar construction, as well as workshops on French polishing and spray-finishing. The courses are scheduled for June, August, September, and October.

Under "construction" by William and Ivon is a fretted instrument-making academy with an advisory board including Michael Gurian, Tim White, and Michael Millard, and a faculty of more than twenty noted professional makers and technicians. They will present guest lectures in just about everything from electronics and finishing, to history and Latin American instruments. They hope to have a really complete program—a world-class academy—by 1998.

For more about class scheduling and pricing, or to register, contact Ivon Schmukler at (413) 582-0034, or write:

Leeds Guitarmakers' School,
8 Easthampton Road,
Northampton, Mass. 01060

Ivon Schmukler (above) and William Cumpiano have opened the Leeds School. Cumpiano (with beard) is pictured in the background of the top photo.

Lindy Fralin Pickups

indy Fralin operates a custom pickup-winding business in Richmond, Virginia, offering replacements for many of the standard magnetic pickups used by guitar builders (Strat, Tele, humbucker, P-90, and Jazz Bass styles). Besides making stock-output reproduction pickups, Lindy and his small crew provide one of the world's best rewinding/repair services for vintage pickups, and will custom-wind new Fralin pickups to suit your needs.

Lindy was one of the key instructors at the Great Northwoods Seminar in October '95. He writes:

We try to custom-wind pickups to give a customer the sound he's looking for. I understand guitar sounds, and I'm a player. I always loved the Strat neck and middle pickup, but thought the bridge pickup was too thin. That's the reason I got into winding in the first place. Our assembly and winding is done by hand from American-made materials, and it's the hand-winding which gives our pickups the authentic vintage tone. We rewind and repair pickups, along with making our own. What we can't do is change a pickup's string spacing, or reproduce missing parts (we're not that type of manufacturer).

Except for Fender, most vintage pickups were not potted, or at least not well-potted (we "pot" pickups to stop microphonic feedback and to protect them from the elements). Some guitar makers pot by brushing on wax, others wrap the coil with tape. All new Fralin pickups come potted, and we pot rewinds that were originally potted. If we're asked, we will pot Gibson and other pickups as long as we think it won't damage them.

I pot with wax because it's non-toxic, easy to deal with, cheap, and you can undo something if it goes wrong. I don't want to work on epoxy-potted pickups because you can't get to the parts to rewind them, and epoxy only coats the parts—it's too thick to penetrate the coil.

wax thin with a hot soldering iron, and press it to the guitar body while it's still warm. You can't see it once the bridge is remounted, and the thin layer of wax acts as a shock absorber between the bridge and the body.

Fender potted most of their pickups in wax, but they also did a number of them in lacquer. Lacquer's okay, but it doesn't penetrate as well as the hot wax

Jenny and Lindy (left), with crew members Dan Roberts, Doug Humphreys, and Tom Brantley (kneeling).

In the photo of Lindy at right, note the Tupperware spool holder sitting on the chair behind him. That's how they feed the wire to the machine.

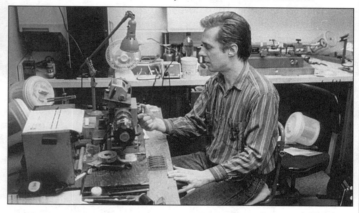

Hot wax is thin enough to penetrate completely into the coil, which is what you're after, and it keeps *everything* from vibrating.

Microphonics is that squealing or knocking sound you hear when you tap on a pickup. A good example of microphonics at its worst would be the Fender Telecaster bridge pickup—not only do you have a coil of wire and magnets, but you have a steel plate under it and a steel bridge around it. Fender used to mount the steel plate after the pickup had been potted, and that's why the Tele is so notoriously microphonic—the steel plate vibrates. For that reason, I pot my Tele-style bridge pickups *after* the plate is mounted.

On my Teles, I also pot the bridge itself! I melt a few drops of hot wax (you could use a candle) onto the bottom of the bridge in the area where it surrounds the pickup, spread the

does, and it's harder to repair a pickup that's been lacquered because you can't peel them for repair ("peeling" is unwinding the layers of copper wire to find a break in the coil or a spot which is rusted or corroded. Rusted steel, corroded copper, or a combination of both, are the most common causes of dead pickups, or pickups which die a slow death.) Wax-potted coils unwind nicely, unlike lacquer-potted coils which might as well be glued together.

You can recognize lacquer by its thin, shiny, wet-looking coat, compared to wax which is thicker and more dull-looking. Fender used wax more often than not, but sometimes they only dipped the pickups—whereas I *soak* mine. Today, most of the modern pickup makers like Seymour Duncan, Van Zandt, myself and others, use wax for potting.

We only charge $10 plus shipping to pot pickups, so of course it's easier for most people to just send them to us rather than doing it themselves. You can pot your own pickups for a minimum investment, however—I tell customers how to do it all the time—but you have to follow certain safety precautions, and probably only the really serious professional shops will set up to do it.

Mix canning paraffin and 20% beeswax by heating them in a pot. Paraffin expands and contracts with temperature changes, and the beeswax nullifies most of that. The heating is the dangerous part—*never try heating your wax on the kitchen stove or in a microwave oven because hot paraffin, and especially paraffin vapors, can ignite.*

Our wax pots are the mid-sized, heavy-duty deep fryers used in some home kitchens and small restaurants thirty years ago. [The wax pots in the photo above are Lindy's.] We leave them at 150°F all day long, and pickups can sit in there for an hour or more without problems (ten or fifteen minutes is our normal potting time). At 150° you won't harm a pickup, but use a kitchen meat thermometer to check the temperature. Stew-Mac's Hot Glue Pot makes a great single-pickup wax-pot for a small shop; it's UL-approved, and is designed to run all day. I had to lower the thermostat a little, though (*see note*).

Experiment with potting by heating the wax outdoors, or maybe in the garage. Once you find the 150° setting, and know what you're doing, then use it in your shop. Provide adequate ventilation, too—we pot under an exhaust hood which vents to the outdoors.

[**Note:** *Stew-Mac's No. 668 Hot Glue Pot has a thermostat designed to heat hide glue to about 145°. The pot, with glue or wax, is meant to be at least 2/3 or 3/4 full. It can operate with less liquid without damage, but it may get too hot (perhaps that was Lindy's problem). Extra metal liners are available (so you could have one for wax and one for glue); ask our phone staff for part No. 668-P, $23.95.*]

Ahhh... Nothing like a nice hot bath.

To Contact Lindy:
Lindy Fralin Pickups,
3415 Floyd Ave,
Richmond, VA 23221
(804)-358-2699

WAX PICKUP POTTING GUIDELINES

■ The wax-pot's metal walls may be hotter than the wax itself, so don't touch the pickup to the walls of the pot; instead, use some sort of hanger to suspend the pickup in the wax. Paul Reed Smith uses a layer of marbles in the bottom of the pot.

■ If the wax is smoking, it's too hot (but you should be checking the temperature with a meat thermometer anyhow—150° or less).

■ "Cook" a pickup until all the air bubbles have stopped coming out, usually in 10 to 20 minutes.

■ Wax is messy, very flammable, and it'll burn you, too. So for safety's sake, stay with the wax-pot and be sensible. It splashes too, so **wear safety glasses!**

■ Don't remove the tape from Gibson-style pickups. The heat may cause the tape to unwrap, so stretch rubber bands around the pickup to hold the tape in place, and only remove them after the pickup has cooled.

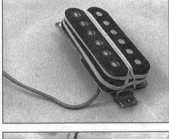

■ Remove the excess wax with paper towel as soon as the pickups are cool enough to touch.

ADJUSTING THE THERMOSTAT ON STEW-MAC'S GLUE POT

We don't suggest that you take the pot apart all the time to adjust, but here's how to do it:
■ Remove the inner basket
■ Remove the two small screws holding the metal liner and then pull the liner out as far as it will go and lay it on its side (photo below). Handle the inner liner gently.

■ Adjust the hex nut counter-clockwise to lower the heat. One-sixth (one hex point) of a turn will change it 20° to 25°.
■ Re-assemble, and let the pot run for about 1-1/2 hours while the thermostat readjusts.

Lindy spends a lot of time trying out new pickup ideas in his many test guitars.

USING A RADIUS GAUGE WITH THE STRINGS ON

After you've read Bill Cumpiano's procedure for calculating correct saddle height (page 84), here's an alternate method:

Follow Bill's steps, but only on the outer two E-strings. Then, use a radius gauge which matches, or is closest to, the fingerboard's arc as a guide to draw a line on the saddle blank between the two points. Shape to that line and you'll get a saddle contour that matches the fretboard exactly, without having to deal with the measurements of the middle four strings.

Notch a set of radius gauges so they drop *over* the strings; then you can determine a fretboard radius with the strings on. This is a real handy way to adjust bridge saddle height on electrics! An advantage of the first method, however, is that you can control the height of the individual strings across the fretboard (if, for example, you don't want them to follow the fretboard radius exactly).

STEP-BLOCK FOR REPETITIVE SETUPS:

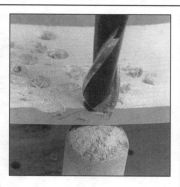

I used the Hacklinger gauge to measure the thicknesses of several vintage archtop guitars before carving a replacement back for a 1958 Gibson L-5 CN (cutaway archtop acoustic guitar). After finishing the outside shape of the back, and working from the measurements, I drilled a series of "depth" holes (to guide me as I carved the inside) using a 1/2" round-bottomed end mill. A wooden post centered under the drill bit supported the work, and the clearance between the two determined the thickness of the new back (photo above).

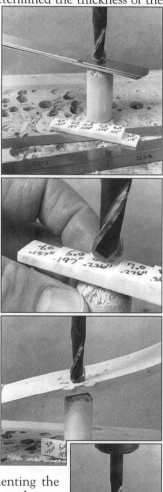

■ To set the depth-stop for drilling the many holes, I tried stacking feeler gauges to set the clearances—what a pain! (*Photo, right.*) The Hacklinger gauge measures in millimeters, and at Don MacRostie's suggestion, I carefully filed steps into a piece of Corian, producing a metric "step block" gauge (*also shown in photo, right*).

■ The step-block made it easy to set the depth (*right*).

■ The round-bottomed end-mill makes a smooth-bottomed, dish-shaped hole with no tear-out. With the tall pin you can tilt the workpiece (i.e. an arched back) without hitting the table (*lower right*).

■ I put a foam block around the pin to support the work (*bottom right*).

This was my first serious attempt at carving either a top or back for a guitar, and thanks to the Hacklinger gauge, it came out well! It was a real learning experience for me, and I'm documenting the repair with photos, drawings, and measurements to help anyone who might want to build in the L-5 style. I should have the guitar re-bound and re-finished by the next issue of Trade Secrets, and I'll report more on it then.

— *Dan Erlewine*

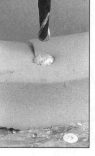

ARE YOU STILL SCRAPIN' NAKED? HERE'S WHAT THE WELL-DRESSED BLADE IS WEARING:

Here's a hot tip we wish we'd known about years ago—try it, and you'll agree. Frank Ford of Gryphon Stringed Instruments in Palo Alto, California comes through with another of his practical trade secrets:

"I use scrapers a lot and make them out of everything. For example, the plane iron from those little Stanley planes makes a great scraper. And for light-duty work my favorite is a heavy-duty, single-edge razor blade (the blade thickness is .012") with a burred edge. It will scrape anything from wood to plastic, and it excels at leveling built-up finish or drop-filled stick shellac during a finish touch-up.

"Hold a fresh blade firmly, and draw its sharp edge at an angle against any piece of hardened steel to turn the edge into a burr. You get a scraper that has incredible sharpness, although it does not have a lot of strength and won't last long. My style is to burn through the work, and replace the blade as soon as it's dull. In boxes of 100,

they only cost a penny or two apiece. Here's the secret to leveling finish with a razor scraper…

"Wrap cellophane tape (it's the thinnest tape I can find) over each end of the blade, leaving as much of the blade's center unwrapped as you need for the job at hand. Go ahead and scrape aggressively—the blade stops cutting when the built-up finish has become the thickness of the masking tape. What remains can be leveled with normal sanding or wet-sanding procedures.

"If I'm really terrified of scratching the surrounding finish I use a layer of tape on the finish surface too. When doing this, it's anybody's guess whether the scraper edge will last longer than the tape—either will wear out quickly, so you have to keep your eye on it.

"And I like the razor blades over any other scraper for scraping spruce. As you all know, spruce doesn't scrape well. But when I scrape 'naked' (without the tape, wise guy) I can scrape even large areas of spruce with ease."

— *Frank Ford*

Binding

This issue we focus on binding, which relates to both repair work and building. Much of what's described here applies to wood binding, but we're really looking at three types of plastic binding: ABS, Bolteron, and Celluloid.

1 SIMPLE, USEFUL JIGS

Dear Stew-Mac:

Of all the jigs I've made (duplicating machine for carving tops and backs, body mold, mold attachment for soundbox binding, etc.) my two favorites are the simplest of all, a side dot drill and a binding gluing jig.

SIDE DOT DRILL

For accurately drilling the small holes for plastic side dots in plastic binding, I find hand-held electric drills hard to control, and my "drill press" is the simple attachment for the hand-held drill-type—not too accurate. Almost as a lark I tried turning a drill bit by hand and it worked great!

Then I dipped the drill bit shank into a pool of epoxy and turned it slowly as the epoxy dried and gathered onto the bit—ending up with an oval handle that gave a better grip for turning (top drawing). If the hole-center is located with a sharp awl, the bit stays on center perfectly once started, and it can make holes through plastic bindings in seconds (a little longer on hardwood).

BINDING GLUING JIG

My archtop has its soundbox binding as shown in the second drawing, and binding strip "A" can be difficult to glue into the cutaway if you haven't glued it to the main binding "B" previously. Gluing A and B was a hassle until I came up with this jig. Here's how to make one:

■ Cut a slot in a long piece of wood (I used a 1/2" x 1/2" piece). The depth of the slot is slightly less than the height of binding B, and is the same width as the binding (shown at right). I use three or four clothes pins to hold the binding into the channel as I glue A to B and "clamp" it with adhesive tape, retiring the clothes pins as I progress. The A piece is wider than B, and I scrape any overhang to final size when it dries (bottom drawing).

Best regards,
Fernando Alonso Jaen
Madrid, Spain

Thanks Fernando! Pre-gluing sections of plastic binding before attempting the actual binding task is the best way to do the job. On next the page is a variation on your technique which I learned from Stew-Mac's Director of R&D Don MacRostie . . .

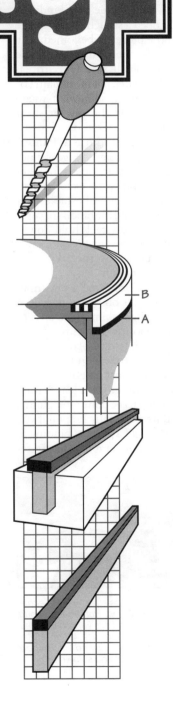

SIZING BINDING WITH A ROUTER

From Don MacRostie...

To edge-glue two bindings, you need a straight, square edge on the pieces to be joined. The smooth (often shiny) factory side of the small side (A) strip is ready to glue, but most main (B) strips have a somewhat rough edge left by the saw or shear which cut it. Don developed a tool that acts both as a "jointer" for truing the sawed edge of bindings, and a thicknesser for trimming a piece to exact height before gluing. Adjustable ball-bearings hold the binding against a fence, and a steel "hold-down" keeps downward pressure on it as it passes by the router bit (photo above).

After "jointing" a few thousandths off one edge to true it using a light skim cut, Don runs the opposite edge through the tool several times—adjusting the cut each time—and trims his pieces to exact height before he glues them in. This leaves little scraping to be done after gluing, and it's especially helpful if you want to get a piece of binding to fit without scraping during repair work.

Don and his assistant, R & D Technician Todd Sams, worked long hours on this tool, and this version is neither the first, nor the last. When all the bugs have been worked out, I hope to see it in our catalog some day. —Dan

ACETONE JOINS BINDINGS INSTANTLY

When not creating new products for the catalog, Don MacRostie builds his "Red Diamond" brand mandolins—bound in plastic. When faced with the problem of keeping the bottom edge-trim of multi-layered bindings in place during gluing, he uses acetone instead of glue to bond the pieces instantly in a "non-stick" glue jig.

We keep a variety of materials around the Stew-Mac shop for jig-making and production purposes. Teflon's one of them. Don took a chunk and table-sawed a precise groove in it.

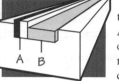

Don makes his piece (A) only slightly wider than (B), and keeps one edge flush during gluing by pressing the strips against the bottom of the channel as he draws them through. When the glue dries, he can either scrape one side flush, or use the tool described below.

The groove is a snug fit to the combined height of the A and B bindings, and other groove sizes accommodate different binding combinations. For example, I used Don's method for laminating b/w/b/w peg-head and fretboard binding on a 1958 Gibson L-5C which was in *major* need of rebinding. After scraping the four pieces of binding to the correct thickness using the methods described in Trade Secrets Vol. 25, I followed these steps:

■ Press the unglued bindings into the block with the ends–about 4"–hanging out (photo at right). Brush a liberal coat of acetone on the mating surfaces of the ends. A tin-handled acid brush works better than the Q-tip that I'm using!

■ Next, pull the strip ends into the channel to squeeze them together. Stop for several seconds to let the pieces set.

■ Reverse the strips in the block, letting their full lengths hang free, and use the glued ends as a "handle" to pull the strips through the block as you glue 4" to 6" at a time (below, right).

[TEFLON, in sheet and block form, is available in a wide variety of sizes from the McMaster Carr Company, P.O. Box 4355, Chicago, IL 60680-4355; (708) 833-0300.]

Continued on next page

I'd say these babies are really in need of rebinding, wouldn't you? —Dan
▼

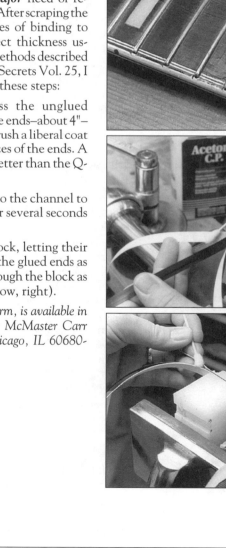

ACETONE JOINS BINDINGS

Continued from page 48

■ You can make most laminates tall enough to provide two strips when sawed in half.

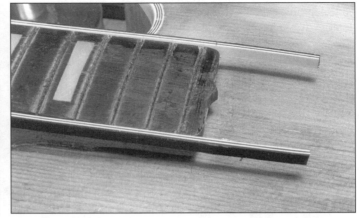

■ "Home-made" binding matches the original exactly.

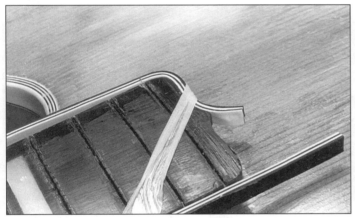

■ Heat the pieces with a heat gun to bend around the end (they won't come apart if you don't overdo it).

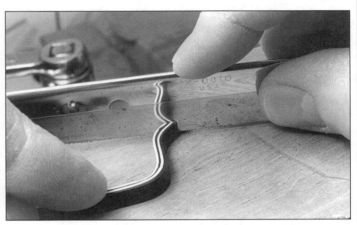

■ Once it's bent, cut the miters with a razor saw.

■ Trim the miter faces clean and glue the strips in place using a 3-way clamp and waxed wooden cauls.

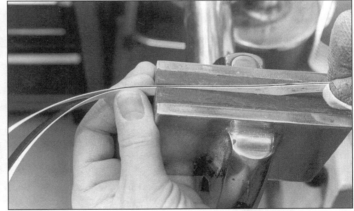

■ I found that the jaws of my "Ultimate Repair Vise" make an *adjustable* acetone-glue jig. The rubber jaw faces are not quite as non-stick as Teflon, but they work fine to *squeeze* strips together. Or, set to just the right pressure you can pull the strips through the corner at an angle—no channel is necessary. (*We've discontinued this vise, but any vise could be adapted for this use. How about a vice with Teflon jaw liners? —Dan*)

TradeSecrets!

ROCKIN' ON THE FINGERBOARD

Dan: Here is a simple and indispensable tool for checking relative fret height before, during, and after fret dressing. Most repairers use different length straightedges to span three frets at a time for an accurate assessment. A single straightedge of any length is limited to spanning only those frets it can reach, but with my modified straightedge you can accommodate any group of three frets on any fretted instrument, from electric bass to mandolin.

On a 4" piece of 3/4" X 1/16" flat steel stock, grind one side down to a 20° angle. I took my idea to a machinist and he turned out accurate edges on his milling machine. This step is a must, because each of the four edges is usable as a fret-checker. With a chamfered hole for hanging, this is one of the most utilized and accessible tools I own, and especially useful to illustrate high frets to a customer—nothing's more effective in showing someone of the need for fret filing.

I told Frank Ford about this idea at the last A.S.I.A. Symposium where he had laid out a whole table of similarly simple but effective tools of his own invention. I thought I saw a light bulb go off over his head!

Yours in lutherie,
Paul Neri
Clinton, CT

OPERATING YOUR SHOP IN A MUSIC STORE: IT PAYS TO BUILD A GOOD WORKING RELATIONSHIP

Some may recall John O'Boyle's crack-repair knife described in Vol. 7 of Trades Secrets Book One. It's a needle file ground thin in width and with a chisel tip. The file teeth on the edge of the file are not ground away so that you can pare a spruce fill flush or below the surface, and further shape the fill for with the file teeth. I made a variation of John's tool from a miniature rat-tail file by grinding it to a uniform, non-tapered width. It's still a chisel, but with a round bottom that gives a slight dish shape to the fill and is able to smooth the brittle finish at

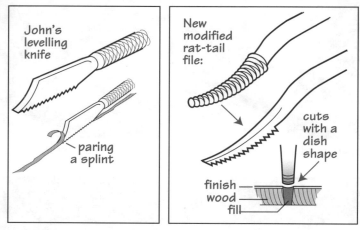

the fill's edges (below, right).

John learned his guitar repair basics, fresh out of high school, in my Ann Arbor, Michigan shop in 1971. Since I'd married his older sister (my wife Joan), it was easy for me to take him on as an apprentice. Around '73, we closed the shop and both of us went to work repairing for the Herb David Guitar Studio. Those were fun times for us, and we made numerous guitar repair discoveries together (like the original 'Neck Jig'). John stayed on with Herb when I moved north to Big Rapids, Michigan to open the "Guitar Hospital" in

1975. Soon John's yearning for a southern clime took him to Tampa, Florida where he opened his own "Guitar Hospital" as the in-house repairman for Thoroughbred Music in 1977.

Today, 18 years later, John is still working as Thoroughbred's main guitar repairman, although the scenery has changed around him. "Man have we grown in 18 years," says John. "Now we're one of the biggest combination retail/mail order music stores in the country. We've even got our own vintage division here in the store, Classic Guitars, managed by Kent Sonenberg and Russell Farrow.

"Our two new stores have repairmen too: Mark Borgmeyer in Sarasota, and Rex Rogers in Clearwater. But our Tampa store's still the hub. The working arrangement I have with

That's John on the right in the photo below—with Kent Sonenberg (left) and Russell Farrow of Thoroughbred's vintage division.

the shop and I go out to meet the customer at the service desk to make the estimate. This keeps 'down time' to a minimum because I can leave when I want. When customers are right in the shop it wastes time, and you're not getting paid for it. At the service desk, the customers expect you to be brief. I return the finished repairs at the service desk, too.

"The percentage arrangement is good because I'm not locked into a fixed salary (I file my own tax returns through my accountant). Of course, this can have its financial ups and downs, but overall it's been great. It's a lot cheaper than having my own shop, and I knew from the beginning that I could never run a business—stocking all the accessories like pickups, strings, hardware, worrying about overhead, and all that—it's just not for me."

John O'Boyle
Thoroughbred Music
Tampa, Florida

Thoroughbred's owner, Elliot Rubinson, has really worked out well, and that's why I've stayed.

"The store gets a percentage of my work each week, and I pay a small fee for the shop space. In return I get the draw of a well-known store, excellent shop space, high visibility, health insurance, and the pride that comes with being a part of a really successful operation. My customers pay the store for the repairs, and when I turn in a worksheet at the end of the week, the store writes me a check.

"When a customer brings in a repair, the desk buzzes me in

INSERTING THE JACK PLATE INTO A TELE

Here's an excerpt from my *Guitar Player* column (Miller-Freeman Publishing), which I thought Trade Secrets readers would appreciate—especially since the tool is now available in our catalog.

Have you ever seen a Telecaster where the output jack, the jack cup, and the jack cup retainer clip (the steel plate fastened into the body) are either loose and wobbly, or else they're hanging from the side of the guitar? It can happen if the guitar is dropped on the output jack with the cord in it, or when someone trips over the cord. A repair shop usually sees this problem *after* everything from drywall screws, duct tape, epoxy glue, or even auto-body filler has been used to fasten the jack and cup back into the body.

The best way to execute this repair, from a vintage standpoint, is to reinstall the original retainer clip solidly into the body by mounting it so the "teeth" bite into new wood, but it's not easy! Out of frustration I made the tool you see here, though it wore out quickly because I made it from aluminum. Afterwards our R&D shop made one of hardened steel. It's destined to become an important new tool which every serious repair shop will appreciate.

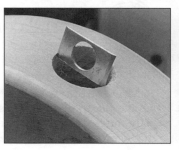

1 The jack retainer plate is as long as the hole is wide, and would slide right in if installed on edge…

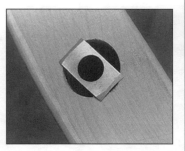

2 …which it isn't. It's installed this way, and the corners "bite" into the wood once the tool installs it.

3 The tool has a stepped-barrel with a clearance hole through it (a bolt slides through the hole). The "nut" has a milled groove to grip the retainer plate. The retainer is bent in a slight U-shape for installation.

4 Tighten the parts together until only snug, and insert it into the hole. The tool, being concentric, keeps the retainer's jack hole on center.

5 Tighten the hex-head bolt until it stops—the plate is flattened and driven into the wood.

6 Remove the tool—the plate's installed!

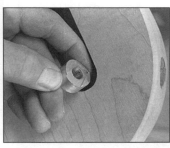

7 The nut comes out through the control cavity.

8 Install the jack and cup, and you're done.

Great Northwoods Building & Repair Seminar 1996

Michigan is gorgeous in September, and there may still be time to sign up for this 4-day repair seminar at Bryan Galloup's Guitar Hospital in Big Rapids, Michigan. There's room for 30 people on a first-come basis. The seminar takes place September 11–14, and this year's instructors are:

- **Frank Ford** (Gryphon Stringed Instruments): *Acoustic Workshop: French-Polishing As A Repair Tool; Fretting; Structural Stuff, and Running A Repair Business.*
- **Roger Fritz** (Gibson Guitar, Nashville): *Gibson Repair Techniques and Authorized Warranty Repairs.*
- **Bryan Galloup**: *Neck Resetting and Problem Resets.*
- **Seymour Duncan** and **Lindy Fralin**: *Pickup Manufacture, Re-winding, and Guitar Electronics—A Combination Workshop.*
- **Yasuhiko Iwanade**: *Vintage Guitar Repair.*
- **Steve Uhrik** (Umanov Guitars): *Finish Restoration and Repair.*
- **Dan Erlewine** (Stewart-MacDonald): *Finish Touch-ups and Antiquing.*
- **Bart Reiter** (Reiter Banjos): *Cutting And Engraving Pearl.*
- **Tim Scheerhorn** (Scheerhorn Resonator Guitars): *Dobro Set-up.*
- **Joe Konkoly** (Elderly Instruments): *Traditional Fretting Techniques & Compression-Fretting Martin Guitars.*

For details, contact Bryan or Susan Galloup at The Guitar Hospital: (616) 796-5611 Fax: (616) 796-3837.

"DO AS I SAY, NOT AS I DO" DEPARTMENT:

I ran into a problem when working with yellow alcohol-soluble dye and superglue that goes to prove once again that one should always test an idea on scrap work first. In this case, I was using yellow Lockwood powdered-aniline stain which had been dissolved in Behkol solvent.

During a neck reset on a late-60s Mossman guitar (bound-fingerboard model), I glued a wedge-shaped basswood shim (a "tongue support") under the tongue, or fingerboard extension to keep the fingerboard in line with the new neck set, and conceal a radical drop-off. I also pieced-in white binding to hide the shim. I used acetone to "melt-in" the slip of binding, and was able to carry on with the work almost immediately.

I color-matched the new plastic to the existing yellowed binding with the yellow alcohol stain, but it turned *pink* when I sealed over it with superglue! It could have been disaster, but I managed to scrape off the pinkish-yellow (and some of the original finish color with it), and then finished the job with lacquer and lacquer shaders.

Conclusion: most stains are mixtures of several colors, and each color can have different solubilities. Be on your toes when using stain, especially an alcohol stain, and particularly the yellows, reds, and ambers. Don't use any finish, especially superglue, over a stain without testing first—testing is much faster than re-doing your work.

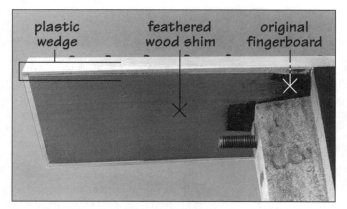

plastic wedge — feathered wood shim — original fingerboard

We now sell the Color-Tone powders instead of Lockwood stains, because we like them better. Our supplier, Jeff Jewitt, is a skilled furniture restorer who is able and willing to formulate colors especially for us. Color-Tone yellow caused me no problem under superglue, but Color-Tone amber (alcohol) "bled" red under lacquer if the dye was dissolved in Behkol solvent (shellac thinner). Jeff advised us to use Color-Tone Reducer to dissolve the alcohol-soluble powders (rather than Behkol), especially with amber, to avoid bleeding. We tested Color-Tone amber powder by dissolving it in both Behkol and Color-Tone Reducer (separate jars) and using each to stain a section of the same maple board. When we sprayed lacquer over them, only the Behkol-thinned stain bled red.

CUTTIN' CORNERS...

Here are two ways to miter corners on plastic bindings, which are especially helpful for b/w/b/w and other laminates . . .

1 MacRostie Method: When Don miters corners in plastic, he does glue the binding strips to the wood, but leave the faces of the mitered corners unglued. Once the glue is dry, he presses the edges of the miter together and acetones them. The result is a cleaner line, because the two edges haven't softened and "smooshed" together, which happens so easily if cement is applied to them. Also, there's no dark "line" of cement between the joint.

2 Gibson-Style Miter Overlap: I did major repairs to the Gibson L-5C mentioned earlier, including rebinding everything. I like the way Gibson miters the bindings on their multi-bound pegheads. If you've ever removed this type of binding you see a joint which looks like the photo shown here. It looks tricky to cut, but it's easy.

First miter and glue the b/w/b/w inner strips (Gibson may do the whole thing together). Then add the outside white strips as in the drawing below, with one strip running past the miter and off the edge (to be trimmed later), and the other strip butting up to it. The result is a type of "lap-joint" which is not in line with the b/w/b/w miter, so that your eye isn't drawn to it. It's a nearly invisible joint!

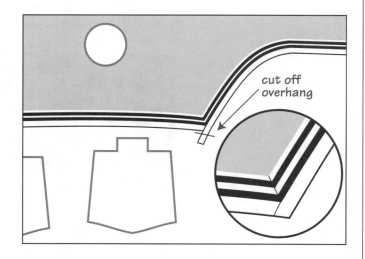

cut off overhang

BRUCE KIZERIEN'S HYBRID HOTROD BELLYCASTER!

Here's a way cool idea from Bruce W. Kizerian in Farmington, Utah:

Dear Stewart-MacDonald:

The quality of your parts, prices, and service are the best I've found. Thanks for an inspiring catalog—I get some wonderful off-beat ideas by reading it backwards! For example, here's a 6-String "Bellycaster" banjo built almost entirely from Stewart-MacDonald parts. I built-up a mahogany heel on one of your vintage necks (because mahogany carves so easily), and mated it to a Whyte Ladie banjo pot. Your dual rim rod set and Vega-style armrest were used on the "banjo" end of the instrument, with Grover tuners at the "guitar" end. The bridge is *two* banjo bridges spliced to form a wider, lightweight 6-string bridge. The only parts which are *not* Stew-Mac are the tailpiece and mounting bracket—both of which I machined from scrap steel and polished to a high luster.

The "Bellycaster" plays like a guitar, sounds like a banjo, and has a balanced sound with a very "live" feeling—and it is loud! The sound quality and playability are exceptional. Reaction from local dealers and fellow musicians has ranged from enthusiasm to accusations of blasphemy—just the response I'd hoped for. Enclosed is a list of all the Stew-Mac parts that I used.

Bruce Kizerian
Farmington, Utah

No. 4276 Neck
No. 910 Whyte Laydie pot outfit
No. 280 Dual rim rod set
No. 1004 Vega-style armrest
No. 908 Grover tuners
No. 266 Banjo bridge
  (2 each, spliced)
No. 672 Behlen Master-Gel
  finish over several shades
  of brown leather dye

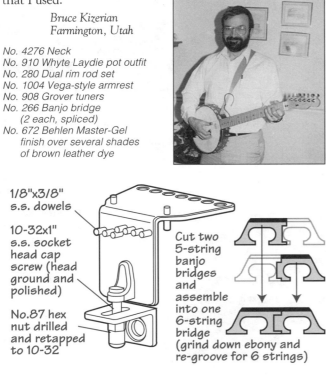

1/8"x3/8"
s.s. dowels

10-32x1"
s.s. socket
head cap
screw (head
ground and
polished)

No.87 hex
nut drilled
and retapped
to 10-32

Cut two 5-string banjo bridges and assemble into one 6-string bridge (grind down ebony and re-groove for 6 strings)

FROM BELGIUM: VERTICAL COLUMN BINDING ROUTER

Hugo Valcke sends this hot tip for routing binding channels:

A metal column is mounted vertically on the workbench. A linear bearing housing carries a wooden block on which the router is fastened—the assembly moves effortlessly up and down the column.

The guitar body rests on a wooden workboard, and is held by the gentle pressure of two threaded bolts touching the endblock and neck block area (use protective cauls). Four threaded levelers, with protective rubber feet, adjust up or down to level the guitar on the workboard. The top (or back) and the sides end up perfectly level and plumb with the router.

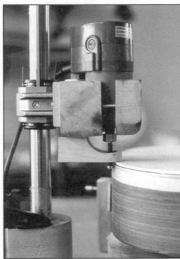

The workboard has casters underneath, and rolls easily in all directions. The cut's width is controlled by a ball bearing on the router bit, and its depth by the small wooden "shoe" under the router. The shoe's contact area is small and close to the edge, so arched surfaces and cutaways can be routed perfectly—the channel is always square to the sides no matter how arched the soundboard or back is!

One hand holds the router, the other hand pushes the "chariot" around. This gives a clean and accurate cut along the entire edge of the guitar. The masking tape along the sides protects against marks of the ball bearing of the router bit touching the wood. This is a very easy set-up that makes cutting channels a non-risky pleasure!

P.S. If any Trade Secrets readers in the U.S. or Canada can help me find a quality magazine(s) on the topic of model railway systems and model scenery, I am grateful. Model railroading is my hobby, and the European magazines are not so good. **Any** help would be great. Contact:

Hugo Valcke
Reparaties Snaarinstrumenten Instrumentenbouw
Munkendoornstraat 62
8500 Kortrijk, Belgium
tel: 056/222102 (from the US: 011 32 56 222 102)

Bearing Supplier: linear bearing assemblies, called "ball-bushing linear motion systems," are available in the U.S. from the Thompson Bearing Co., Inc. of Port Washington, New York. Tel: (800) 645-9357

How (and why) to sharpen the fret slot cleaning knife

Even the best chisels usually need final sharpening and honing when new. The same holds true for the curved blade of our # 4851 fret slot cleaning tool (page 11). The .019"-thick blade is quality tempered steel that has been photochemically machined to the perfect shape needed for prying, levering, and hooking dust and dried glue from fret slots. However, you must sharpen it to remove the ridge left by the manufacturing process. In the photo above, the blade on the left is the way it looks when you receive it; the blade on the right is how you want it to look after final sharpening (like a small claw-shaped scraper with a sharp chisel tip). Here's how to do it:

Important: Cool the blade by dipping it frequently in cold water, to keep from removing the temper.

■ Put a fine (220-grit) belt on your belt sander. Hold the knife handle firmly, and square to the moving belt in the direction shown. Roll the back side of the knife's blade lightly against the belt to flatten and square it, following the curve of the blade.

■ Next, mount a clean sharp 3/8"-diameter grindstone into your Dremel Moto-Tool or other handheld grinder. Run the stone across the inside edge of the curved blade, flattening and squaring it as you did the backside.

Note: Using your Dremel's router base, you can lay the blade on the table for grinding and keep it at 90° to the stone at all times. You can also use this set-up for the backside of the blade and skip the 220-grit belt sanding if you choose.

There are LOTS ways to use the slot cleaning knife...

If you're interested in fretting and would like to learn more about it, you should read our book, *Fretwork Step-By-Step*. It'll get you thinking and doing on your own, while showing you the right way to use a variety of specialty tools such as our #4851 Fret Slot Cleaning Knife (page 11).

Whether you're hammering, pressing, or gluing in frets, there's nothing more annoying than a fret that won't go down because the fret slot's too shallow or dirty. After first measuring a clean fret slot's depth, we often deepen it, and remove debris, using any or all of three tools. These include small saws, small cutterbits powered by a Dremel Moto-Tool, or a fret slot cleaning knife.

Years ago, I sacrificed a chip carving knife to the grinder to make a hooked blade for cleaning fret slots. Then when I visited my friend Frank Ford at Gryphon Stringed Instruments in Palo Alto, California, I found that he also lived by the knife. Soon Stew-Mac's Don MacRostie and Todd Sams combined the advantages of both our knives to make our #4851 fret slot cleaning knife, handle and all. With its replaceable blades, it's one fretting tool that I couldn't be without. Here's how to use it:

■ As a glue prying tool. Both hands are needed, as a lever for prying the hardened glue, and to control the blade and keep it from slipping up and onto the fretboard.
■ As a slot bottom scraper. Lever it like a steamshovel.
■ As a corner cleaner on bound fingerboards. Scrape and hook down into the corner or scoop upward like a steam shovel.

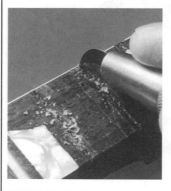

■ As a fret slot wall cleaner. Work both sides of the slot separately to remove glue.

YOU'LL FIND EXTRA TRADE SECRETS
THROUGHOUT THE CATALOG!

TradeSecrets!
Hot tips & inside scoops. Editor: Dan Erlewine

VOLUME 27

Finishing

As part of our "Shop Guide Series," we've been working on a finishing book for some time. Though the book is titled *Guitar Finishing Step By Step*, it's also a method book for finishing banjos, mandolins, dulcimers, and other instruments.

The book describes lacquer finishing (either nitrocellulose or waterborne), but the same techniques and schedules apply to other media. The first half of the book boils finishing down to the **ten basic steps** listed here, and explains each one clearly. The second half follows these steps, giving schedules and recipes for specific finishes.

1. Wood preparation
2. Stains on bare wood
3. Wash coating
4. Filling open-pored wood
5. Primer for solid color
6. Solid color coats
7. Sealer coats
8. Sunbursts, shaders, toners & touch-ups
9. Clear topcoats
10. Final sanding & rub-out

From the pages of **Guitar Finishing Step-By-Step**, *the upcoming addition to the Stewart-Macdonald ShopGuide Series.*

1 **Wood preparation:** As you'll see, the last step of the wood prep stage is to blow the guitar clean and then degrease it using a rag dampened with an appropriate cleaner, usually naphtha. It doesn't hurt to *start* the wood prep stage with a light cleaning either since many lumber mills spray wax or silicone lubricants on the beds and blades of saws, jointers, planers, knives and cutter heads. Traces of these lubricants can remain on the wood throughout the building process, and lacquer sprayed over wax or silicone may crawl, shrivel, or fisheye (crater) as in the photos shown here.

To clean new wood, wipe the surfaces using three separate clean rags, dampened (not dripping wet) with:

- Naphtha to remove waxes;
- Mineral spirits to remove silicone;
- Ammonia and water to remove any mineral spirits and silicone left on the surface (a cup of ammonia in a gallon of warm water is the right mix). Clean the wood in that order, and you'll probably never have fisheyes in the finish, or poor adhesion.

Stripping and refinishing: Follow the instructions for whichever stripper you use, and let it do its work. How you clean the work *after* the stripping, however, can effect the finish. Follow the cleaning steps listed here. Rinse off any remaining stripper gunk with a rag dampened in warm water, then wipe the guitar with these five chemicals:

- An appropriate thinner for the old finish, to remove any slight finish residue and stripper remaining on the surface (lacquer thinner would be most common, so avoid plastic binding.
- Alcohol to remove any dye or shellac which may be present.
- Naphtha for wax.
- Mineral spirits for silicone.
- Ammonia and water. **Use five different rags!**

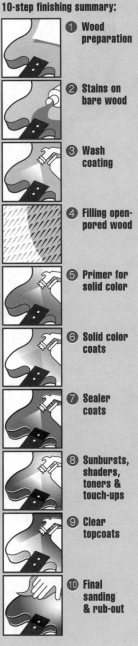

10-step finishing summary:

1. Wood preparation
2. Stains on bare wood
3. Wash coating
4. Filling open-pored wood
5. Primer for solid color
6. Solid color coats
7. Sealer coats
8. Sunbursts, shaders, toners & touch-ups
9. Clear topcoats
10. Final sanding & rub-out

Silicone

Wax

*From the pages of **Guitar Finishing Step-By-Step**,
the upcoming addition to the Stewart-Macdonald ShopGuide Series.*

① **Wood prep/cleaning (continued):** A clean brush will remove most sawdust trapped in open-pore woods, but compressed air is best. Once the piece is clean, never handle it without gloves or at least very clean hands. If you scratch your nose or face, wash the oil off your hand. Although it's said that body oil is not a problem to finishing as are petroleum-based oils, it should still make you nervous to transfer body oil onto bare wood or a finish. If you're finishing something, use naphtha to degrease door handles, telephone receivers, lamps, and anything that might be touched by someone who just ate a hamburger and a bag of chips before dropping by to visit—or even worse, used Armor-All on their guitar case…

*Excerpted from **Guitar Finishing Step-By-Step**.*

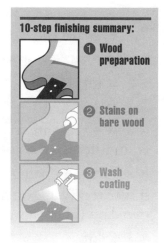

10-step finishing summary:

① Wood preparation

② Stains on bare wood

③ Wash coating

We researched *Guitar Finishing Step-By-Step* by speaking with fellow builders, repair techs, and lutherie teachers: "What part of finishing was hardest for you to master?" "Where do you think a beginner should start?," etc. As time goes by, we'll print their observations here in Trade Secrets—like this advice from John Reuter, director of training at the Roberto-Venn School Of Luthiery in Phoenix:

"Being able to control gun distance, and laying on a good even finish, *that's* the key. Good gun technique takes a lot of practice, and finishing in general takes really good hand skills. If a student can sand decently (some need to develop an eye for it), the prep stuff is pretty well laid out for them. The hardest part of the finishing process is laying down even coats, and the final sanding and rub-out.

"Our spraying method is very close to that used by the Santa Cruz Guitar Company. SCGC's Richard Hoover has helped our program immensely,

and some of our graduates work at Santa Cruz. Our students finish their acoustic instruments in a clear natural finish, without stain or other colorants. Any student who can learn to prep the wood and apply a clean, flat, professional finish, will then be able to tackle colored finishes. Once the instrument has been prepped, wash coated, and grain-filled, we spray the nitrocellulose lacquer finish in three days. Of course Phoenix is very dry, and one of the better climates for finishing.

"We use McFadden ready-to-spray lacquer

John Reuter (right) at the Roberto-Venn School of Luthiery

which requires very little thinning (about 1/2 gallon thinner to 5 gallons of lacquer), so each coat has a high solids content. Using a different brand of lacquer, such as Behlen which is thinned 50/50, it might take you a couple of days longer."

Guitar Finishing Step-By-Step teaches exact finish recipes by following the ten basic finishing steps. Here's how the Roberto-Venn School's finishing schedule follows these ten steps:

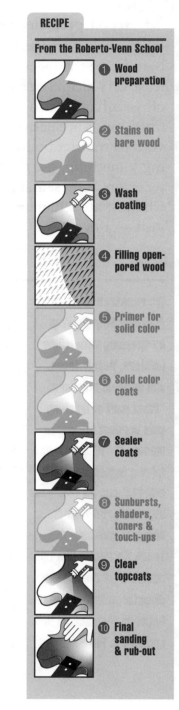

RECIPE

From the Roberto-Venn School

1. Wood preparation
2. Stains on bare wood
3. Wash coating
4. Filling open-pored wood
5. Primer for solid color
6. Solid color coats
7. Sealer coats
8. Sunbursts, shaders, toners & touch-ups
9. Clear topcoats
10. Final sanding & rub-out

① **Prepare** the wood. *[This step is detailed at length in the book, but we don't have the space for that detail here in Trade Secrets—Ed.]*

② (Skip.) *[This is a basic clear finish—the color is the wood itself.]*

③ **Wash coat** with vinyl sealer using two well-thinned coats (allow 45 minutes drying between coats). The wash coat keeps the grain filler from coloring the wood and the wood bindings we use.

④ **Fill** the open grain on the sides, neck, and back, but avoid the spruce top! Wipe off the excess filler and hang the instrument to dry for two days (allow a week if you have time).

⑤ (Skip.)

⑥ (Skip.)

⑦ **Seal** in the filler by spraying one light coat of vinyl sealer (the light coat avoids bleeding the filler). Let dry one-half to one hour, then go to Step 9.

⑧ (Skip.)

⑨ **Top coat** with lacquer. This is the same day as Step 7, and the first day of three days of spraying four coats a day...

▪ **Day One:** Spray the first coat of lacquer light, let it dry 1/2 hour, then spray three wet coats one hour apart. Let dry overnight.

▪ **Day Two:** In the morning, level-sand the finish half way with 150- or 180-grit "fre-cut" (open-coat stearated) paper on the orbital sander. This "scuff sanding" will give today's coats more to bite into. Spray four wet coats of lacquer with one hour drying time between each coat. Spray the last coat (coat 4) only on the back, sides, and neck—not the top (it doesn't need any more lacquer).

At day's end evaluate the finish, look for any "drop fills" that may be needed, and apply them with a brush. Allow overnight drying.

▪ **Day Three:** Level the finish completely using the orbital sander and 150- or 180-grit fre-cut. Spray four wet coats on everything but the top, allowing one hour drying between coats.

Let instrument sit for two weeks.

⑩ **Final Sanding & Buffing:** Wet-sand out all imperfections with 600-grit using a palm sander. Follow with 1000- or 1200- grit, or use both. Next, buff (we use Stew-Mac's buffer—we have two of them), using Menzerna fine compound (tan), and follow with the extra-fine (white) only if you feel it's necessary.

Elliot John-Conry lives a mile from Stewart-MacDonald's Guitar Shop Supply in Athens, Ohio—the perfect location for a 15-year old guitar lover and do-it-yourselfer. When he's not playing guitar, studying, or odd-jobbing for "tool money," Elliot can be found in his bedroom

"The fingerboard had way too much relief. With the truss rod and strings loose, I forced a backbow into it by clamping near the center with my dad's carpenter's level for leverage. It's better now, but it needs to be leveled and refretted—it'll be my first fret job. I'm also doing

Cyanide & Superglue

Elliot's parents let his band "Cyanide" practice in their basement daily—with about a million friends hanging out! From left to right are Elliot (bass), Jeremy Valeda (guitar), Nate Gates (guitar), and Ben Evans (drums).

With a razor-knife, Elliot cleans up the "gold leaf" before spraying clear.

workshop hot-rodding and repairing guitars. "Stewart-MacDonald was a great discovery," he says. "I've already owned at least six instruments since starting to play four years ago, and that's *only* because I can fix them myself. What started as a necessity turned into the most fun thing I've ever done.

"Now all the guys in our band, 'Cyanide,' are starting to work on their guitars too, but I'm the most serious. I just *found* a 'Phantom' bass in a trash can downtown that was covered in paint and nail polish, but with the original finish still there. The paint flaked off easily, and the nail polish came off with nail polish remover which I diluted with water.

my first complete refinish, on a little plywood-topped Jose Masymas classical guitar made in Valencia, Spain.

"The finish was gone and there were two areas in the upper bouts of the top where the spruce had been sanded-through into the plies below. I hid the blemishes with a camouflage design painted in Testor's gold metallic enamel. It looks kind of like a fancy Ovation I saw in *Guitar Player* magazine.

"After reading about testing on scrap in Trade Secrets Volume 26, I was afraid that Behlen lacquer might not work over enamel. So I put gold on a test board, dried it two weeks, and sprayed lacquer on that first—spraying the first coats pretty dry before building up a gloss. It worked, so now I'm gonna spray the guitar."

HOT TIP!! A friend, Andre Bohren, applies superglue to slivers of white plastic (cut from a Fender guitar pick) which Elliot presses into the worn plastic nut slots of his "Tele Star" guitar.

Elliot uses a clamp, caul, two blocks of wood, and a long level to force backbow into the neck of his "found" guitar. Notice the custom-made workboard/neck rest. It was a recent birthday present from a friend, it helps keep the table clean enough to do schoolwork between repairs.

TradeSecrets!

From the CONSTRUCTION BUSINESS to the CONSTRUCTION OF A BUSINESS

Frank Mirigliano owns and operates "Music Repair Service" from his basement shop in Greensburg, Pennsylvania. Though he'd been fixing guitars since age 14, Frank (now 40) didn't go full-time until four years ago. Frank and his wife Cindy have a three-year old daughter, Katie, and twins on the way—the makings of a nice little family band. Frank's an active professional bass player, and he also teaches a half-dozen students weekly.

"Having been in the construction business for years as a general contractor, I approached repairing like a professional—with a business plan and marketing strategy for music stores without an in-store repairman. I introduced myself to stores over the phone, sent them a letter detailing my business plan, and followed-up quickly with a second phone call to set up an in-person interview. I didn't just waltz in wearing jeans with holes in the knees and say 'I fix guitars, man.' You must offer a firm handshake, look 'em in the eye, and let them know you're the real thing.

"I began by picking up and delivering to a number of stores, but as people heard about me, walk-in business developed. Now a yellow pages advertisement begun seven months ago has finally started bringing in work, too. I had to cull the stores down to just a few very active ones that I'm glad to be associated with. Currently, sixty percent of my work is direct, and forty percent is from the stores. A store gets twenty percent of the labor, and sells the parts and strings. In return, I get a good volume of work, name recognition with the store, and there's no time lost talking to customers.

"My partner, Rick Struzzi, is an electronics wizard. Together we hold a patent on a design for the SMR pickups which we build—pickups with exceptional lows and highs, and a pretty flat response against the whole audio spectrum. Rick has his own shop, but we advertise jointly, and together we can fix any kind of guitar or amplifier. We've both made more money in our lives, but we're able to make a living doing what we love.

"Your Trade Secrets 'Blue Book' of repair prices helped me set my pricing. I didn't want to start too cheap and give the perception that my *work* was cheap. I wasn't new to fixing guitars, just charging for it, and you gotta start high enough to be legitimate. A few of the bread-and-butter jobs like nuts, saddles, set-up, and fretwork, I kept low for awhile so I could get *lots* of experience on such good money makers. Here's my basic price list as of summer, 1996:"

Frank Mirigliano,
"Music Repair Service,"
Greensburg, PA

Nut (Bone, 6-string)
Shape, fit, material included $42
Saddle (Bone)
Shape, fit, material included $48

Neck
Truss rod adjustments .... $18 – $24
Warp or bow Heat treatment $54
Plane and refret .... $180 – $220
Reset w/o binding $250
Reset w/binding $300
New neck (Martin style) $240

Bridge
Reglue .... $36 – $60
Replacement
(Factory bridge (bridge+labor, bone saddle extra) $78
Custom-made bridge (saddle included) $120
Custom-made with compensated saddle $180

Top Repairs
Bridge plate veneer (retainer) .... $24 – $36
Replace small bridge plate $84
Replace large bridge plate $144
Level existing plate/top .... $42 – $60

Fret work (Set-up, nut work, etc. extra)
File fret ends (new guitars) $24
Dress existing frets (level, crown, polish) .... $42 – $60

Maple fingerboard
Refinish $120
Touch-up .... (price on request)

Refret
With binding $180
Without binding $150
Replace single frets .... first fret: $15
With binding (each) $10
Without binding (each) $7.50
Repair worn fretboard .... $36 – $60
                                                    (additional)

Acoustic bracing, back, side, and top repair
Reglue loose braces .... $30 – $90
Crack repair (first inch $10.00) .... $6 – $12/inch

Pickguard
Reglue/replace (includes parts) .... $30 – $60

Intonation/Action
Realign archtop bridge $24

Height adjustments
Nut or saddle, raise or lower .... $18 – $36
Lower bridge and saddle (shave bridge) .... $36 – $60
Compensated saddle $60

Clean and polish instrument $24/hour

Tuners
Replace with retrofit .... $24.
Redrill and bore .... $24—$60

FRANK'S CUSTOMIZED CLAMP PUTS THE HEAT ON A CRACKED GUITAR TOP

Frank Mirigliano (photo at right—also see related story on page 60) recently undid a less-than-perfect top crack repair (the two sides of the crack had not been glued level with each other) by heating a block of aluminum and clamping it against the crack from the inside to loosen the glue. To quickly and accurately locate the heated caul along the crack's length and in between the angled tone bars, he fastened the caul to a long Waverly clamp with the bottom "foot" inverted:

"Drill a hole in the back side of the caul and thread it onto the exposed threaded rod so it can't swivel out of the way at the wrong moment. You'll notice in the photo that I had to spring the clamp open some, but it worked and now it's a 'dedicated' tool.

"Before becoming a contractor, I was a liberal arts major in college; in other words, trained to do absolutely nothing. What I did learn in college was how to talk to people, and especially how to listen—a most important skill in business, since you must be able to communicate with your customers."

superglue here

HOT TIP: HOT STUFF ON THE TIP!

Frank Mirigliano (see related story on page 60) has a clever method for fastening battery clips to the neck block on the inside of an acoustic guitar: "I've never been happy with double-stick tape to hold the battery clip," says Frank. "I screw the clip to the endblock. After starting the hole with a gimlet, I use yellow-label 'Hot-Stuff' to superglue the screw to the tip of a small phillips screwdriver—accelerating it for added strength. Then I power-drive the screw right in without slipping, and snap the screwdriver free. For some reason the glue always seems to stay with the screwdriver when it breaks free—and I don't care why. The glue scrapes off the tip easily.

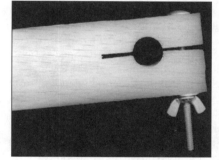

"Here's my simplest tool (at left). It's a round object holder for the drill press. It holds objects flat on the drill press table. Make one each time you drill a hole into a round object, and eventually you'll have a good selection.

"The most important tool in my shop is in this box —it's my customer mailing list. With it I can track each customer and every job that I've done for them. Occasionally I do small mailings offering specials, parts discounts, new services, or just encouraging them to visit. It works for me!"

The Greatest Neck-Jig

Mitchell Miller operates "Gatorhead Guitars" in San Rafael, Ca, where he lives with his wife Mary and their seven-year-old daughter Dana. A builder and repairman since the late 1970s, the 43-year-old luthier is also at home in a machine shop—proof is the awesome neck-jig which he designed and built. While Mitch hasn't said he'll make more, he said he *might*, so anyone interested may contact him. *[If he makes a run of these, I'm buying one! — Dan]*

Along with his own workload, Mitch spends two days a week at "The Magic Flute," a music store owned by his friend Mike Mitchell (Mitchells are coming and going here). "Mike specialized in brass and woodwinds for years," says Mitch, "then six years ago he opened a guitar department. Now we're dealers for Martin, Gibson, Fender, Washburn, and others. I handle the small repairs and set-up on both store stock and customer instruments. Hard stuff like neck resets, fret jobs, and broken necks, I take to my shop. I'm good friends with Mike Mitchell, general manager Tom Holmes, and Mike Kramer, who heads the guitar department, which makes the 'Flute' a great place to work. Here's Mitch:

"I build what I call 'road' instruments. They're stand-ins for vintage guitars that players are afraid to take on the road. By combining the favorite aspects of a customer's vintage piece—neck shape, weight, feel, or sound—and using my own design ideas, I satisfy them without building a direct copy. The neck-jig idea is from you, Dan, though I changed it to suit my needs.

"Mine's not a bench, it's a welded frame of special lightweight 1"-square tubing mounted on two steel L-beams extending from my bench. I'm making a second jig mount from two free-standing poles, or stanchions (shown below). I'll drill holes in the shop floor to drop the poles into when the jig's in use. It'll be nice to walk completely around it, don't you think?

"The 3/8" steel jig-rods are capped with thin cork glued to the slightly-domed tops. I've used up to three dial indicators at a time on the jig to measure the deflection and twist of the peghead and neck. A difference of .004" to .008" in twist, from treble to bass side, is not unusual. Once jigged, the *slightest* pressure on the neck makes the indicator needles jump. It was only then that I realized how sensitive a guitar neck is, and why the neck-jig is so valuable."

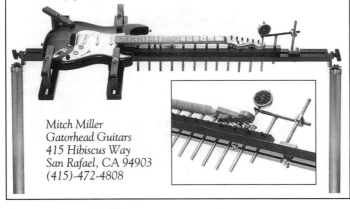

Mitch Miller
Gatorhead Guitars
415 Hibiscus Way
San Rafael, CA 94903
(415)-472-4808

From the Luthier's tacklebox

Dear Dan: Realizing the difficulties of wiring a hollow body guitar, I'd like to tell Trade Secrets readers how I proceed. Let me call this method the "Puppet-On-Strings Theatre In Lutherie," because it's like working a marionette.

As I am a fly angler, I make use of fishing line and fishing lead weights (covered in rubber for finish protection), to guide potentiometers into their exact position after soldering. There are many useful fishing knots, and this particular one is a 'ring knot,' which expands when you pull on one side, and shrinks if you pull on the other (shown above).

■ Loosen the hex nut with a wrench, but don't remove it completely.
■ Tighten the knots onto the respective potentiometer shafts.
■ Remove the hex nut and slip it over the line toward the weight.
■ Extract the pots one at a time, pulling the fishing line with it. I solder the pots on a 'pallette' made from fishing cork.
■ Pull the lines, and each pot goes back where it belongs—pull all the lines at the same time. The nuts will slide down the line toward the pots.

My real love is building mandolins. In Italy F-5 style mandolins are very rare, and I've built this according to the Roger Siminoff book!

Cordially yours,
Carlo Doria,
Genoa, ITALY

YOU'LL FIND EXTRA TRADE SECRETS
THROUGHOUT THE CATALOG!

TradeSecrets!
Hot tips & inside scoops. Editor: Dan Erlewine

VOLUME 28

A pickup winder from down under!

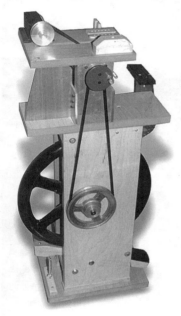

Kevin O'Brien, of Victoria, Australia, credits Gary Brawer in the video "Shoppin in San Franciso," and Lindy Fralin in the "Pickups & Guitar Electronics" video (from the 1995 Northwoods Seminar), for inspiring him to build the pickup winder you see here. Says Kevin: "This machine, for all its peculiarity, winds beautifully with lots of control, and the gentle torque reminiscent of an old steam engine."

Yours faithfully,
Kevin O'Brien
28 Citriodora Walk
Vermont South, Melbourne,
Victoria 3133, Australia

A footbrake (left pedal) can slow, or stop instantly, the treadle-operated flywheel (right pedal) without breaking the wire. Note the adjustable hand rest (black walnut), and mechanical counter*. The white acrylic back screen is an "eyesaver," and the vertical nylon fingers are "limiters" to keep the hand-traversed wire on course. (These details are best seen in the photo at upper left.)

The thin drilled wooden plates on top of the machine are used as spacers when Kevin mounts the bobbin holder (thick wood blocks w/beveled edges in the photos) for winding. "If I add a spacer and mount the bobbin's *top* plate to the bobbin holder," writes Kevin, "I get a clockwise wind. If I mount the bobbin's *bottom* plate to the bobbin holder *without* the spacer, I get a counterclockwise wind. The spacer's only purpose is to compensate for the projecting mangets at the top plate and hold them captive. A center screw holds everything in place, and a catchplate on the side of the bobbin holder grabs the bobbin and stops it from free-spinning."

* We found a variety of counters available from the Grainger Company: Call (800) 323-0620 for a dealer near you.

12-string tuners

Ralph Bown is one of England's finest luthiers, and renowned for the Stella-type 12-strings he builds. He also builds other custom instruments—such as Martin Simpson's Koa-wood baritone guitar. Wanting high quality 12-string tuners which would be appropriate for his guitars, Ralph had to make his own. He credits fellow UK luthier Bill Dinsdale for showing him this trick…

"We join two sets of Schaller A-style mandolin machines. They are a nice quality open-geared tuner with small round pearl buttons and a compact spacing. The innermost gear is removed from each set and the plates mated with sort of a jigsaw-shaped dovetail. Follow the lines in the engraving for an almost invisible joint. Cut the 'male' plate first, and then set both sets into the headstock for correct spacing before scribing around the male to get a nice clean fit with the second plate."

Ralph S. Bown Luthier
The Old Coach House,
1, Paver Lane,
Walmgate, York
YO1 2TS, England

The Guitar Medic Has A Quick Way To Heal A Bad Break!

Dear Stew-Mac:

I've had my share of broken or cracked headstocks, and have grown weary of using clamps, blocks and cauls, etc. At the local Home Depot I found a "rachet cargo strap," which makes a great new repair tool.

1. Run a loop of heavy-gauge wire through two tuner holes, and another at the bottom strap button (like a violin tailpiece strap).

2. Glue the cracked area on the head stock, fasten the rachet strap to the cables, and then rachet the strap until the glue oozes out of the cracks and the head stock is perfectly in line.

3. Let this sit for twenty four hours, add she's done!

Ed Essayen, Guitar Medic, Lake Park, Florida

1929 Binding Restored!

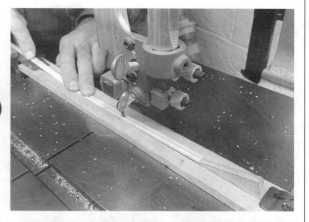

From Ken Fallon:

Dear Trade Secrets Readers,

No sooner had I read about the router table binding trimmer in Trade Secrets Volume 26 (see pages 47-54), than a 1929 Gibson L-5 guitar waltzes in the door needing its fingerboard binding replaced. Most of the original binding was missing, but enough remained to show me what to look for: a white/black/white laminate (.090"/.030"/.060" from the top down) measuring .034" thick.

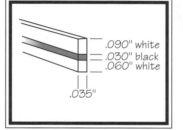

.090" white
.030" black
.060" white
.035"

As verification, I looked at several other L-5s from the same period (I live in New York, you know) only to find that *their* fingerboard binding had already been replaced—and not with anything close to the scraps I had. Apparently, finding the old-style L-5 binding unavailable, whoever rebound those fingerboards made do with what they could find. I was determined to *restore* this binding, not just replace it!

When Stew-Mac's R&D shop offered to let me test-drive the most recent prototype of their binding trimmer, I was in luck! Here's how it can turn two pieces of ordinary 1/4" x .090" binding (No. 3331 white and No. 3338 black) into vintage L-5 w/b/w binding right before your very eyes…

■ Lay the strips flat and saw them down the middle. Cut a groove (a "rabbet") of approximately the binding's size into a long strip of wood. Push the strip into the running saw blade, then spring-clamp this fixture to the bandsaw table. The jig centers the binding to the saw blade and supports the cut as the binding is pushed through (photo 1). The wedge-shaped "ramp" at the rear of the saw blade guides the sawed strips up and over the spring clamp. The result: four strips measuring .090" x (*approximately*) .125".

■ Rout ("joint") the sawed edges smooth, put these jointed edges against the router fence, and trim them to .090". The result: two white and two black strips measuring .090" x .090" and with perfect edges.

①

②

③

④

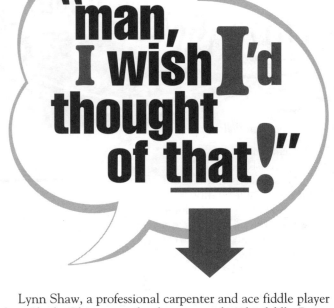

"**man, I wish I'd thought of that!**"

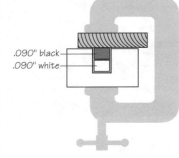

.090" black
.090" white

■ Glue the black to the white with acetone. Cut a slot .090" wide and .170" deep in a block of teflon and clamp a scrap of wood on top to put downward pressure on the strips as you acetone them and pull them through (see left). The result: two w/b strips .090" X .180". Let dry several hours or overnight.

■ Run the glued strips through the trimmer, removing black until it measures .120" (photo 2). Next, edge-glue another .090" white to the black and let it dry. The result is a w/b/w strip measuring .210" tall.

■ Trim the bottom white until the piece measures .180"—the desired binding height in this case.

■ Thickness the binding by standing it on edge (photo 3) and trimming one side smooth. Flip the smooth side against the fence and trim the other side. Work the .090" thickness down to around .035" to .040" (which is as thin as this trimmer can accurately thickness strips). The result: a final thickness of .035", easily scraped to fit by hand (photo 4).

Be careful! As the binding gets thin, don't try to remove more than .005" or .010" per pass.

That's it—now I've gotta choose a binding glue that won't damage the finish too much. Hot hide glue will do a good job of holding plastic to wood and metal (the fret ends) in a case like this and it cleans up easily. Dan, we *must* have that tool!

Ken Fallon

Thanks, Ken!
Ken Fallon repairs and builds guitars at Sadowsky Guitars in New York City, where he has worked since 1989.

Lynn Shaw, a professional carpenter and ace fiddle player from Shade, Ohio, wanted to fix a top crack on his fiddle. Being an old friend and bandmate of Elderly Instrument's President Stan Werbin, Lynn is familiar with stringed instrument repair work, although not a professional. Since he'd have to remove the top to execute the repair properly and then reglue it, he mixed fresh hot hide glue for the job and planned to borrow a number of clamps from a luthier living next door.

On glue-up night, the pot was hot and waiting, but Lynn found that his neighbor wouldn't be home until late. Not wanting to wait, and using real country ingenuity, Lynn made his own clamps by cutting 3/4" cross-sections from "Schedule 40" thick-walled (1/4") PVC pipe, slicing them open, and spreading them apart for clamp pressure. Try this—the possibilities are endless!

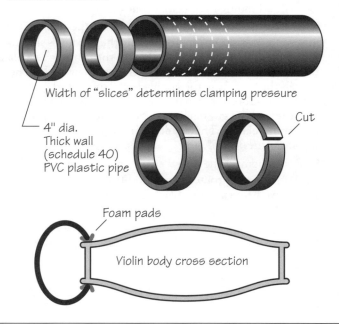

Width of "slices" determines clamping pressure

4" dia.
Thick wall
(schedule 40)
PVC plastic pipe

Cut

Foam pads

Violin body cross section

"Erle's breakdown"

Here's a spray booth that can be set up or broken down in seconds. Easy to make and reasonably inexpensive, the "booth" works well for limited-spraying in a tight space like my basement shop. A window on the far side of the basement *must* be left open to create an air flow, however, so the weather controls my spraying. I've included a floorplan of my basement to show this air flow.

Solvent-based finishes need hanging time in a room with good air movement to evacuate the solvents. I won't work in the room if I can *smell* the finish, since it's not healthy to breathe solvent vapors. That's why professionals use dedicated spray rooms and booths. So, after spraying, I exit the room for at least a half-hour, leaving the fan on and the window open. (Those of you with outbuildings and garages are lucky!)

Recently, I converted the old cement and brick-walled coal room in my basement to a room where I hang instruments to cure. That room also has an explosion-proof fan. I could even spray in there if I wanted, but the low ceiling and slanted "coal chute" floor make it difficult.

My vent fan is the Model 7F448 fan assembly from the Grainger Company. It has a totally enclosed explosion-proof motor (6K7340), a spark-proof aluminum blade (46386), and a steel venturi (4C545). It sold for $281.25 dealer price. You can contact Grainger at (800) 323-0620 for a dealer near you.

Dan Erlewine, Editor

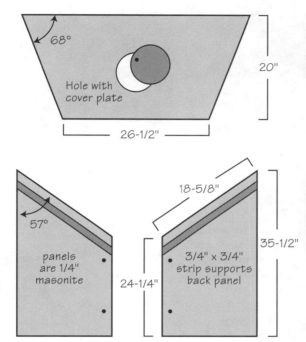

This drawing is of my current "booth" which is smaller than the one in the photos, and has no top. An access hole, with cover, allows me to reach through the back to open or shut the window.

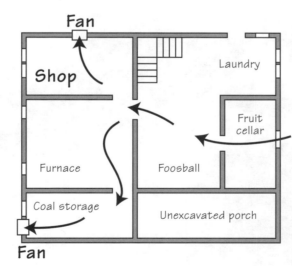

Layout of basement showing air flow.

The invisible spray booth.

The fan is "boxed" into the outside of the window frame with wire mesh (1/2" squares) on both sides, to keep animals, or humans from the blades.

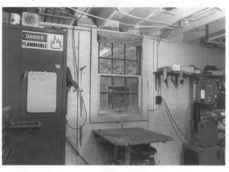

Inside, the window sash shuts normally. A general purpose worktable for sanding, stripping, mixing, etc. sits over the belt-sander, and lifts off easily.

Each wing hangs on two pins. The wooden rails support the angled back and the top. With the back and top in place, one elastic "bungee" cord stretched between the top two corners (not visible in photo) holds them in place. A filter-frame is placed in front of the opening to collect overspray. Crude, eh?

Making a new "old" neck for a vintage Les Paul

Rod Hannah, of Hannah Guitars in Saint John, New Brunswick, Canada has built and repaired guitars since 1980. Rod shares a well-equipped woodworking shop with cabinetmakers Brad Smith, Joe Bartlett, and Fred Whelply. Hannah combined his cabinetmaking and lutherie skills to build a replacement neck for the 1956 Gibson Les Paul "Black Beauty" shown here. Although the neck had disappeared, the body and parts were in perfect shape

and luckily the original serial number had been recorded and left in the case! Here are a few of the tricks Rod used for a great reproduction . . .

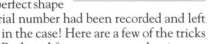

■ He glued the neck drawing from Stew-Mac's No. 857 Les Paul plans to a 1/4" piece of plywood to make a "storyboard" of all neck measurements, then fit the storyboard's tenon to find the right neck angle before touching the actual neck blank.

■ "I had a '58 'TV'-Finish Les Paul Special in the shop to make comparisons with as I worked, and one of our larger router bits fit its neck shape perfectly," said Hannah. "I hadn't realized that the neck's shape was part of a perfect circle. Next I laid out three circles (1-7/8", 2", 2-1/4") in a piece of cardboard and slid them along the Les Paul special neck until they fit snugly at the 1st, 4th, and 9th frets respectively. I used the template often to shape the new neck. (Photo, upper right.)

■ "Before gluing in the new neck, I carved channels into the tenon to help any future luthier steam the neck out if it ever breaks again.

■ "Later, I traced the Les Paul Special's serial number along with several other vintage Gibson numbers, then cut and pasted the numbers together into the correct serial number. A local print shop scanned my paste-up to make a rubber stamp that looks original. (Middle photo at far right.)

"According to an expert at Mandolin Brothers, the serial number color of a '56 black Les Paul was the same yellowish 'Limed Mahogany,' or 'TV'

#857 plan glued onto 1/4" plywood

Easier to see and fit a plywood blank to determine neck angle

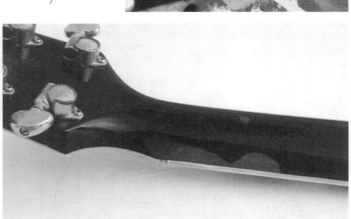

finish of many Les Paul Specials, so I was in luck! Into lacquer sanding sealer I mixed Stew-Mac's 'Tints-All' universal colors in yellow, burnt umber, and white to create the yellow."

■ "I antiqued the finish with shellac for an aged color, and then created appropriate 'wear spots' on the neck (photo above) by copying the neck finish of a well-worn Gibson J-45."

OK out there, who's got the original neck?

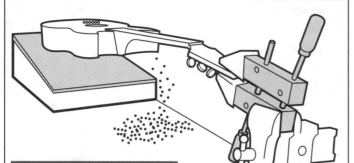

Keeping the guitar body up and away from benchtop debris

After working at the Gibson Guitar Company from 1976 til 1984 on an R&D team with Richard Schneider and Tim Shaw, Abraham ("Abe") Wechter, of Wechter Guitars in Paw Paw, Michigan, became world-renowned as a builder/ artist who combined great sound and playability with super tasteful and incredibly-executed ornamentation. He has built guitars for John McLaughlin, Steve Howe, Al DiMeola, B.B. King, John Denver, Earl Klugh, and Jonaf Hellborg, to name a few.

Now, the "Pathmaker," an acoustic-electric guitar recently unveiled by Abe and his partner Michael Davidson, will most likely encourage acoustic guitar lovers to try an electric, and vice-versa. While retaining the quality sound and striking good looks for which Abe's guitars are known, the Pathmaker can be set up to play like the best elec-

Abe and the Pathmaker with Frank Ford.

tric guitars. This is thanks to a revolutionary (patent applied for) neck-to-body design which allows the player access to 19 frets clear of the body!

With the guitars about to start "rolling off the line" Abe's ready for the fret work, nut work, and set-up which make or break any guitar. His setup benches are unique—and it's a guarantee that he won't get any shavings, bone dust, or powdered fretwire on his shiny new guitars.

BENCHTOP TIP FROM ABE WECHTER:

A padded parallel-jawed wooden screw clamp in a VersaVise holds the peghead, while an angled ramp contacts the body at only one point. All residue falls onto the workbench.

Balloon jack for guitar top braces

"Dear Stew-Mac:

Enclosed are photos of two devices that I frequently use in my shop. One is a fixture for holding necks to be sprayed— it uses four long wood screws with brass tubing to provide a "stand-off" from the handle. The third is a brace repair jack fabricated from a blood pressure cuff. The PVC cylinder contains a water balloon which inflates to push the piston upward, putting pressure on a brace. A football-shaped base allows placement in almost any location while affording a fairly large footprint."

*Dave Wellman
Guitar Works,
Albuquerque, New Mexico*

GUITAR WORKS

Fretted-instrument
repair & modification
20 years experience

David Wellman: Luthier

4300 Hilton NE
Albuquerque, NM 87110
505-884-6950

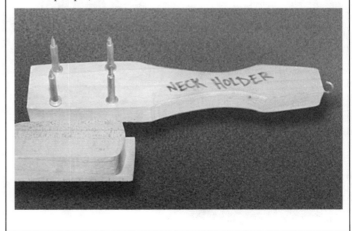

Scarf-joint creates longer binding

Here's a Hot Tip from the '96 Great Northwoods Building and Repair Seminar. Resophonic guitar expert Tim Scheerhorn was describing the inconvenience of having to stop in the middle of the binding process to butt-joint two pieces of the ivoroid edge-binding he wraps around a top or back. Immediately a seminar student walked into the tool room and with a table-saw, a router, and a half-hour's time, made the simple jig shown here. It's a tool for trimming and scarf-jointing two lengths of binding. It works great, and produces an invisible line! Do this the day before you need the binding, and you can treat the joined strips as one!

1 A table-sawed groove the width of the binding thickness holds the plastic as it's chiseled to the desired scarf angle (a 25° to 30° angle is good).

2 The ledge created with the router accommodates the lengths of scarfed binding as they're mated and acetoned.

3 The groove holds them neatly in position.

4 When pushed together, they dry into one strip!

Frank Ford's step-by-step fretting checklist

Here's the fretting checklist Frank Ford handed out after his fretting demonstration at the Great Northwoods Guitar Repair Seminar this past September. The drawing at right shows Frank's trusty "hooked blade," with which he picks the fret slot clean.

.020" wide at tip — regular violin knife (.050" thick) hollow ground to clear fret slots — 3/8"

#	Task	✓
1	Plug in soldering iron.	✓
2	Evaluate neck straightness and stiffness; sight fingerboard for evenness, relief, neck angle, etc.	✓
3	Loosen and lubricate truss rod nut, then tighten slightly.	✓
4	Remove strings, saddle, bridge pins and nut.	✓
5	Check tuning posts for sanding clearance, remove tuners if necessary.	✓
6	Lube open gears, check for loose tuners or gear parts.	✓
7	Protect top around end of fingerboard.	✓
8	Heat and remove frets, using soldering iron and flush-cutting end nippers.	✓
9	Saw or pick (tool above) fret slots to clean; deepen if needed.	✓
10	Sand fingerboard level with long block (I use the flat sole of a steel jackplane). Use 180 grit on rosewood, 220 on ebony.	✓
11	Apply 4 layers masking tape at 6th fret to raise end of long sanding block.	✓
12	With the end raised, sand the end of fingerboard (tongue) with a half-sheet of sandpaper in the same grit sequence. This eliminates any rise and produces slight "drop-off."	✓
13	Check for neck straightness and a drop-off starting at the 12th fret (on 14 fret guitars).	✓
14	Trial fit fretwire and select appropriate gauge.	✓
15	Cut all frets to length; trim to overhang binding if necessary.	✓
16	Tap in frets with plastic hammer, using ballast inside body where possible.	✓
17	Sight down fingerboard for uneven and unseated frets.	✓
18	Level and seat frets with steel hammer and steel plate; test for rocking with short straightedge.	✓
19	Check for loose tuner parts again.	✓
20	Trim fret ends with diagonal flush cutter.	✓
21	Unbound fingerboard: dab catalyst (accelerator) at fret slot ends and fill with medium superglue.	✓
22	Run thin superglue under frets if desired and clean up with acetone.	✓
23	File fret ends flush and bevel with mill file.	✓
24	Finish fret ends using "cant saw file."	✓
25	Sand tops of frets level: use jack plane body and 600 grit wet-or-dry sandpaper.	✓
26	Sand fret tops and ends with 600-grit backed by fingers only.	✓
27	Buff frets with 0000 steel wool or Micro Mesh paper (3200 to 12,000 final grit depending on guitar).	✓
28	Buff edge of fingerboard by hand with Micro Mesh or machine buffer.	✓
29	Set up and adjust action.	✓

ENGLAND SWINGS!

LONDON

In November, Stew-Mac International attended England's National Music Show held at Wembley Stadium on the outskirts of London, England. Though newcomers to the UK, the three of us (Kris Thomas, Jay Hostetler, and myself) felt right at home thanks to the many nice folks we met. Thanks for the hospitality!

— Dan Erlewine

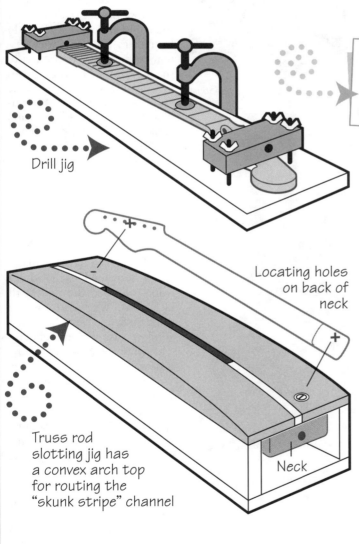

Drill jig

Locating holes on back of neck

Truss rod slotting jig has a convex arch top for routing the "skunk stripe" channel

Neck

THE *TRADE* SECRET OF THE ENGLISH CHANNEL!

Ted Lee

The English are renowned craftsmen with a colorful history of instrument making and woodworking. Most senior British tradesman (age 45 or older) studied under the apprentice system as joiners, tinsmiths, cabinetmakers, carpenters, boat builders, etc., where they received extensive training in the use of traditional hand tools. Take for example Ted Lee, a 56 year-old engineer who's been building and repairing guitars since the 1950s...and professionally from 1961.

In 1986 Ted began teaching guitarmaking part-time at the 'City of Leeds College of Music' in Leeds, England. Five years later he assumed a full-time position heading the school's Musical Instrument Technology program. The MIT program is a two-year course offering specialization in one of four categories: General Musical Instrument Repair; Acoustic/Classical Guitar Manufacture & Violin Repair; Electric Guitar Manufacture & Repair; Musical Instrument Electronics. Students also gain a strong background in Wood/Metalwork (toolmaking); Wood Metal Sciences (theory); Acoustics; Music Theory, Instrumental Studies; Business; and First Aid.

"Along with heading our MIT program," says Ted, "I teach the electric guitar construction and repair courses. Several part-time instructors teach the other areas of specialization, such as the course in classical guitar construction, which is taught by our friend Peter Barton. From West Yorkshire, Peter is among England's finest classical builders.

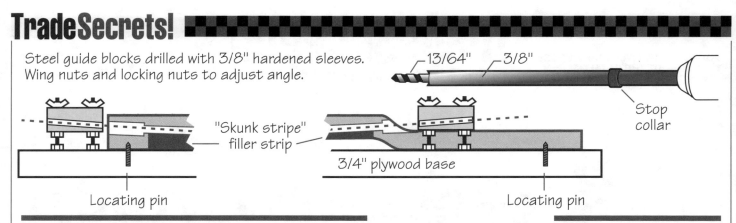

Steel guide blocks drilled with 3/8" hardened sleeves. Wing nuts and locking nuts to adjust angle.

13/64" 3/8"

Stop collar

"Skunk stripe" filler strip

3/4" plywood base

Locating pin

Locating pin

"Since we teach advanced courses in guitar building and repair, of course we've the usual stationery power tools, but the students must master the basic hand tools first. Speaking of hand tools, here's a funny story…When I visited the USA I toured your museums. I was surprised to see an 'antique' hand plane on display in a glass showcase. 'Antique,' I said, 'it's *exactly* like the one I still use every day, and that was used by my father and his father before him.' After three generations it still planes a surface perfectly!

"I love American electric guitars, and have a particular fondness for Fender instruments. Perhaps that's because when I toured the G&L factory in the late '70s, I spent an entire afternoon visiting with Leo Fender and George Fullerton. Although we encourage the students to design and build their own guitars, they learn how the great ones are built—especially the innovators like Gibson and Fender. Then when they go out on their own, they're building on solid ground.

"Take truss rod installation for example. One way that we're set up to install a truss rod is 'Fender-style,' with a rear-routed truss rod channel, skunk-stripe filler strip, and blind holes from each end. Your 'Trade Secrets' readers might appreciate the simple jigs we've made for routing the channel, and boring the holes…

■ The Drill-Jig has 3/8" drill guides at each end made from steel blocks with tempered drill bushing sleeves pressed in.

■ The neck is drilled from the rear to locate on two small pins (one "locating" hole later becomes a tuner-screw hole, the other small hole remains empty, on the part of the heel which is never seen (just like a vintage Fender neck). The neck slides under the peghead drill guide, onto the pins, and is clamped tight.

■ The drill guides are angled at 3°, but they're also adjustable at the four corners for correct height and to fine tune the angle.

■ The drill bit is a 3/8" outside diameter counterbore with a 3/16" center bit (it's actually 13/64" to give a little play for a 3/16" truss rod). The center bit contacts first and is followed by the 3/8" cutting edge which leaves a flat-bottomed hole. A stop-collar on the bit controls the depth.

"Our truss rod slotting jigs are simply boxes with a slot in the top for a router bit guide collar. A concave-topped box routs a curved slot from the front of the neck (under-the-fingerboard installation), and a convex top routs from the back of the neck ('skunk-stripe' style). The neck is held in the router box with two small screws fastened into the locating holes through countersunk brass inserts mounted in the box.

"Our school is located well north of London in one of the more lovely areas of England. We welcome inquiries from interested students in the USA."

Ted Lee, City of Leeds College Of Music, Cookridge Street, Leeds LS2 8BH, TEL 0113 243 2491 FAX 0113 243 8798

Sid Poole and two of his handbuilt guitars

OLD-SCHOOL JOINERY SKILLS FIND NEW USE

Another traditional craftsman we met is Sid Poole, of 'Poole Custom Guitars' in Kent, England, whose hand-built guitars rival anything on this side of the pond. Here's Sid:

"Most British tradesmen in their mid to late 40s (I'm 51) learned in the apprentice system, although we're the last of the old school. From age fifteen to twenty I was an apprentice joiner—training to make window frames, doors, furniture, bank counters, and such. Then in college, we improved our knowledge of the construction industry by studying engineering, drafting and business.

"I had years of experience be*fore* mass-produced joinery like pre-fab door and window kits finally made our trade obsolete. In the old days my mates and I respected each other's work—admired the perfect fit of a joint. We were proud to stand back and say 'I built that window casing from scratch!' The younger guys aren't getting it now.

"I built my first guitar at age 17. It was an EB-2 style hollow-body bass, and I nearly lost my apprenticeship over it because the shop foreman caught me working on it during a shift. (I couldn't keep my hands off it!) Over the years I continued to do guitar work on the side, repairs and refrets, as sort of a hobby turned part-time job. Then around '86 I hurt my back on a

job and used the opportunity to get into guitar work full-time. The good joinery jobs had all gone to hell anyway—if a door shut and locked, that was good enough, and it mattered little how *well* it was hung or how nice the casing looked. Nobody cared about quality anymore. So, the idea of guitarmaking full-time appealed to me, and I reasoned that a skilled joiner, with given guidelines, could make a good guitar—and I've been making a go of it for the ten years since."

*Sid Poole, Poole Custom Guitars
Kent, England*

Sid Poole's only power tools are a bandsaw and a router, and he does all the jointing and carving by hand; the tops of many Poole solidbodies are carved in the traditional European violin-style "recurve" which was adopted and made popular in America by Gibson, Grestch, and so many others. Sid prefers to spend his time handcrafting beautiful instruments—not making jigs, fixtures, and specialty tools in order to make more guitars faster. For example, he cuts each fretboard by hand. We liked Sid's tip for for grinding a knife-edge on the tip of his fret saw blade to keep it on dead center to a line scribed across the fretboard:

"With a modeling knife and a square, I scribe sharp lines at each fret location, then start the sawcut with my custom fret saw. The knife edge centers on the scribed line, and as the sawblade begins to cut I slide the square against it for support.

"Grind the teeth off at the tip of the saw at a slight curve, then sharpen it like a knife. The knife edge will center on your scribed line and hold the blade's position as you start the cut."

From Mr. Roger's Neighborhood
The Neck Fritzer

Roger Fritz heads the Warranty Repair Department for Gibson USA in Nashville. Before joining Gibson in 1993, Roger's "Fritz Brothers" guitar company in Mobile, Alabama built high-end solidbody electric guitars, including the 'Roy Buchanan' model which Roy favored before his tragic death.

When Gibson owner Henry Juszkiewicz asked his Customer Service Director, Wayne Greene, to create a professional in-house repair department, Wayne called Roger. "We're old friends," said Roger, "and even though my business was doing well, the chance of working with Wayne to create Gibson's USA repair department was too good to miss. And to be truthful, I'm a repairman at heart.

"So you like our 'Mr. Coffee Neck Steamer?' Great! All of us in the repair department are glad to give something back in return for all the Trade Secrets you send our way—and the tools. Stew-Mac tools are used all over the plant. For neck removal, I've used pressure-cookers, and even a felt hat-steamer, but Mr. Coffee's the best. I got the idea from the GAL's Datasheet #285, which has a transcription of Michael Dresdner's 1982 lecture on neck resetting.

■ The fretboard over the body is removed to expose the neck joint, and a series of holes are drilled in the tenon right next to the glue line (shown at right). This will leave the walls of the mortise in the body clean.

■ The steam goes in one hole and soon comes out the others—if it doesn't, we'll put steam in those holes too. Typically, the neck comes out in a very short time—a minute or two. It's easy when you don't need to save the neck!

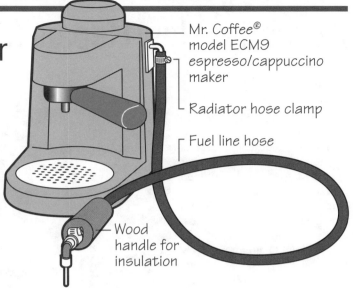

Mr. Coffee® model ECM9 espresso/cappuccino maker

Radiator hose clamp

Fuel line hose

Wood handle for insulation

"This is the method we use on the newer guitars. But if we're saving the neck, say on a vintage instrument, we steam the neck out intact by removing the frets over the body and steaming down through some fret slots. Also, those older instruments are a different animal since the tenon goes right into the pickup cavity, which makes them more difficult to get out (Les Paul Customs are still made that way, too). But we'll talk about that another time!"

*Roger Fritz
Gibson USA*

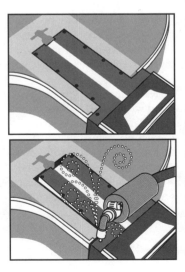

Top photo: Roger shows off a Les Paul built for the Hard Rock Cafe. Lower photo: The Gibson shop crew. Front row: Sean Benjamin, Gypsy Carnes, and Tony Nagy. Back: Todd Money, Rich Grace, Bob Bearden, Rick Goodwin, Dan Erlewine (visiting from Stew-Mac), and Roger Fritz.

Safety note: When working with steam, be sure to use hosing that is rated for heat and pressure (we use fuel line hose from the auto parts store).

Hot Tip! Thanks to Roger and crew, our neck steamer needle, hose, and adapter has been re-designed to fit the "Mister Coffee" Neck Fritzer.

Attractive New Repair Techniques!

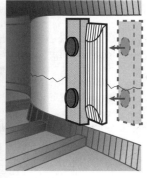

Magnets are helping me do better, more accurate, and cleaner stuctural acoustic repairs (especially interior) than ever before. Magnets can be fastened onto or inlaid into a variety of cauls and shapes made from wood, teflon, plexiglass, or brass. Cauls in matched sets of two (photo, right) align perfectly when faced together (magnetically attracting). With a top, side, or back separating them you know exactly which direction the caul is running on the inside of an instrument, and where it is. This is a big help in lining up such things as patches, crack reinforcement, and side struts. For example, here's how I'd use magnets to locate the bridge clamping caul Tom Humphrey describes on page 78.

Once glue has been applied to the bridge, you must *quickly* locate the notched bridge clamping caul over the braces at right angles to the top's centerline so that it parallels the bridge and ends up in the correct position for the clamps. The classical guitar's somewhat small soundhole (3-1/4" dia. average) makes such maneuvers more difficult than in a steel-string guitar. Magnetic "caul stops," and a magnet taped temporarily to the caul itself, made the job easier…

■ Protect the top around the bridge.

■ Place interior magnets at (A) and (B) (illustration at right) and attracting magnets (or steel blocks) on the outside. The caul will align as it butts against these interior "stops," and if the magnets are strong enough, they won't be pushed out of location while you work the caul into position.

Left: placing a spruce reinforcement strip next to a magnetic alignment caul.

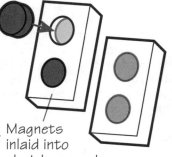

Magnetic cauls in matched sets help accurately align a crack reinforcement strip inside a guitar. When the exterior caul is moved into position, its mate follows. Position the strip next to the caul when gluing.

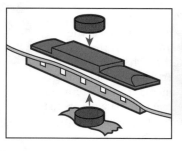

■ I taped a strong magnet to the underside of the caul and with the bridge set in place used an outside magnet to hold the caul in place while I applied the first couple of clamps!

CAUTIONS:

■ Keep a firm hold on magnets—they'll break and shatter, or damage delicate tonewoods, if you lose your grip and let them fly together

■ Keep magnet "pairs" separated with a 1/4" piece of wood

■ Wear safety glasses when using strong magnets!

■ Keep them away from computers, watches, and TV sets!

■ Practice your techniques on scrap wood or yard sale guitars!

Dan

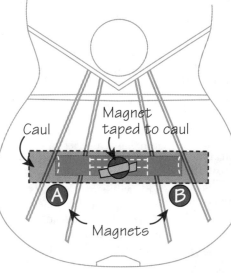

Magnets inlaid into plexiglass cauls (matched set)

Caul

Magnet taped to caul

Ⓐ   Ⓑ

Magnets

Want magnets? Keep your eyes on these pages—once we find a reliable source for the magnets of the right kind, size, and strength we'll make them available to our customers.

Trade Secrets International
From Japan: a Perfect Fit

Akiyoshi Sakamoto, from Nakatsugawa City, Japan, visited the Stew-Mac booth at the '96 NAMM show in Anaheim, California. He showed us a great acoustic guitar which he'd just completed (photo, upper right).

Before learning to build guitars, Akiyoshi learned to build and repair roads. From 1977 to 1980 he worked for the public works department, and eventually became department manager. In 1980 road-building gave way to guitar-building and a job at the Terada Instrument Company making acoustic guitar parts, spray-finishing completed instruments, and setting-up electric guitars. Nine years later, looking to get even deeper into guitar building, Akiyoshi was fortunate to enter the great Takamine Instrument Company as an acoustic guitar builder, where today he remains happily employed. And when he's not at *work* building guitars, Akiyoshi is at *play* building guitars in his "hobby house," the home shop which he built in 1994. Here he designs and builds his own guitars for relaxation!

Here's Akiyoshi's secret for the perfect mating of the bridge to the top before gluing.

■ An adjustable screw-post, with protective rubber caps, supports the top.

■ A .5mm sheet of supple vinyl protects the top (left).

Akioshi Sakamoto with Dan Erlewine at the StewMac booth at the '96 NAMM show in Anaheim.

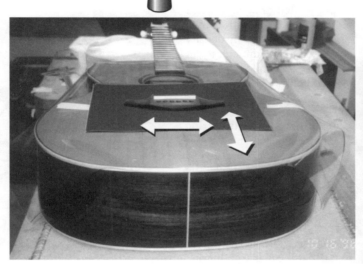

■ Very sharp 180-grit sandpaper is double-stick-taped onto the vinyl, and the bridge is moved in both directions with very short strokes (below).

■ After a proper fit is determined , scribe the lacquer around the bridge and remove the unwanted top finish with a "dog leg" chisel (left) using a small straightedge as a guide.

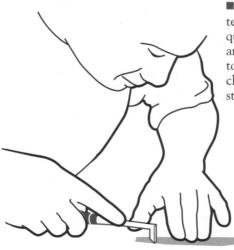

■ The final test is a "tap tone" (right). The perfect gluing surface produces a solid tap (no rattle).

Fitting a Saddle in a Resonator Bridge

The 1996 Northwoods Building & Repair Seminar held in September at Bryan Galloup's Guitar Hospital in Big Rapids, Michigan was a big success. Watch for Hot Tips and Trade Secrets from the NBRS on these pages—like this advice from resophonic guitar expert Tim Scheerhorn, of Scheerhorn Resonator Guitars, in Kentwood, Michigan.

Tim Scheerhorn builds some of the world's premier wood-bodied resonator guitars on a limited-production basis (Tim builds in batches of two). Before going full-time into instrument building in 1994, Tim worked at the Steelcase Company as an engineer, tool and die maker, and supervisor of special machine and automation engineering. A skilled dobroist who plays in three bands, and a power boat racer who's built his own boats and motors, Scheerhorn's combined skills enable him to build at a very high level. "After designing equipment to make a desk drawer every 15 seconds, it was natural for me to find the most effective ways of manufacturing guitars," says Tim, "although my setup is surprisingly simple." Tim's lecture on both Dobro and National setup was a highlight of the seminar, and watching him work, we all knew that his way was the "right" way! Here's how Tim fits a saddle in a spider bridge …

"The fit of the saddle to the bridge is so very critical to your sound. For a Dobro-style, spider-bridged instrument, I friction-fit the saddle by squeezing it into the spider bridge slot. I use a Wilton machinist's vise that I equipped with customized extended jaws to reach the center of the bridge, while avoiding the delicate spider leg support system (top drawing).

"I prefer a friction fit over the more common press fit. A press-fit shaves off excess wood as the maple saddle blank is forced into the bridge slot, and in my opinion, destroys the wood fiber. I hand-sand the saddle on 180-grit sandpaper stuck to my work surface until it measures .005" oversize.

"The old style instruments have saddles made entirely of maple, which isn't *bad*, but I prefer to cap them with ebony. Since maple varies in density and hardness, it's difficult to get a consistent sound. That's why my saddle choice is a base of select maple with an ebony top—putting a consistent dense material right under the string where it's needed. Ebony has great wear resistance and gives a clear distinct note, while the maple on the bottom brings in the woodiness and warmth of the old tone. At the customer's request, I have made saddles in maple for a warmer, mushier sound, but the maple and ebony is my favorite—it's a great combination.

"I cut the saddle's string slots with what may look like a 'feather edge' file or maybe the old Ibanez nut-slotting file. It's actually a mill-bastard file which I ground, so that only a thin edge of file teeth remain. Holding a small ruler against the bridge for spacing, I start each slot with a small nick from the file (middle drawing).

"Next, I shape and finish the slots with Dobro strings (bottom drawing). For the 6th, 5th, 4th, and 3rd I use the actual string type and gauge I intend to set the guitar up with; for the 2nd and 1st I use a .026" wound

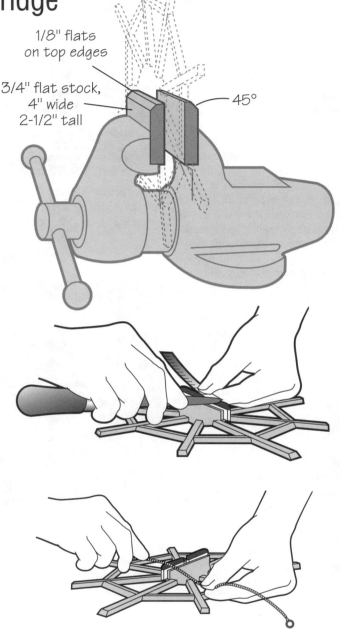

1/8" flats on top edges

3/4" flat stock, 4" wide 2-1/2" tall

45°

for the initial shaping and then burnish the slots with the proper size plain strings. I recommend the D'Addario J-42 Phosphor Bronze strings which Mike Auldridge uses. They measure: .016", .018", .026W; .035", .045", and .056".

You can use this technique on any guitar saddle or nut. Shaping the saddle slots with strings accomplishes three things:

1. It makes a really nice-fitting string slot.

2. It gives the proper back angle and draft off the saddle's back edge.

3. It improves the sound by compressing and burnishing the wood the way strings do over time (and there are none of the rough edges which files leave)."

From Feline Guitars:
The Purrfect Fret Job

Jonathan Law owns and operates Feline Guitars in South Croydon, England. A 31-year-old veteran rocker and inveterate luthier who found that building and repairing guitars was as satisfying as playing them, Jon's handbuilt solidbody electrics are surpassed only by his vast knowledge of absolutely everything to do with guitars. Jon, Jay and I spent two evenings over dinner and deep guitar talk. Here's one of Jon's many Trade Secrets:

"Often, when fretting with the jumbo (wide) fretwires, I switch to a narrower wire for the high frets (frets 14 and up). This gives extra 'finger room' at the top end, especially on a Gibson 24-3/4" scale. Two fretwires which combine well for this technique are Stew-Mac's new #154 wide high-crown (.100" wide x .050" tall) and the #155 medium width high-crown wire (.080" x .050")."

Jon Law,
Feline Guitars

From left to right in the photo: Jon Law, Simon Farmer of 'Gus Guitars,' and Dan Erlewine admiring Simon's Gus G4 electric bass. At right: Simon's "Gus G1."

Building a Better
Binding Block...

Dear Dan:

The Trade Secrets issue on binding inspired me to make the binding laminating jig shown below. It's put together from stuff lying around the shop—a scrap aluminum billet with two 1/8" x 3/4" flat aluminum bars screwed to it. I screwed one bar down tight, and the other is slotted for adjustment and held with wing nuts. This lets the bars remain flat on the surface, but loose enough to clamp with spring clamps. It works great, although I plan to replace the flat bars with taller ones. The jig is a little over 6" long because that's how big the aluminum bar happened to be, but you can't glue up much more than that at once anyhow. The main thing I found is to really soak your joints with acetone if you don't want to be going back and joining them again. Thanks for the Trade Secrets!

Jim Hilburn,
Louisville, Colorado

Jim: Thanks for the input, and the Trade Secret!!
— Dan Erlewine

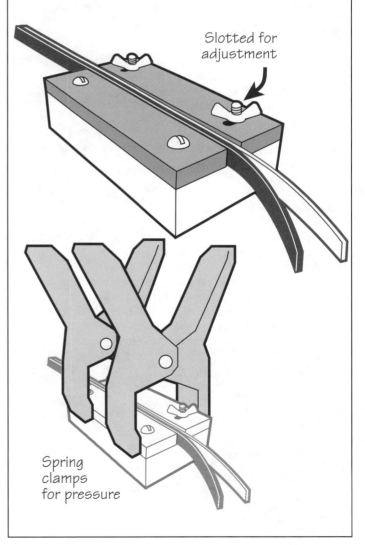

Slotted for adjustment

Spring clamps for pressure

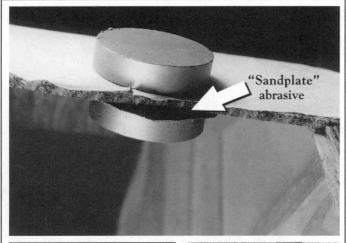

"Sandplate" abrasive

Still attracted to magnets…

On page 74 we describe some uses for magnets in guitar repair. There are more uses—lots more—and the following are just a few examples:

■ A padded magnet wrapped in cloth and tied-off can be dipped in warm water, squeezed-out, and used wet, can be drawn along a brace to clean hard-to-reach interior glue squeeze-out during a brace repair (upper right).

■ Magnets are perfect for locating and then clamping interior patches along glued cracks and seams (lower right).

■ Magnets with either sandpaper or the Sandvik "Sandplate" abrasive superglued to their surface do the best job ever of removing old dried glue from an interior surface (top photo).

■ They're also great for removing dried glue squeeze-out and rough spots from along a repaired crack (below).

Always use protective tape on the outside of the instrument when you're dragging a magnet over the surface!

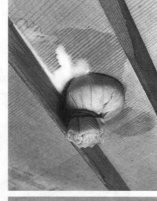

This Technique's a Classic!

Classical guitar maker Thomas Humphrey is a hard worker. In '96 he *almost* built his annual quota of 21 "Millennium" guitars, *plus* he taught two-week-long guitar building course/lectures at The "Club De Lauderos" in Paracho, Mexico, the "International Festival De Agosto" in Caracas, Venezuela; and "Gitarrenfestspiele" in Nurtingen, Germany. All that, and Tom still had time for Trade Secrets—like this trick for clamping a classical bridge, and determining bracing alignment on cedar-topped instruments…

"When you're clamping the bridge on a classical guitar you must have a well-fit caul on the inside for the clamps to contact. Cedar tops in particular keep me on pins and needles because they're so fragile; they dent and ding easily, and excess clamping pressure can crush the wood fibers. Also, with cedar tops you can't use the old light bulb-inside-the box trick to see through the top to locate the braces (for making a caul) because cedar doesn't illuminate like spruce does. I use styrofoam to take an imprint of the top bracing before transferring it to a wooden caul.

"Make a caul from a piece of wood 7" to 9" long x 1-1/2" wide x 3/4" thick (or whatever goes in and out of the soundhole easily). Then double-stick tape a 1/8" to 1/4" thickness of styrofoam to the block. When the block's clamped lightly in place, the styrofoam takes an imprint of the bracing pattern. Remove the block and saw along the imprint marks, right into the wood. Remove the styrofoam, deepen your saw cuts to match the height of the braces, and chisel out the waste to make channels which fit over the bracing. Chamfer the sharp hard edges of the caul to keep them from denting the wood, and be sure that the caul matches the curve of the top and/or the bottom of the bridge if there is a curve.

Tom Humphrey,
New York City

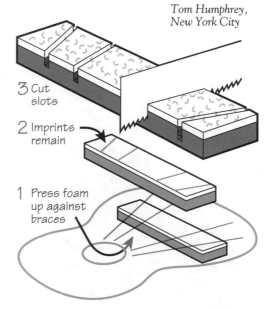

3 Cut slots

2 Imprints remain

1 Press foam up against braces

NEWS FLASH!
We've just learned that at the '97 NAMM show, C.F. Martin & Co. unveiled their new high-end classical guitar designed by Thomas Humphrey and handcrafted at the Martin factory to the exact specifications of his "Millennium" design. Congratulations Tom, your guitar is in good hands!

YOU'LL FIND EXTRA TRADE SECRETS THROUGHOUT THE CATALOG!

TradeSecrets!
Hot tips & inside scoops. Editor: Dan Erlewine

VOLUME 30

After over twenty years as a builder, Gernot Wagner, of Frankfurt, Germany is gaining a reputation that is sure to rank him as a world-class maker of classical guitars. With an annual production of only a dozen instruments or so, quality, not quantity, is clearly his main focus. We visited with Gernot and his family, and came home with these great shop tips!

During last winter's Musik Messe international trade show held in Frankfurt,

Stew-Mac's Sally Stredny, Kris Thomas, and Jay Hostetler visited Gernot's shop and were awed by his work. Later, after dinner and a pleasant evening at his home with Gernot, his wife Edeltraud, and their children Andi and Martina, they vowed to return the hospitality in American fashion: California wine for the parents, and ball caps for the kids. When he got home, Jay showed no jet lag in his eagerness to get these Trade Secrets into print…

Gernot's son Andi is a big fan of US basketball teams, and he gave Jay this great picture!

The 48-year old Wagner started building steel-string guitars, switched to renaissance and baroque instruments, and now builds only classical guitars, made to order, in two models. One is a modern, powerful, cedar-topped concert-stage instrument; the other is a spruce-topped traditional model built in the Hauser style. "I learned that you have to concentrate on one kind of instrument if you want to build a good instrument," said Gernot.

Gernot's shop is comprised of the power tool room (including wood storage and a corner spray booth) and the building room with workbenches, hand tools, forms, jigs, and finishing material storage. Each tool has its place on the handsome, hardwood racks lining the shop walls. An inveterate toolmaker skilled with hand tools in true European fashion, Gernot has an open mind to high-tech luthiery as well, evidenced by his

vacuum bridge clamp, and his passion for polyurethane glue…

"I only use vacuum-clamping for the bridge," says Gernot, "because (and I never hear this discussed) the top deforms under the weight and torque of bridge clamps, and *I don't want it to cure in that state!* Over-tightened clamps can also crush delicate wood fibers. Vacuum-clamping eliminated these worries for me. However, vacuum-clamping didn't have enough pressure to get the squeeze-out needed for a good joint when I used Titebond yellow aliphatic-resin glue. Also, in a vacuum, glue squeeze-out can't be cleaned up. I needed a glue that had great strength in a thin layer, and that would make a good joint without the pressure of traditional metal bridge clamps.

"I discovered polyurethane glue, a high-tech industrial glue made without water. It makes a stronger bond in a much thinner layer than Titebond yellow

Gernot's laminating jig is made of segments of MDF-board glued to a rubber sheet, and looks a lot like a building mold.

glue, so I was in luck! I quickly learned how much glue to use for minimal squeeze-out. I apply glue to both surfaces and immediately wipe off almost all of it, until only a thin layer, or 'shine' remains. If you use the normal amount of glue, as per Titebond yellow, there'd be too much squeeze-out, because polyurethane glue swells to four times its size. If you use traditional bridge clamps, and you are worried about a 'starved' glue joint, use more glue if you wish. It doesn't have to be spread so thin if you have the pressure needed for good squeeze-out and are able to clean it up.

"Since it has no water, polyurethane glue creates less tension in the bridge area than any water-base glue. Spruce or cedar tops absorb moisture (and therefore swell) more than bridges, which are made of hardwood. The two parts dry differently and tension is created, when you *want* the parts to be in a state of equilibrium. The opposite direction of the wood fibers (bridge going one way, top going another) is a problem, and moisture only adds to it.

"Soon, I was using polyurethane glue for almost all situations where I wanted to avoid introducing water to the wood: jointing tops, laminating kerfing, gluing veneers, gluing the sides to the back and top, installing the neck—and especially the fingerboard. I'm not sure if others feel this way, but when I glued fingerboards or laminated linings with Titebond I learned from bitter experience to wait a week for the water to leave before doing any close tolerance work. With polyurethane, you can do as you please the next day and things will remain stable.

"Yellow Titebond is an excellent glue, but I simply like polyurethane glue better. I still use yellow glue for inlaying purflings, because it's less messy and cleans up easily with water, and assembling necks (gluing the peghead and laminating the heel), because the glue lines are invisible. Most of my necks are mahogany, with an occasional Spanish cedar, and the polyurethane glue line is too dark for mahogany. On spruce, the color of the glue is perfect because it resembles the darker wintergrowth lines.

Follow these rules with polyurethane glue

- Don't use it when the humidity is below 45 percent at normal room temperature. Every builder or repairperson needs an accurate, precision-made hygrometer!
- In dry conditions, leave the joint clamped longer at 45 percent humidity (I leave joints clamped for three hours).
- One of the glue surfaces must be porous.
- Naphtha will clean the glue until it hardens.
- Spread the glue on one surface only (except when gluing bridges—then spread both surfaces).

Laminated lining

Choosing from mahogany, Spanish cedar, and basswood (basswood does not tear out as spruce does when you notch for the struts), Wagner laminates his linings from three pieces 2" wide, .080" thick, and as long as the guitar's sides. A humble man, Gernot's quick to point out that he did not invent this technique. Sometimes he uses a layer of rosewood in the center because it looks attractive. Once dry, the wide laminate is bandsawed into strips—a tricky maneuver through the waist, no doubt—and dimensioned with a thickness sander to produce strips of unkerfed lining, pre-bent to fit the sides! Linings made this way have great strength, and the thickness is good for supporting the extra-wide Hauser-style purfling Gernot uses.

Ebony reinforcing strip is slightly longer than the channel between two inlaid end blocks

Steel-string tip

Wagner doesn't feel any reinforcement is necessary in a classical guitar neck if it's made from good, well-seasoned wood and built in stable conditions. He agrees that a steel-string neck needs reinforcement however, but not necessarily adjustable reinforcement.

In his steel-string guitar building days, he used the method shown below. "It's nothing new," says Gernot, "surely many have done this, but it counters string tension very nicely...

"Inlay an ebony strip down the neck's center, but with small ebony buttress strips crossing at 90° to the main strip at each end.

Then, if the ebony strip is made slightly longer than its channel and glued in with pressure, it creates a counter-tension that can withstand considerable string-pull."

More Trade Secrets from Gernot Wagner on the next page...

More shop tips from Gernot Wagner

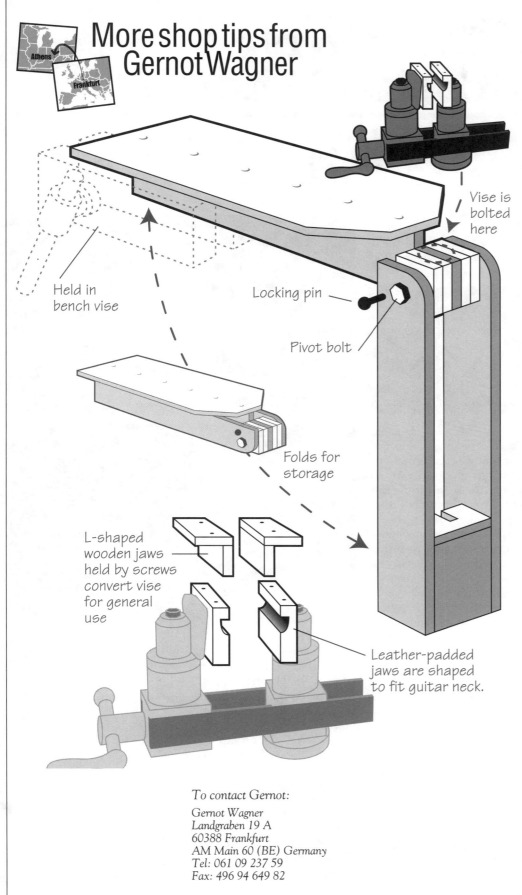

Held in bench vise

Vise is bolted here

Locking pin

Pivot bolt

Folds for storage

L-shaped wooden jaws held by screws convert vise for general use

Leather-padded jaws are shaped to fit guitar neck.

To contact Gernot:

Gernot Wagner
Landgraben 19 A
60388 Frankfurt
AM Main 60 (BE) Germany
Tel: 061 09 237 59
Fax: 496 94 649 82

Jigs and fixtures

Gernot built the storable workbench/vise shown here to mount in the shoulder vise of his European-style woodworker's bench. The bench sets up almost instantly and he can walk around it, working on both sides of an instrument.

The extra-thick vise jaws are notched and leather-padded to accept a neck contour, guaranteeing that a guitar won't fall, even with the vise swiveled to hang the instrument out over the floor. L-shaped "normal" jaws screw to the permanent jaws to cover the notches when not in use.

Natural drying

Wagner hangs prospective spruce or cedar topwood on a wire through drilled holes. This way, the boards dry naturally.

A skilled French-polisher, Gernot fills the open pores in the traditional manner: he French-polishes with shellac and a dusting of rottenstone, which cuts minute fibers of wood from

the surface, takes on the wood's color, and fills the pores with the slurry of shellac and wood dust. (For more on this technique see Jeff Jewitt's new book *Hand-Applied Finishes* in this catalog.)

Why didn't *I* think of that?!

Bruce McLaren, of McLaren Products in San Diego, California, displayed his distinctive electric basses two booths away from us at the '97 NAMM (National Association of Music Merchants) trade show in Anaheim, California. He impressed us with his luthiery skills, and as a tool designer, too.

Bruce's background in mechanical design engineering prepared him well for turning his hobby into a career. At 56, McLaren took an early retirement from industry ("they stopped making things I like to build," said Bruce), to pursue electric bassmaking as more than just a weekend endeavor. He plunged in headfirst by displaying his instruments at the '96 NAMM show. At this year's show he described the clever measuring device shown here . .

An easy and accurate way to measure neck relief

"Make a feeler gauge using guitar strings as shown in the photo. Choose strings with diameters increasing in .002" increments, beginning and ending with string sizes that suit your needs. Relief in the .011" to .020" range suits me as a bassplayer and builder. Tape the strings to a piece of wood or cardboard to hold them in place while you epoxy them to a wooden holder board.

"With a capo installed at the 1st fret and the string depressed at the 15th or 17th, measure neck relief in the 5th, 7th, and 9th fret area. Slide the gauge

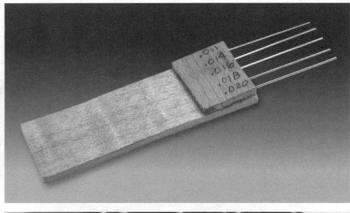

along the fretboard, then up and over a fret until one of the strings resists going through the gap (start with the smallest string first of course). If a string *barely* resists, the string diameter is probably the same as the gap. If there's a lot of resistance, but the previous smaller string went through easily, then the gap is one thousandth less than the string diameter.

"Because of its delicate nature, this is also a useful tool for measuring string clearance over the first fret when filing nut slots. Measurements with this tool are accurate to the nearest .001"."

Sideways fretting

Gernot installs his frets sideways, a la Leo Fender, holding the fret down with a hardwood block curved to match the slight fretboard radius, and hammering it in from the bass side. The hammerhead must have no facets; otherwise the hammer would miss those frets in the fretboard extension over the top of the guitar body. The fret should be filed flat where the hammer hits it, and sharpened as in the drawing at right.

The crucial point is to press the fretwire down correctly where it enters the fret slot. Too much pressure will cause the fret to bend from the hammer blow; too little pressure, and the fret may rise up and chip the fretboard! Gernot installs Stew-Mac #155 and #147 wires into a 0.6mm (.0235") slot, and protects the topwood from his hammer blows by first covering this part of the top with a thin steel cabinetscraper lined with leather on the underside.

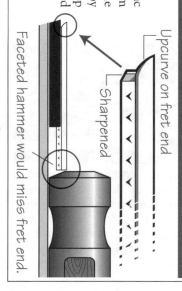

Upcurve on fret end

Sharpened

Faceted hammer would miss fret end.

TradeSecrets!

Beck Boogies!

Way out in Arizona, 'midst the desert heat and scorpions, Phoenix-area musicians have an oasis: Beck's Guitar Specialty Services. Luthier Richard Beck's client list includes such notables as the Gin Blossoms, Meat Puppets, Lyle Lovett's Band, Glen Campbell's band, and even Glen himself (Beck does his personal instruments). Recently, enroute to the '97 Namm show, I visited Richard to see if he had any old Trade Secrets laying around that he wasn't using . . .

Located in a modern shopping center near Arizona State University, Beck's Guitar Specialty Services is far more than the guitar repair shop I'd expected. Customers enter a retail showroom where well-stocked

parts and accessory counters block access to the rear shop, which is visible through a wide connecting doorway.

Walls can speak, and the showroom tells you of Beck's meticulous nature, and attention to detail. "This guy's successful" say the many framed photo-collages of customers and their guitars; "He's hip. Has a sense of humor" adds the zebra-

patterned carpet; "A professional works here," states the tasteful interior-decorating; "You can trust your guitar with this man, he takes good care of stuff," guarantee the clean safety-padded countertop workboard and guitar neck-rest.

Although Beck's direct approach might seem almost blunt to some, what you see is what you get, and he's as refreshing as a cold Gatorade on nearby South Mountain. A man who obviously enjoys people, Richard entertains with his quick sense of humor. While unlocking the front door he says, "See the sign? It says 'No food or drinks inside please.' That's the first clue, if you can't read this sign—*if you come in with a sandwich*—then I'll know you're not smart enough to have me work on your guitar.

"I like this plaque," he continues as we step inside and he points to "Picks Of The Rich And Famous" in a red-lacquered frame, "it's a reminder to me of where I've been and what I've gone through. For years I'd go try to sell people guitars. A lot of times they wouldn't buy a guitar, but I always got to steal some of their picks.

"But the main purpose of all this 'artwork'—and this *is* my Trade Secret—is to entertain customers and occupy them while I do my 'Be right with you' number. So because the entrance looks real nice, with all the photos and stuff—that's the Meat Puppets gold album which they presented to me—the customer is pleasantly entertained long enough for me to *carefully* set aside my work before hustling

up front."

In Beck's 15'x28' shop, a drill-press stands at the far end by the rear service door; the buffing machine is along the right-hand wall between the bathroom and a small "sawdust room" used for template-routing and wood planing. Most of the power tools, a tablesaw, thickness-planer, jointer, dust-collector, and drum-sander—stand in the center of the room. When not in use, the power tool surfaces all become building stations, hosting a side bender and numerous molds and parts.

The repair bench extends the entire length of the left-hand wall (a wall covered with tools), and though it's *covered* with small tools and work in progress, the bench is amazingly uncluttered. Rich is neat, and a clever organizer. Triple-tiered "Magna-bar" magnetic tool-holders secure *hundreds* of small steel tools—from drill bits to chisels in an easy-to-reach fashion.

Along with a heavy repair load, Beck and his co-workers Tim Fox (a graduate of Tempe's nearby Roberto-Venn School of Luthiery), and Rico Mei produce a dozen guitars a year. "Mostly we build our maple Mini-Jumbo model patterned after an old Gibson Everly Brothers guitar I loved," Beck says. "Ours differs from the J-185 model (the basis for the Everly

BECK'S

Brothers model) in that it has a tighter waist, is slightly longer overall, and it's quite a bit deeper too. My biggest influence was John Greven of Bloomington Indiana, who answered 2000 of my first questions.

"After repairing guitars for twenty years, and seeing lots of cracks in the top along the fretboard, I build the area from the waist downward quite delicately, but I beef-up the bracing in the upper bout. It hasn't hurt

the sound, because our guitars sound great, and are bought by customers who've done serious comparison-shopping before placing an order. Now, along with building guitars for customers, which makes money to help keep the shop running, we need to start building some guitars for the store, too. People need to see our work, and we don't always have one to show them.

On table-saw safety

"I love my fingers, but it took a table-saw mishap before I knew it. Sitting there looking at the ten stitches in my thumb I thought 'Man, those power tools, they don't care—they'll cut

wood, they'll cut flesh!' So I built a shut-off frame from hardware-store PVC tubing that hangs from two large eye-bolts mounted to the front rail. It swings, so a nudge from the knee pushes the PVC 'finger' against the 'Off' button instantly. I also insist on eye protection, ear protection, and certainly pushsticks. If you can't do it with a push-stick, don't do it. I like this triangular one with the handle cut-out."

Beck on fretting

"After I put the frets in (assuming they're round, perfectly installed, and with very little removed from the tops during levelling), I shape them using one of four different-sized triangle files ranging in width from 1/8" to 1/4", and in overalllength from 5" to 7". The #1698 and #1680 files in the Stew-Mac catalog look about right—send me some so the guys can have their own!

"I choose from seven files actually, because some are more worn than others. I just keep grabbing files 'til one feels right. There's no science to it. The reason I have four sizes is that

frets of different thickness and height require different-width files to get the right 'attack.'

"I don't want the frets to be round. I like 'em to be sort of little mini-pyramids, for the best intonation. Fret slots are calculated to be within thousandths-of-an-inch, and someone with really good ears is gonna hear it if a string contacts off-center. As for whether or not triangulated frets wear faster, I get plenty of dresses out my fret jobs, and face it—everything's a compromise. So unless requested not to, I file a slight pyramid shape into any of the four standard fret sizes which I rely on most. The next time somebody wants really large frets I'm gonna try your #3392 triangular-shaped wire and save myself some work."

Beck's favorite fret sizes
1. .078" x .043" narrow vintage for Fender, Martin, and some Gibsons;
2. .102" x .042" wide vintage for Gibson "wide oval";
3. .118" x .058" jumbo rock 'n roll;
4. .055" x .090" medium/tall.

See page 85 for Rich's great trade secret for polishing frets!

Guitar building school

"I've enjoyed working with Tim and Rico so much—others call it 'mentoring'—that I've developed a program for persons wanting to learn practical guitar repair and luthiery skills from a working repairman and luthier. Anyone interested in a one-on-one, hands-on course tailored to their needs should call me."

Richard Beck
Beck's Guitar Specialty Services
930 W. Broadway Road, Suite 3
Tempe, Arizona, 85282
(602) 829-9630

Blue Book of Repair Prices

"I don't put too much stock in price lists because even a simple nut job can turn into a nightmare that you wish you'd never quoted a price on. When that happens I don't like the customer quoting me prices from my own price list, so I don't post my prices. But here's a list of my charges for some common repair jobs."

- Basic set-up (adjust neck, nut, bridge arch, intonation—includes strings) $45
- Fret level (Includes basic set-up) $65/up
- New bone nut (Strat, acoustic, bass); no plastic $45
- New bone nut (Martin) $65
- New ivory nut (Martin) $75
- Reglue bridge, adjust action; includes strings $65
- Shave bridge, deepen saddle slot, adjust action (acoustic) $75/up
- Install Fishman-style pickup, re-slot saddle $75/up
- Fabricate compensated saddle $55/up
- Simple broken headstock, no touch-up $35/up
- Repair badly broken headstock, touch-up $150/up
- Repair loose brace, top or back $25/up
- Glue and cleat basic crack, no touch-up $35/up
- Refret plain rosewood board with adjustable neck (Strat, Les Paul Junior, etc.); use existing nut; set-up $200
- Refret maple board, lacquer, set-up $235
- Refret bound fretboard (ebony or rosewood) $275
- Refret unbound, non-adjustable neck (Martin, etc.) $250 With/binding (D-35 style) $300
- Refinish natural spruce-top acoustic, reglue bridge, set-up $275
- Refinish basic bolt-on neck (Strat, Tele, etc.) $65
- Lacquer touch-ups (acoustic or electric) Start at $50

A new spin on polishing frets

Rich Beck writes:

"Around 1990 I began polishing frets with Cratex rubberized abrasive wheels mounted in a flexible-shaft tool. I hold the tool horizontally, for a low right-angle approach to the fret. This is done, mind you, *after* the frets have been levelled and filed to shape—to remove filing marks and polish the surface to a diamond shine.

"I use an old miniature rat-tail file to shape the fret's contour into the wheel, then draw the coarse gray wheel along the length of the fret—*polishing, not grinding!* The trick is to let the shape follow the fret, removing the file marks without disturbing the top of the fret. Once you get the feel you *can* touch the fret tops if you do it right—but use the next grit (pink) wheel.

"Repeat the trick using the softer (pink) wheel and a little higher speed for this second pass. You never want to go more than two times because it will get the fret hot. I do worry about overheating the fret and perhaps loosening it, but it hasn't been a problem.

"Then as a final trick we use the little cloth Dremel buffing wheel loaded with an extra-fine green jeweler's rouge called 'ZAM'. Much experimentation went into the choosing of the Cratex gray and pink wheels, and the green rouge, so trust me—they work."

[See pages 83–84 for more Trade Secrets from Rich Beck – Ed.]

Magical Mystery Tool

Dear Stew-Mac: I have often seen people installing springs in the Strat tremolo by levering with a scriber or small screwdriver (I have also seen such tools stuck into the body, shot like an arrow). I have even used my fingers, with the mystery of the Orient, to do this.

Akifumi Koyanagi and Hayashi-San

But finally, here is a fine tool for this job: a "tremolo spring setter." The one enclosed is a gift to you from the tool's "inventor," my friend Hayashi-San of the ESP Musical Academy in Tokyo, Japan. Originally, this tool was designed for fishermen to remove fish hooks. The small gap allows the tool to slide over the fishing line to the hook where, with a dexterous twist, the hook can be removed.

For Hayashi San's purpose, he widened the gap to slide over the bent "hook" of a guitar's tremolo spring, allowing easy installation of the spring:

■ Hook the spring setter onto the spring.
■ Pull the spring to the block.
■ Set the spring into the block.
■ Remove the spring setter by pushing it sideways as you press the spring into the block!

*Best Wishes from
Akifumi Koyanagi and
Hayashi-San*

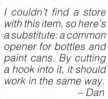

*I couldn't find a store with this item, so here's a substitute: a common opener for bottles and paint cans. By cutting a hook into it, it should work in the same way.
– Dan*

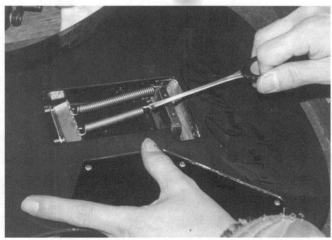

TradeSecrets!

"Art dear, where are all the clothespins?"

Dear Dan:

"After attending Charles Fox's class in '95, I'm now building guitars as my day job permits. I want to go full-time eventually. Anyway, here's a Trade Secret for you.

"I found that clothespins don't make the best lining clamp because their built-in "clothesline grooves" leave a gap on the inside edge. Irving Sloane recommends using clothespins in his book *Guitar Construction* after filling these grooves with glue. I did this on my first three guitars. After pondering the situation however, I decided the problem is in the fulcrum/pressure point of the standard clothespin.

"By gluing a piece of 1/4" dowel into the large groove on one side of a clothespin, you shift the pressure point to bear on a better spot on the lining. You can make 75 clamps at once by placing dabs of glue equal distances apart on a dowel rod, and clamping the clothespins on it overnight. Then on a bandsaw, just cut them apart, wrap rubber bands around them, and there you are—no gaps! I hope you find this useful.

Regards,
Art Collins,
Luthier (In My Mind).

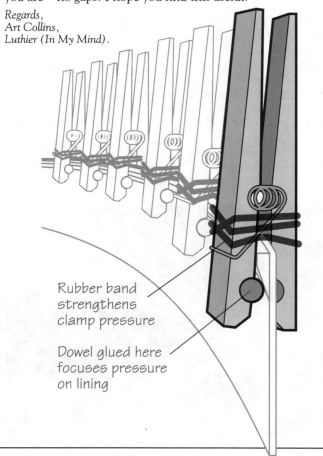

Rubber band strengthens clamp pressure

Dowel glued here focuses pressure on lining

TradeSecrets!

Hot tips & inside scoops. Editor: Dan Erlewine

Here's a great shop that makes big-time use of floor space!

From Australia: Gabriel Ochoteco writes with hot tips and a detailed workshop layout

"We're very happy to contribute to *Trade Secrets*, because back in the '70s when I was going professional, information could only be had by communicating with other local guitar techs. Today, thanks to the many books, magazine articles, videotapes, and of course *Trade Secrets*, we have global access to lutherie information, and everyone is building better instruments and achieving higher repair standards because of it. Stewart-MacDonald is a leader in this information-sharing, so as we say here in Australia, 'Good on ya mate!'"

Gabriel Ochoteco

We liked Gabriel's shop plan and photos so much we hope it starts a new series in *Trade Secrets* to accompany our *Blue Books*: shop plans showing tips on making workspaces really work. Let's compare notes and learn from each others' successes and mistakes this way.

Dan

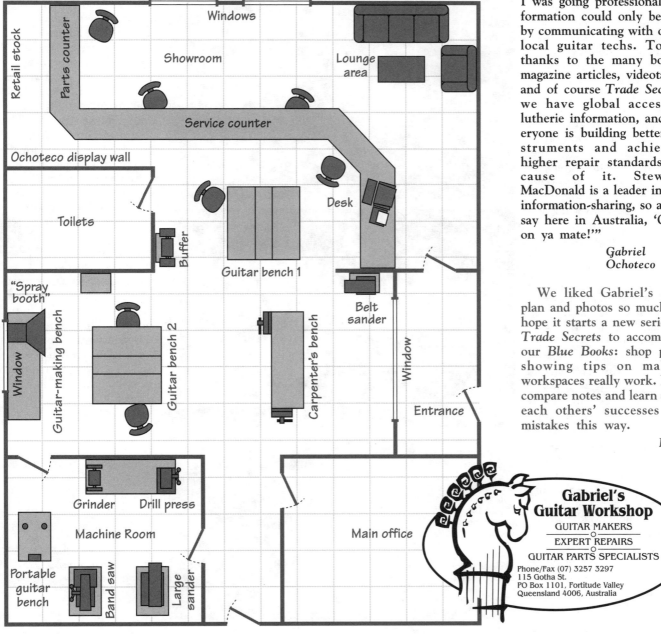

Gabriel's Guitar Workshop

GUITAR MAKERS
○
EXPERT REPAIRS
○
GUITAR PARTS SPECIALISTS

Phone/Fax (07) 3257 3297
115 Gotha St.
PO Box 1101, Fortitude Valley
Queensland 4006, Australia

"Our shop," says Gabriel, "measures 65' x 23' (1500 sq. ft.), and it's laid out so that all the messy work is done in the machine room. And the larger machines are on wheeled trolleys so we can move them out onto our parking lot for really big sawdusty jobs. Every wall in the workshop area has shelving or tool racks for storage.

"The building has air conditioning which I supplement with a dehumidifier—keeping the temperature about 20° C, and humidity at 45% at all times. Big spray jobs are done on rented premises, but touchups are done through an 'Erlewine-inspired' spray booth setup which is a portable, two-foot square box with motor, filter, and a folding shroud—on the fashion of the one you showed in an earlier *Trade Secrets*. The shroud, or funnel, folds double, so it's quite large. We can place the 'spraybooth' in front of any window or door.

"Guitar bench #1 is used mostly for setup and routine jobs. It's in my 'nerve center,' where we have access to the phone, computer, stereo, fax, etc.—all from one stool! The second guitar bench is mainly for fretwork and major repairs."

"I employ an apprentice, Ivan Aird," says the 47 year-old Gabriel, "and my wife Sacha runs the business end, keeping our paperwork at bay. Making a living in this game requires high efficiency, and quality results, so here are several useful tools for achieving this. We hope they will be as useful to others as they are to us."

"This double workbench design (photo above) was inspired by Michael Wichman's bench which was simply a long, wide, carpet-topped bench with a tool rack in the center. I worked on

Gabriel Ochoteco's apprentice, Ivan Aird is shown second from right in the photo above. That's Gabriel playing one of his flattops in the photo at right. Gabriel started repairing guitars in his home country, Uruguay, in 1968. During the mid-seventies he studied guitarmaking under Michael Wichman in Hamburg, Germany. In 1984 he moved to Brisbane, Australia, and he's been running his own guitar repair and construction business there ever since. His shop is a warranty service center for Martin, Fender, Ovation, Ochoteco, Takamine, PRS, and most major brands.

one side, Michael worked on the other (keeping an eye on me), and we shared the same tools. Sociable people, Ivan and I enjoy talking whilst dressing our 15 millionth fret, so the bench makes for good communication. We have two such benches, and can keep four guitars going at once with a minimum of tools.

"The center console holds the most-used tools as well as tuners, soldering iron, test amp, electric drivers, straight edges, etc. Each side has its own lights, and a 6" space under the tabletop stores smaller clamped-up work while drying. Two sets of drawers (one facing each side) contain more tools and give weight to the structure. That's Calvin Lim in the foreground (he completed my guitarmaking course last year and has stayed on, part-time, to gain experience).

"The bench's neck rest features a V-shaped caul, padded with non-slip rubber, that swivels on an axle to accommodate any neck angle (a different, *solid* rest is used for fretting, though). The rest can be removed instantly by unclamping the C-clamp/bench-dog. Guitar bodies rest on two adjustable pads which swivel to make solid contact."

more

Regards!

Gabriel Ochoteco

Send inquiries to:
Gabriel's Guitar Workshop
Ochoteco Guitars
115 Gotha St.
PO Box 1101
Fortitude Valley
Queensland 4006
Australia
Phone/Fax: (07) 3257 3297
International: 61 7 3257 3297

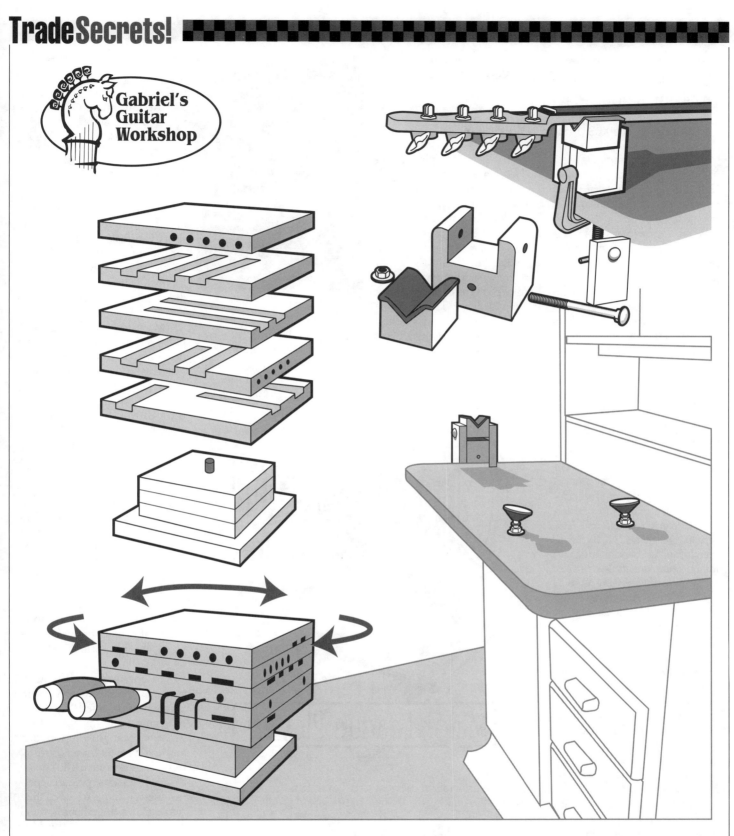

Gabriel's Guitar Workshop

Gabriel Ochoteco's "tool turret" is a clever design. Glued pieces create a solid "butcher block" construction, but before assembling, each layer is drilled and grooved to hold specific shapes. Planned carefully, this can hold a remarkable number of items. The rotating design is particularly good on the center shelf of Gabriel's double workbench because two workers can share it.

Gabriel's benches feature neck rests with V-shaped padded cauls that swivel to accommodate any angle. The neck rests can be removed by unclamping the C-clamp/bench-dog. Guitar bodies rest on two adjustable pads which swivel to make solid contact. (See story on preceding page.)

Cincinnati Is The Home Of Major League Players

Ex-accountant Mixes Business With Pleasure.

ASIA's Symposium '97, held in June in Burlington, Vermont, had a strong turnout, and was a huge success, as usual. A highlight for me came during the repair panel on "Getting Started In Luthiery." The subject of apprenticeships, and how difficult they are to find, was under discussion when a man stood up and said, "I've been fortunate to have served an indepth apprenticeship with Dan Erlewine. He got me started in this business. . ." (Everyone looked at me and applauded, but I was thinking: 'Who is this guy? I've never seen him before. What's he saying?') . . . "in his videotapes," the man continued, "Dan took me right into his shop and showed me how!"

Oh, videotapes! That's where he knew me from! (I wasn't going crazy after all). My "apprentice" was Neil Harrell, from Cincinnati, Ohio. We met after the lecture, became friends, and have kept in touch since. Neil's a good friend of another Cincinnati luthier, Jamon Zeiler, and the two traveled to Symposium together. When I got home from Symposium I realized it was Neil who had sent me this letter a week earlier:

"Dear Dan:

When reviewing your Color Finishing video the other day it occured to me that I feel I know you from your books, videos, *Guitar Player* column, articles in the GAL and ASIA magazines, and of course *Trade Secrets*. I want to thank you, and StewMac, for my new career as a luthier. I love it so much that I feel like this is what I was meant to do—like I've searched my whole life, and this is the perfect thing. Thanks to your help and inspiration, I started working full-time as a luthier in June, 1996.

"My shop is called 'Neil

Harrell's String Hospital' (Guitar Hospital was already taken!). I'm located in Cincinnati, Ohio, and work out of my home shop and a shop in Cincinnati's biggest and best vintage guitar store—'Mike's Music'—owned by Mike and Kelly Reeder. I pattern my working habits after Frank Ford's (after seeing Frank in the videotape 'Trade Secrets On The Road,' and reading about him in a GAL article this past year), by working on the major repairs at my home shop, and the others at the store. So far, things are going really well, and I expect my repair business

Neil Harrell

children are behind me too—Justin (18), Matt (15), and Anne (15). No, Matt and Anne aren't twins—Matt's my stepson.

"My father is a CPA and was president of a cabinet company,

to continue growing for the next few years. I'm making my living right now doing guitar repair, but I'm on the edge, for sure, and right now I'm just glad I have, as Bob Taylor says, 'The first requirement for this career path: a wife (Connie) with a good job and benefits.' Our three

so I was exposed to both the business and production side of cabinetmaking. My mother is an artist and art teacher, and that's where I get my 'artistic side.' I'm 42 years old, and after working as an accountant for 15 years, I got laid off in 1993. A friend, Vernon McIntyre at 'Fa-

mous Old Town Music,' had a repair opening and he offered me the job. He knew that I'd been repairing guitars as a hobby since my teens, and that I'd gotten pretty good at it. Needing an income, I said 'yeah, I can do it,' and jumped right in.

"A year later I left to take a job repairing furniture so that I could improve my finishing skills. Having a particular interest in vintage repair and finish touchups, I thought I could learn lots by repairing furniture—and did. I even took the 'Mohawk Finishing Course.'

"My accounting background helps me understand the business side of things, but a big obstacle has been learning how to do quality work *efficiently*,—keeping the jobs moving through the shop. I'm living a completely different lifestyle now, with regard to how my days are constructed. Without a 9 to 5 routine (I work more hours than that, but it's work and leisure combined), I tend to get lost down in the shop and just lose track of time; this doesn't always translate into making money! So even we ex-accountants have to struggle with setting prices and learning how to charge for our work!

"When I work for the store, Mike takes a cut of my labor—we're experimenting with the amount, but it's been as high as 50 percent, may go as low as 20 percent, or else somewhere in the middle—something that'll be comfortable for both of us. Mike makes any markup on parts and hardware like tuners, strings, tremolos, and etc., while I make a buck on repair-type stuff which he doesn't want to stock like nuts, saddles, fingerboards, wood bridges, fretwire, and the like. And on the work I take home, we do an 80/20 split. Whenever finishing's involved I take the work home because I have a spraybooth in the basement.

Continues...

TradeSecrets!

Luthier's Blue Book:
Neil Harrell's String Hospital Repair Price List

As of July 1997, based on a rate of $50/hour.

Electric Guitar Repairs:

Basic Set-up (Set action, relief, intonation, lube keys, clean fingerboard):

Normal electric	$35 plus strings
With locking tremolo	$55 plus strings

Electronics Repairs:

(Initial charges—range estimates are given for each repair)

Solid body guitar	$25 and up
F-hole electric	$45 and up
Repair pickup	$50 and up
Clean and lube pots/jack	$15 and up
Custom pickguard	$70 plus materials
Install aftermarket bolt-on neck	$25 and up
Fretless bass conversion (replace frets w/wood markers)	$200
Level and "hard seal" rosewood fretboard on fretless bass	$150 and up

Acoustic Guitar Repairs:

Basic Set-up (Set action, relief, lube keys, clean fingerboard):	$30 plus strings
Custom saddle	$25 plus materials

Remove/reglue bridge:

Normal bridge	$60 and up
Bridge with internal pickup (may require pickup repair)	$60 and up
Repair bridge pin holes	$30 and up
Custom bridge	$100 and up
Replace bridge plate	$150 and up
Repair/reinforce bridge plate	$50 and up
Top or back crack	$35 and up
Glue loose braces	$25 per brace
Replace pickguard	$15 and up
Install thinline (or other internal pickup)	$35 and up
Acoustic top replacement	$500 and up
Custom neck to match original	$500 and up
Install 'Bridge Doctor'	$50 plus parts

Neck reset (may require fretwork, finish touchup, etc.):

Basic loose neck on inexpensive guitar	$150 and up
Tight neck on expensive guitar	$250 and up

Common Repairs:

Re-string and tune

6-string	$15 plus strings
12-string	$30 plus strings
Adust truss rod only	$15 and up

Custom nut

6-string	$40 plus materials
12-string	$60 plus materials

Broken headstock:

Reglue (no finish touch-up)	$50 and up
Reglue-finish to match	$125 and up
Reglue, spline or other reinforcement, match finish)	$175 and up

Headstock replacement:

Replace headstock and part of neck—finish to match)	$300 and up

Tuner replacement:

Direct replacement (no drilling, reaming, finish repair)	$15
With drilling, reaming, fill screw holes, finish work)	$35 to $75
Fret dress (level, re-crown, and polish)	$50 and up
Refret (setup, new nut, fretboard leveling additional)	$170
Level fretboard during refret	$50

Partial refret:

First fret	$25
Additional frets	$10 each

Repair broken-out jack in hollowbody:

Basic repair with finish match	$75 and up
Replace part of side, finish to match	$125 and up
Install strap button	$10 with button

Finish Work:

Refinish—New Look

Strat body	$250 and up
Strat neck—rosewood board (no decal)	$150 and up
Les Paul—complete (no decal)	$450 and up
Acoustic	$500 and up
Maple fretboard during refret	$150 and up
Complete maple neck	$250 and up

Finish stripping: hand strip prior to refinishing (decals saved when possible)

Strat body	$100 and up
Strat neck rosewood fretboard	$50 and up
Les Paul complete	$150 and up
Acoustic	$175 and up
Maple fretboard during refret	$50 and up
Complete maple neck	$75 and up

Antique Finish (to restore vintage look)	Add 75% to refinish cost
Install decal during refinishing	$20 plus decal
Touch up finish nicks and dings	$30 and up

Other Stringed Instruments:

Over the years I have worked on many other stringed instruments, including upright basses, violins, mandolins, banjos, autoharps, and even a sitar. Repair prices for such instruments can be provided upon request.

Notes:

Due to the nature of finishes used for guitars, most refinishes require 8 to 12 weeks to complete.

Most vintage guitars are worth more with their old finish—regardless of how badly-damaged it is. Refinishes to vintage guitars are only done to restore finishes already poorly refinished, or ruined in some other way.

Discounts are given for instruments that need multiple repairs done at the same time.

This price list is a guideline only. All repair estimates are made after careful evaluation of each instrument. In many cases, price estimates are given in a range to cover best-to-worst-case scenarios. Every effort is made to treat each customer as fairly as possible and to provide the best service for a fair price.

Prices subject to change without notice

"I have full-sized stationary power tools at home, and small ones (a drill press, sander, and bandsaw) at Mike's. My most-used specialty handtools—fret files, nut files, straight edges, knives, files, rasps, chisels, and others—I carry back and forth between home and the store in a toolbox. That little 'Rolykit' you're selling looks very interesting.

"When I first started, I did a phone survey of the area to determine locally-competitive prices, and used the 'Blue Book' prices in the Stew-Mac catalog. Then Jamon Zeiler and I began sharing our pricing with each other, to get an idea of whether our prices are competitive or not for this area. It's not that we're 'price fixing,' because we don't agree to set a certain price—we just talk about what we think is fair.

"I've tried to pattern my repair business and my prices after the most successful repair business I've been associated with: auto mechanics. One advantage an auto mechanic has is industry-published guidelines that set time and cost standards for various jobs. In the future I'd like to do a survey of guitar repair prices throughout the country, and then establish some published guidelines for our industry. By describing each repair in detail, and then using published cost of living data, we can balance the prices among different locales. Now, here's my price list for 'Blue Book,' and a couple of repair ideas that have worked for me that you may wish to use in *Trade Secrets*.

Neil Harrell
Cincinnati, Ohio

TradeSecrets!

Hot Tips From Neil Harrell's String Hospital

■ I use the Stew-Mac fret guard when I dress frets. For additional protection, I extend each side of the guard with two pieces of the brown "Binding Tape" attached face to face. Then I bend the edges of the guard, and instead of using a rubber band to hold it to the neck, I use a nylon cord tied to one side and clamped to the other side with a mini spring clamp.

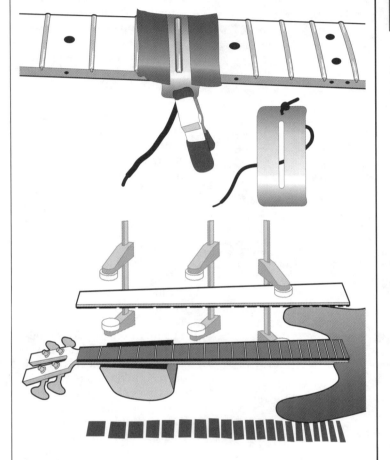

■ Leather cut to fit exactly in-between each fret made an excellent pressure-pad and caul for regluing the fretboard on this Travis Bean bass guitar. By the way, I used the new Titebond Polyurethane glue to glue the rosewood fretboard to the aluminum neck—it worked very well.

■ I use leather to pad clamps and vises around my shop. Most leather shops sell scraps for about $2.00 per grab bag. Besides padding the faces of the jaws on my repair vise, I've added leather safety straps which hang below the jaws to catch a guitar neck if the vise should ever happen to be loosened inadvertantly.

■ Small leather pads glued onto the bottom jaw of my Waverly bridge and brace clamps often make it unnecessary to use specially-shaped protective cauls.

Super-Simple Screw Storage and Squeeze-Out Scraper Secret: Soda Straws!

Frank Ford sends his regards, and passes on this great idea which he learned from Larry Cohea, of California—one of the West Coast's finest banjo pickers, Larry is a well-respected repairman and a master banjo neck maker. Here's Frank:

"Trim a drinking straw at a sharp angle, and use it to clean glue squeeze-out whenever two glue surfaces create a hard-to-clean corner (bridges, finger-boards, and the like). Scoop along with your straw, and as it fills with glue, clip it off and start again! Crease the straw for a very sharp scooper!

"Then, since I had these clear straws laying around, I got the idea of storing small parts in them! Now if I remove a set of tuners, for example, I slide the screws into a straw, staple the ends shut, and throw the straw in the case while I work!"

Frank Ford
Gryphon Stringed Instruments
Palo, Alto, California

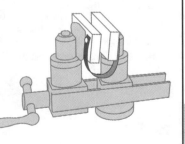

Gettin' In The Groove

Recently, a guitar in for a refret had fret slots which were far too deep (well over 5/32" in the center), and the frets pulled out with very little resistance—there wasn't good "fret-compression" in *this* fretboard! I think Leo Fender's approach to cutting fret slots is best: maintain neck integrity by cutting the slots in an arc to match the fretboard radius, and only as deep as the tang.

Anyhow, I just didn't feel right about leaving all that air space underneath the frets, so I filled the slots with wood up to the depth of the fret tang. Here's how:

Clean the fretslots well. Next, thickness a piece of ebony to match the fretslot's width (these were .024" wide). Then, cut 1/8"-wide strips from it with a razor-knife.

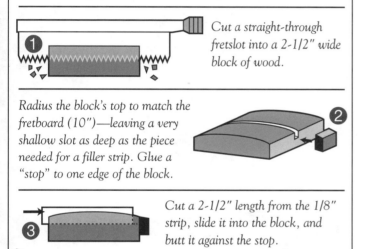

1 *Cut a straight-through fretslot into a 2-1/2" wide block of wood.*

2 *Radius the block's top to match the fretboard (10")—leaving a very shallow slot as deep as the piece needed for a filler strip. Glue a "stop" to one edge of the block.*

3 *Cut a 2-1/2" length from the 1/8" strip, slide it into the block, and butt it against the stop.*

4 *Trim it close to flush with a chisel.*

5 *Final sand it with a 10" radius sanding block.*

6 *You'll end up with a tiny, pre-radiused, fret slot filler strip which, if you're careful, will be just slightly lower than the depth of the tang.*

7 *Center the strip to the fretboard and trim off the excess at each end. I glued my filler strips in with hide glue as I installed each fret. What a difference it made!* *Dan*

TradeSecrets!

Magician Turns Guitar Into Tool Chests!

My father was a magician, and famous magicians often visited our house. I grew up around magic, so it was natural for me to attempt a trick which I learned from Frank Ford of Gryphon Stringed Instruments in Palo Alto, California.

My shop takes up much of the basement for storage, but the actual work area (the ex-garage) is fairly small (9' x 16'). I'd try to keep it neat, but often every flat surface was covered with tools, parts, and jigs by day's end. Important stuff cluttered the belt sander, the mill-drill machine table, the buffer, the bandsaw, my cassette player, and even my chair. Just getting work done was a real trick.

Ralph Erlewine

I had too many tools to fit in the one stack of Sears Craftsman tool chests which I owned, and traipsing back and forth to the other rooms with dozens of tools was really time-consuming. When I discovered "Rolykit" tool organizers things got better: I set up several of the versatile plastic roll-up tool boxes, each holding related tools. My trips to fetch and store tools were fewer, the clutter lessened, I got more work done, and I was happier.

But I found true happiness when I turned a single flattop guitar into four more stacks of mid-priced Craftsman chests to go with the one I already had. I'd paid $1400 for that guitar, but I seldom played it. Now my shop is transformed: it has an entire wall of drawers, housing hundreds of tools within reach, that can be put away after I use them—just like Frank Ford had when I visited his shop in 'Trade Secrets On The Road.'"

This has been the best major "tool" investment I've ever made. I still love Rolykits, and they're an excellent, inexpensive, stackable, way to organize tools (mine are relegated to parts-storage now). But frankly, I don't miss the guitar at all—I'm having too much fun working in an organized shop!

Dan Erlewine, Magician

Three-point support for routing binding on archtop instruments

Don MacRostie showed his technique for routing the binding ledge on his 'Red Diamond' mandolins in the video *Shop Talk 4*. He uses two spring-loaded "spool clamps" on the body to support it up off the table at a uniform height (1/2") which matches the support ring around the cutter bit. The two clamps, plus the support ring, keep the instrument resting on three points at all times—solid, and unlikely to rock. By moving the clamps once, he can rout the entire perimeter of the top or back. The instrument is always level, and the sides maintain the correct right angle to the cutter bit.

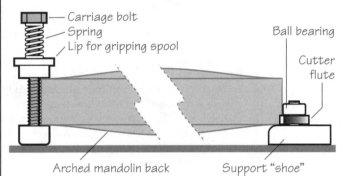

Carriage bolt
Spring
Lip for gripping spool
Ball bearing
Cutter flute
Arched mandolin back
Support "shoe"

Each of Don's clamps is made from two spools of wood cut with a hole-saw. He slides a spring over a carriage bolt, runs the bolt through one spool (the "top"), and threads it into the remaining (bottom) spool. Much of the bolt sits well above the instrument. When Don rests his palm on the bolt head and pulls up on the spring-loaded top spool with his fingers, the clamp releases so he can slide it along to a new spot and release it instantly.

Don drills the top spool halfway through with one hole saw, then switches to a larger hole saw to finish the job. After chipping away the excess, a "lip" is left which he can grab when he wants to release a spool.

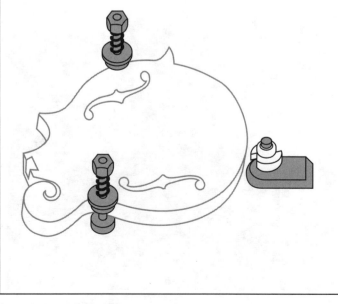

Nashville cats: visiting Gibson's repair team

LAST MONTH I SPENT two weeks in Nashville, Tennessee visiting Gibson USA, at the invitation of Wayne Green, Gibson's Worldwide Director of Customer Service. Under Wayne's command is the Warranty Repair Division, with a team of five repair techs guided by his friend and mine, Roger Fritz. Wayne and Roger enlisted me to instruct the repair crew in the fine points of using the warranty shop's new neck-jig, a '90s version of the tool I designed in the early 1970s for holding a neck under simulated string tension while the fretboard is trued and fretted.

Standing, left to right: Wayne Green, Todd Money, Forrest Smith, Roger Fritz, and Rick Goodwin; kneeling: Jennifer Quigley, Tony Nagy. Not pictured are Service Coordinator Gypsy Carnes, and Shipping and Receiving's Bob Bearden.

Gibson's "industrial" all-steel neck-jig was built by Wally Boswell, a machinist from Easton, Pennsylvania. Wally's "cold-steel" version of my old wooden bench took some getting used to, and some custom alterations, but I ended up wanting one (it's riddled with tapped 3/8"-16 holes for mounting jigs and accessories). Like my neck-jig workbench table, the guitar body is clamped firmly and is then rotated into the "jigging," or "playing" position, where adjustments are made, and the neck support rods are set, before bringing the instrument to the level position for work.

Wally Boswell with the neck jig he made for Gibson's repair shop.

My neck-jig is featured in the video "Don't Fret," and in the books *Fretwork Step By Step*, and the *Guitar Player Repair Guide*. Or check out Don Teeter's version in his book *The Acoustic Guitar—Volume II*, and also Dan Kelchak's variation in Trade Secrets Volume 22. An aluminum and steel neck-jig attachment (#328-J), for mounting on your own benchtop, is available from us at Stew-Mac, as well as plans for building the entire tilting-top guitar workstation that I use (#328-P). And Wally Boswell will be glad to build more of his Super Neck-Jigs. Contact:

The Maya Corporation
attn: Wally Boswell
1310 Knox Ave.
Easton, PA 18042
Phone: (610)-253-4042.

Recently, my wife Joan found an "over-bed" table (used to slide under and over a hospital bed to serve patients) at a yard sale and she knew that I'd want it—which I did! It makes a great tool caddy because its height-adjustable tabletop, which has 14" of travel, brings tools, or lacquer and colors during touch-up, right next to the work. Or, I can sit comfortably in my chair and swing the table over my lap to dress frets. One end of the table tilts, on a split hinge to either side (for reading a book in bed), so it's easy to clamp my surrogate body to it and tilt the guitar toward me or away from me for working on fret ends. Clamping guitars into it other than the bolt-on-neck variety is not so easy however, because the table is rather narrow. I highly recommend an over-bed table for any shop.

For years, the clamping aspect of my rotating neck-jig table has allowed me to hold guitars in almost any position for all repairwork—not just fretwork. With it, and my new over-bed

Sonny Thomas goes from gear-jammin' to guitar repair

Sonny Thomas repairs guitars in Antioch, Tennessee, on the outskirts of Nashville. Sonny and his good friend Leon Rhodes visited Gibson's neck-jig fretting seminar as our guests. Leon Rhodes played and recorded with Ernest Tubb's Texas Troubadors from 1960 until 1967. He's been a staff guitarist for the Grand Ole Opry Band since 1967, and is one of Nashville's finest studio musicians. He's recorded with nearly everyone, including George Jones, Kenny Rogers, Connie Smith, Loretta Lynn, George Strait, Ricky Skaggs, John Denver, and Larry Gatlin. Leon likes repairing guitars, and he and Sonny enjoy working on them together.

table, I thought I was pretty cool until I saw Gibson's fixture for holding guitars in production during parts assembly and final setup. A close relative to both my tilt-table and the tool caddy, Gibson's fixture was conceived by owner Henry Jusckiewicz and built by his head of engineering at the time, Lynn Matthews.

Henry's fixture has a quick-lock handle at the guitar's butt end which allows the guitar to tilt on its side in either direction—or be rotated face down for tuner and electronics installation—while the neck is supported by a U-shaped, felt-lined "yoke." Immediately I saw this fixture as the ideal tool for putting a guitar into the "playing" position for neck adjustment, final nut-slotting, and as the most accessible, user-friendly way to dress frets.

The fixture mounts on a rolling table which, much like my "tool caddy," could swing over the lap of a fret dresser sitting in

Gibson owner Henry Jusckiewicz does the pickin' while Dan Erlewine demonstrates a G-demolished chord.

a back-supporting chair or stool, without his or her shoulders "hunched" painfully. The guitar can be tipped into the perfect fret-dressing positions as metal filings, steel-wool, and sanding dust fall harmlessly onto the table or the floor. I'm hoping to build one for myself soon, and when I do you'll read about it here.

There's lots more to tell about Roger Fritz and the Gibson crew in future issues, because I learned as much as they did as we "Traded Secrets." Thanks, Roger!

That's Sonny Thomas (left) in the Gibson repair shop with Roger Fritz and Leon Rhodes. The impromptu jam session between Sonny and Leon was a highlight of the seminar.

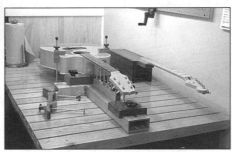

Sonny's "hold-down" clamps, the T-slotted jigging table, and his solid cherry "Luthier's Workstation" were built for him by Tom Owens, a veteran woodworker and cabinetmaker who lives nearby.

Sonny's a great guitarist too, and he played the Opry many times in Leroy "Just Walk On By" Van Dyke's band. After 24 years of driving for Roadway Truck Lines, the 54 year-old repairman will retire next year with a full pension and plenty of time to spend in his well-outfitted shop.

Sonny's version of the neck-jig combines my jig design with Don Teeter's. Although Sonny doesn't tilt the guitar into the "playing" position to set the jig rods, he may be considering that option after talking with me.

Whether tilted or horizontal, most necks lift off the jig rods when the strings are removed, and for years we've been loosening the truss rod to let the neck settle back down on the jig rods. Sonny discovered (as have I) that it isn't usually necessary

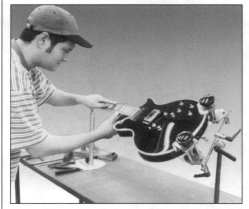

Rick Goodwin using Gibson's high-tech guitar holder for dressing frets.

Continues...

Sonny Thomas
Continued

Sonny's neck jig applies upward stress on the peghead to simulate string tension.

to loosen the truss rod to recontact the neck with the jig rods. He jigs the guitar with the truss rod in its tightened position, and then recreates the string tension by pushing *up* on the peghead until the neck recontacts the jig rods.

Often the problem areas in a fretboard, such as humps or dips, disappear when you remove the strings and loosen the truss rod. Then, since you didn't remove what "wasn't there," the problems reappear after you string the guitar back up.

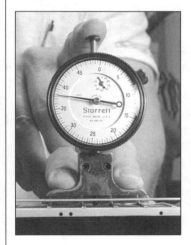

Sonny uses a custom-ground Starret anvil depth-micrometer to measure fret height. The anvil base was ground to fit in between the strings (left).

In his shop (below), he has a "Speedo" tool display from an auto parts store. The rugged four-sided unit rotates on a floor stand and holds loads of parts. Sonny plans on customizing it to hold tools—a great idea!

At Gibson we added two more neck control measures by mounting fixtures to pull *down* near the nut, and push *lengthwise* on the peghead (illustrated below). All you neck-jiggers should try this, because any humps or problems in the fretboard are more noticeable and easier to remove during levelling when the neck is jigged under truss rod tension.

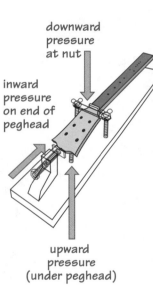

downward
pressure
at nut

inward
pressure
on end of
peghead

upward
pressure
(under peghead)

More Major League Action From Cincinnati

In the last Trade Secrets we interviewed Cincinnati, Ohio repairman Neil Harrell. This issue, we visit his friend Jamon Zeiler, another of Cincinnati's major-league repairmen.

Jamon Zeiler is the guitar repair technician for Buddy Rogers Music, a chain of four music stores in Cincinnati owned by Dave Miller and Bill Harvey. Buddy Rogers is a full-line music store that sells and services horns, drums, keyboards, guitars, amps, and all

the accessories. In guitars alone, they're dealers for Fender, PRS, Parker, Taylor, Guild, Ibanez, Gibson, Seagull, Godin, and Tacoma.

A 1992 graduate of the Building & Repair program at the Red Wing Technical School in Red Wing, Minnesota, Jamon credits good training, a little luck, and mostly hard work for getting him the job at Buddy Rogers, and he feels well rewarded for his efforts...

"The training I received at Red Wing served me well although I was a little impatient at times during the long 11-month course—wanting things to go at a *faster* pace, to *keep up with me*. Later, after getting out in the field I found I learned a whole lot more than I realized at the time, and I credit Dave Vincent for that. Thanks, for your patience, Dave!"

"The lucky part of it, or let's say good fortune, is that I was in the right place at the right time when our repair department manager Scott Snyder—a skilled horn technician—called Red Wing looking to hire a guitar tech.

"Hard work is really what got me this job. I *worked* really hard at Red Wing—along with all the repair training, I built four guitars during my stay! And I've had to work hard since I came to Buddy Rogers in order to keep up with the demands of working in a professional service center.

"The reward is that I can make a living working with guitars. It's a real 'family man's job,' and I appreciate it every day! We have a 401K retirement plan, medical and dental insurance, and along with a 50/50 split of the labor on all repairs, I get a guaranteed salary of $400 a week. My wife, Wendy, and our daughter Rebecca love this area, and we're happy here.

"Wendy and I went to Red Wing together by the way, and that's why it cost us our life savings. Our double-enrollment, and family living expenses for a year came to $30,000! Wendy graduated from the professional-level violin course, and although she's not pursuing the trade, she's good. Wendy trained me in servicing violins. We didn't really know it would work out that way, but what luck!

"I've developed this job to the point where I can make my living and still have time for myself. I'm not so burned-out when I get home that I don't feel like building. I build and sell about five guitars a year."

Dave Miller, Jamon Zeiler and Bill Harvey. Dave and Bill own Cincinnati's Buddy Rogers Music stores.

Jamon with Scott Snyder, repair department manager for Buddy Rogers Music.

Repair tips from the Buddy Rogers service center:

1 "Suppose you're making a new nut for a guitar that also needs fret dressing—the frets have mild grooves worn in them, almost like dents, but they don't buzz. If the owner can't or won't afford fretwork, you must be careful to cut the new string slots in exactly the same position as the old, or you'll get fret buzz instantly, as soon as the strings are out of alignment to the gentle grooves worn in the frets. Here's a tip: put a piece of tape on the fingerboard, and carefully mark the old slot spacing onto it before removing the nut. Fit the new nut blank, then copy the marks onto it.

2 "In the winter, the top of many acoustics will "sink" as the guitar loses moisture in the dry heat. The action lowers and the strings buzz. Instead of making two saddles (winter and summer versions) I make a *winter saddle shim*. I can quickly make a rosewood shim for a reasonable $15, and customers like being able to install it themselves.

3 "When removing a Fender nut, the finish behind the nut tends to chip. I take the Stew-Mac brown "binding" tape (#677), stretch it really tight across the area, and wrap it around the neck. After removing the nut, I remove the tape carefully—that stuff is strong! (I wouldn't advise this on an old

dry maple-neck finish). I've not had one fretboard chip in the two years I've been following this advice.

4 "Sometimes with rosewood fingerboards after I get the neck and frets set up just so, a customer gets a buzz later on that night—on the job. I figured out that the rosewood board is absorbing moisture and backbowing. One fix for this is to rub a coat or two of lacquer into the bare rosewood fretboard and then steelwool it to de-gloss it. This has worked for me on numerous occasions."

Jamon Zeiler

Backbow caused by sweating playing hands seems probable. Thanks, Jamon! Any comments on this from other Trade Secrets readers?
—Dan

Luthier's Blue Book PRICES & RATES

Guitar repair price guidelines from the Buddy Rogers service center:

Minimum bench charge:	$15

Maintenance and setup:
Includes string removal, clean and polish fingerboard and frets, clean body, check tuners, bridge, nut, tailpiece, and electronics, set action, adjust truss rod, balance tremolo, lube, test and play .... $40 plus strings

Maintenance and setup with fret dress, clean and fit nut .... $80 plus strings

Restring and tune only (6-string) .... $15 plus strings

Restring and tune only (12-string) .... $20 plus strings

Adjust neck $15

Set intonation $15

Fret dressing $15

Complete refret .... $40—$60

Partial refret .... $225—$300

dressing, too) (add on $40 .... $17 ea. + $40

Install new nut (6 string) $45

Install new nut (12 string) $65

Saddle (custom made) $45

Install tuners .... $15 - $40 plus parts

Neck repairs:

Heat-straighten neck $40

Plane and refret .... $275 - $350

Reset neck (acoustic) $225

Repair broken peghead .... $50 - $80

(with touch-up) .... $125 - $150

Top repairs (Acoustic)

Replace entire top .... $750 - $1000

Replace bridge plate .... $150 - $200

Remove and reglue bridge $60

Custom-make new bridge, install (6 string) $80

(12 string) $115

Crack repairs .... $40–$220 ($20 per inch)

Set-up acoustic guitar .... $25 plus strings

Electric Guitar Repairs:

Replace potentiometer .... $25 plus pot

Replace selector switch .... $30 plus switch

Install mini-toggle switch $35

Install push-pull pot .... $35 plus pot

Install output jack $20

Replace toggle switch (Strat or Les Paul) .... $25 plus parts

Acoustic pickup installation:

Transducer under saddle (Gold Plus, 332 Thinline) $50

Soundhole w/endpin jack $35

Preamp (cut side hole, install pickup) .... $100 and up

Electric guitar pickup installation:

One pickup $30

Two pickups $35

Three pickups $40

Buddy Rogers Music

Bill Antel's vintage clay dots start with custom-made dowels

Bill Antel, 39, of Monrovia, California, is a veteran woodworker, vintage guitar expert, and guitarist who specializes in building and repairing electric guitars. Upon graduating from high school in 1977, Bill's first job was at the Thomas Guitar Company, where he learned the basics of solidbody guitar building from owner Richard Thomas. Thomas, along with Carl Sandeval, had previously been

one of the top guys in Wayne Charvel's shop. Next, Bill moved on to Anvil Cases to learn a different side of woodworking. Today, and since the early 1980s, Antel works, with an occasional apprentice, at his home shop in Monrovia.

"You asked about my clay dots," says Bill, "but first I should tell you how I make dowels without a lathe, because I 'turn' clay dots the same way:

■ "Chuck a dowel, that you want to downsize accurately, into the drill-press quill.

■ "Clamp a flexible-shaft rotary tool (or Dremel Tool) into an auxiliary compound 'milling' vise clamped onto the drill-press table. My rotary tool is Dremel's 1/5 h.p. version, but you could

use a regular Dremel MultiPro/Moto Tool, or the Moto-Tool driven Flex Shaft Stew-Mac sells (page 21, Part No.1273).

■ "Using a 1/2" drum sander in the rotary tool's collet, and with both the sander and the drill-press running (the sanding drum is turning upward, toward the quill), just run the spinning dowel down along the sanding drum. The milling vise lets you 'feed' the sanding drum into the dowel slowly and accurately. It works great!

"As for imitating vintage clay dots, I've heard that they were originally made from old floor tiles (linoleum perhaps?), but I use a slow-curing, white dollmaker's epoxy that has a ceramic powder additive which gives it a putty-like consistency. I mix a little bit of yellow fresco powder into it, and then form it into little 'snakes'—rolling it in my hands like modeling clay. When the snakes are dry, I chuck them in the drill-press quill, 'turn' them to size, and slice off the 'clay-dots'. The epoxy is manufactured by Martin R. Carbone Inc., 1227 DeLavina St., Santa Barbara, CA 93101 (805) 965-5574.

"Then I tint the dots by rubbing them with a concoction made by soaking brazilian rosewood shavings in lacquer thinner until the reddish pitch colors the thinner. After throwing the shavings away, I leave the container open to evaporate into a thick liquid that colors the epoxy perfectly. Here's a jar of my mix for you, Dan."

Bill Antel
Antel Guitars
Monrovia, California

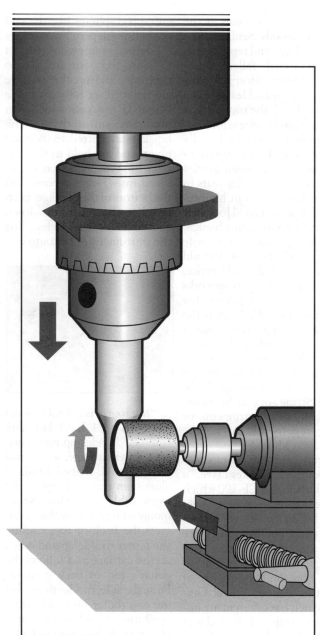

The flexible-shaft tool is clamped into a milling vise with a cross-feed; this allows the upward-turning drum sander to be moved slowly and precisely into the rotating dowel — "turning" it to the required diameter.

From Dave Jones: a router table that follows any contour

We met Dave Jones at the '96 Northwoods Seminar, the guitar building and repair workshop held each fall at Bryan Galloup's Guitar Hospital in Big Rapids, Michigan. He impressed the crowd with the travel guitar he'd built, and a system for routing binding channels. Equally impressive is the $15.00 shop-made repair vise shown here!

After serving seven years in the Air Force Aircraft Maintenance Division, David Jones left the service to study mechanical engineering. Now Dave, his wife Debby, and their 14-year-old daughter Nicole live in Florence, South Carolina, where he works as a project engineer for Wellman, Inc. Wellman is the polyester manufacturer known for Fortrel®. Debby also works for Wellman, as a microcomputer analyst. At night and on weekends, Dave operates Traditional Stringwork in his home shop, building instruments or doing repairwork for nearby McFadyen Music.

"I ruined my first vintage guitar about 1982," jokes Dave, "a beautiful Gibson CF-100 which I drilled for Grover tuners. However, I didn't really get serious about guitar building until three years ago, and since then I've built perhaps sixteen guitars. Right now I'm building five of my little 'Bigfoot Travel Guitars' which have seen many improvements since I showed it at the Northwoods Seminar!

"I got the router-table idea from Tom Ribbecke, and then in Stew-Mac's Summer 1996 catalog (**Trade Secrets** Volume 26, page 27) I saw a similar setup used by Hugo Valcke of Belgium.

"The flat plywood carriage which holds the guitar rides on industrial ball casters, which are entrapped spheres like the end of a ball-point pen. The carriage is shaped somewhat like a Gibson SG, for access to cutaways, and on the carriage are fastened six fully adjustable L-shaped brackets which can hold any guitar shape. The brackets are slotted, to slide and pivot, and are held to the carriage by Acme wing screws fastened into T-nuts mounted in the bottom of the carriage. Each bracket has up-and-down adjustable "levelers" for levelling the instrument to be routed.

Left: the carriage with its adjustable levelers moves the guitar body in relation to the router bit. A large, flat worktable allows plenty of room.

Center: the underside of the carriage shows the roller casters and T-nuts.

Right: a level is placed on the guitar top for careful adjustment before routing.

"My router is a Ryobi model TR30UII (3/4 h.p.) laminate trimmer. It rides up and down on a roller carriage, which fastens to an L-shaped hunk of aluminum that I clamp to the work table. A nylon 'shoe' mounted to the baseplate contacts the back or top, causing the router to ride up and down on the carriage as it follows the guitar's top or back contour. From the side, the depth-guide I use is a router bit/ball-bearing combination, although a simple finger or follower would also work. Anyone interested in this setup should contact:

Linear Motion Components
2101 Jericho Turnpike
Box 5416, New Hyde Park, NY
11042-5416
Phone: (516) 328-3970

Ask for information on the Techno isel, Series 2, Dual-Rail Roller carriage."

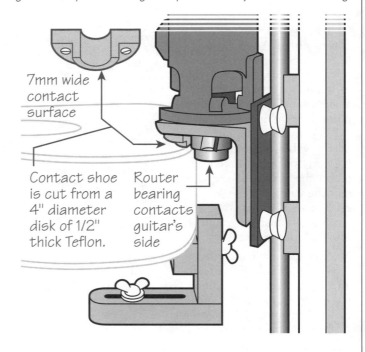

7mm wide contact surface

Contact shoe is cut from a 4" diameter disk of 1/2" thick Teflon.

Router bearing contacts guitar's side

How to heat up just a small amount of hide glue? Here's a cheesy idea!

In searching for the ideal way to keep a small amount of hot hide glue at working temperature without a fuss, I've built my own heater out of insulated coffee cans, used a baby bottle warmer, and fussed with a double boiler. All the while the perfect solution was right under my nose: adapting Stew-Mac's one-quart Hold-Heet Electric Glue Pot for a smaller amount of glue.

The manufacturer recommends that the glue pot be kept at least half full for proper function, but that much glue would last me three months or more, and would go bad within a couple of weeks. The solution is to build a lid that suspends a jar in the chamber of the pot. The jar can hold only a couple of ounces of hide glue that can be used up before it goes bad. I leave the pot empty, and heat only the air.

The lid is two circular pieces of 1/2" plywood, with one smaller than the other to create a step, or "flange," to hold the lid firmly on the pot. In the center a 2-5/8" diameter hole accepts a recycled 8-ounce Cheez-Whiz jar. The jar suspends well into the glue pot, but since it's tapered, doesn't fall through the hole, and has a good fitting "bayonet-style" lid.

The thermometer pictured is important. It's simply a $6-$8 meat thermometer, but it measures the temperature inside the pot. When thermometer reads 160°F, the glue in the jar will be the correct working temperature of 140-145°F. The explanation for this is that the jar is partially outside of the heated glue pot and thus loses a little of its heat. The cover is a tin can, trimmed to an appropriate size, and it helps reduce heat loss through the exposed top of the glue jar.

Periodically I'll remove the thermometer from the air cavity and use it to check the actual temperature of the glue—which should be around 145°.

Don MacRostie
Stew-Mac Research & Development
and maker of Red Diamond mandolins

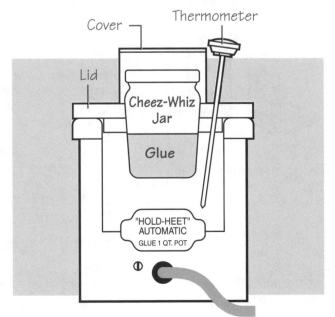

Direct mail advertising nets a big payback

Dave Cassotta, 45, who operates SonFather Guitar Works in Rocklin, California, hired a direct mail company to send 10,000 Guitar Adjustment discount coupons to his local area, with big results. "I paid for the $310 mailing the first day," says Dave, "and within three weeks had made an additional $800! I only mailed to one small zone, but that was 10,000 people. It continued to work throughout the summer, so this Fall I mailed the exact same flyer again—with the same results!"

"The mailer reads:

SonFather Guitar Works, Dave Cassota
Guitar Repair & Modifications
Custom Handcrafted Guitars
Licensed & Insured.

"The coupon includes the phone number, and reads:
"Guitar Adjustment—Acoustic & Electric—$25 (Reg. $30), including: remove strings, clean & polish fingerboard & frets, inspect tuners, bridge, nut, tailpiece, and electronics, restring, adjust truss rod, set action, balance tremolo, tune & intonate. INCLUDES FREE SET OF S.I.T. STRINGS!

"Look in the yellow pages under 'Advertising/Direct Mail.' Two big companies are Adworks, and Val-Pak. AdWorks took my logo on computer disc (a JPEG file), along with a color photo of a guitar I'd built, and made a four-color coupon which I approved before they mailed it along with a number of other coupons (individual mailers cost five or six times as much).

"Like most of us, my shop is at home in a residential area, so it's important to look good. Printing your logo on repair tags, receipt books, and business cards, along with the phone, fax, and e-mail address, makes you look professional. A glance at the wall tells customers I'm a member of the G.A.L., A.S.I.A., and N.A.M.M., and that I'm licensed and insured (that simply means I'm licensed to do business in the city, and I have homeowner's insurance—but it looks good).

"My logo-imprinted office supplies come from the Retailer's Success and Reference Guide at New England Business Service (800) 225-6380. They have everything from checks and accounting systems to business cards, and repair tags."

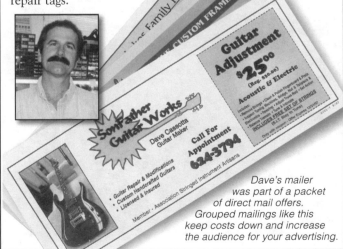

Dave's mailer was part of a packet of direct mail offers. Grouped mailings like this keep costs down and increase the audience for your advertising.

Making wooden bushings on a drill press

Bill Antel was introduced on page 99, where he described using a drill-press as a vertical "lathe." Here's a variation on that setup which Bill uses for making wooden bushings.

"A good way of tightening tuning key holes is to use 'bushings,' or wooden sleeves," writes Bill, "Let's say you want to bush, or tighten up, oversize holes on a Strat that had Grovers installed, and go back down to vintage 11/32" holes. You can use Stew-Mac's conversion bushings (see catalog page 76), but often we find holes that were so crudely enlarged that even conversion bushings won't fit. Or maybe you just want to use wood, or need an accurate wood bushing for another task."

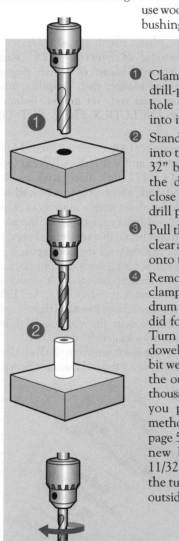

❶ Clamp a block of maple to your drill-press table and drill a 1/2" hole (or other nominal size) into it, about an inch deep.

❷ Stand a length of 1/2" dowel into the hole, switch to an 11/32" bit, and drill a hole into the dowel—you'll be pretty close to center. Turn off the drill press.

❸ Pull the dowel out of the hole, clear any chips, and shove it up onto the drill-bit.

❹ Remove the block of wood and clamp your FlexShaft sanding drum tool on the table, as we did for making the clay dots. Turn on the drill-press—the dowel will stick on the turning bit well enough for you to trim the outside diameter to a few thousandths or so over the hole you plan to fill using the method I showed earlier (see page 52). Cut off slices of your new bushings—they'll have 11/32" inside diameter to fit the tuning keys, and whatever outside diameter you make.

Versatile repair vise from a screw clamp

Here's a great shop-made repair vise designed by Dave Jones (see related story on page 100). He's used an 8" wooden Jorgenson hand-screw clamp and a mount made of angle iron bolted to the workbench.

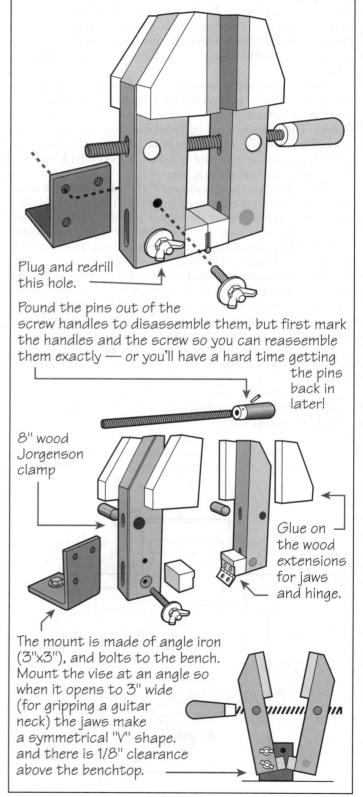

Plug and redrill this hole.

Pound the pins out of the screw handles to disassemble them, but first mark the handles and the screw so you can reassemble them exactly — or you'll have a hard time getting the pins back in later!

8" wood Jorgenson clamp

Glue on the wood extensions for jaws and hinge.

The mount is made of angle iron (3"x3"), and bolts to the bench. Mount the vise at an angle so when it opens to 3" wide (for gripping a guitar neck) the jaws make a symmetrical "V" shape. and there is 1/8" clearance above the benchtop.

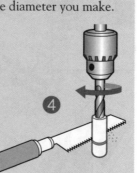

TradeSecrets!

Hot tips & inside scoops. Editor: Dan Erlewine

Fiddlin' Around In The Repair Shop!

Jeff Hostetter, of Stringed Instrument Repair in New Freedom, Pennsylvania, began repairing guitars in 1975. His partner Amy Hopkins started in 1986 when she dropped into Jeff's shop to get her fiddle fixed, and never left (he must've fixed it right). "We've been together ever since," says Amy, "repairing everything from electric and acoustic guitars, banjos, and violins to those strange whatchamacallits from the era of invention, such as ukelins and zithers (that's a double-top mando-cello in the photo of Jeff and Amy on the facing page). We like to build as much as we can, but the repair work keeps us swamped with everything from neck sets and major restorations, to cleaning out the guitar for the lady whose pet tomcat peed in the soundhole. She'd dumped a whole box of baking soda in it—it was so gross. That was the worst *smelling* job we ever did!

Amy's dog howls each time she plays. "We didn't teach him this trick," says Amy, "he learned it on his own."

Jeff and Amy's homemade thickness sander.

In 1990 we bought the barn that houses our shop, and built an upstairs apartment. The shop is separated into three parts. The wood shop is separate from the bench area, which helps to keep dust down, and the spray room is upstairs. The spray room's walls taper back to a 20" explosion-proof fan. For air intake there are four 16" x 20" openings which hold standard furnace filters. Truthfully, it could use more intake because the fan draws hard when the door's closed.

"The retail and the central work area are the only humidity-controlled areas, so our finishing work depends on outside humidity. This will change as the rest of the building is finished.

"Our main workbench is pretty basic. It's a twelve-foot-long plywood bench with a carpeted top. All the small handtools hang above it on pegboard. Storage is a problem, even though we have two three-level, four foot metal shelves along the wall for work in progress (facing page, right).

"The woodworking shop is pretty standard: drill press, sanders, bandsaws, tablesaw, and jointer. The thickness sander (left) we made ourselves. It was inspired by Richard Hoover of the Santa Cruz Guitar Company. It's very basic, with a hinged table that raises and lowers with wingnuts on heavy 5/8" bolts, and an 'Armstrong' feed mechanism. We originally built it for thicknessing tops and sides, but mostly use it for replacement bridges, fingerboard extension shims, neck reset shims, and the like. It didn't take long to build, and it provides all that a small shop needs at little cost. We make dedicated jigs for most jobs that come up in the shop, and these we label and store—that's more shelf space needed! Hey, one of a luthier's most important woodworking talents is the ability to build shelves!

"We met Frank Ford, from Gryphon Stringed Instruments, at the Northwoods Seminar. Frank's a time-study whiz bang, and he inspired us to start keeping track of our work. Now every instrument on the bench gets clocked in and out—not only the overall time, but each phase of the repair. We put the info on computer in Quickbooks Pro, but it all starts out on index cards. (You don't have to be too modern to see where the time goes). Most repair jobs have set prices; however, some have to be based on time and materials.

"Jeff and I can't stress enough the importance of resources such as Northwoods, or the ASIA and GAL conventions, as a means of exchanging information and learning. There's no reason to do a poor job on an instrument through ignorance. There are people out there whom you can learn from, so ask! We couldn't begin to list the folks who've helped us on tough problems. I, for instance, will gladly tell anyone who needs to know the very *best* way to clean cat pee out of an acoustic guitar!"

Amy Hopkins and Jeff Hostetter
Stringed Instrument Repair, New Freedom, PA

Shop tips from Jeff Hostetter and Amy Hopkins, Stringed Instrument Repair, New Freedom, PA

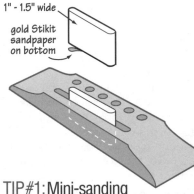

1" - 1.5" wide

gold Stikit sandpaper on bottom

TIP #1: Mini-sanding block for saddle slot bottoms

Flatten the bottom of a 1" to 1-1/2" scrap of bone saddle blank perfectly (we use sandpaper laid on plate glass). The bone should be slightly less than the thickness of the saddle slot, so it slides freely. Fasten a bit of 220 to 320-grit sandpaper to the flat bottom with superglue, and trim the edges with a razor blade (the gold mylar-backed 3M Stikit sandpaper is good for this and many other sanding operations). Now you can sand the bottom of the slot quite precisely.

TIP #2: Easy color matching

For easy color matching in finish touch-ups, we set a piece of glass over the area to be touched-up, and mix colors on the glass.

Amy Hopkins and Jeff Hostetter

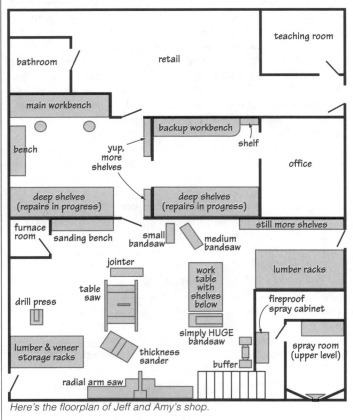

Here's the floorplan of Jeff and Amy's shop.

TIP #3: Patching glitter binding

Need to replace some missing gold "sparkle" binding, such as that used on some Gibson and Gretsch guitars and the Style-6 Gibson banjo? Sparkle binding is hard to come by. We reproduced it with the two-part epoxy "bar finish" often used as a wall-clock finish. Here's how it worked…

■ Mix the epoxy, and tint it with water-soluble vintage amber ColorTone powdered stain.

■ Lay a 3" wide sheet of wax paper onto an acrylic sheet. It should be a little longer than you'd like the strip to be. Stick the wax paper to the acrylic sheet with carpet tape to keep it flat.

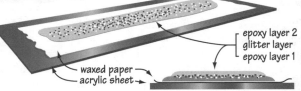

epoxy layer 2
glitter layer
epoxy layer 1

waxed paper
acrylic sheet

■ Run a long trail of the tinted epoxy down on the wax paper.

■ When it has set a little, sprinkle it well with dime store glitter and let it dry overnight. I used gold but any color sparkle would be fine, I'm sure.

■ Run another thick epoxy layer over the glitter, and let it dry.

■ Once dry, true the edges on the bandsaw and belt sander, and thickness the top to the bottom (the bottom is already flat from being spread on the acrylic) on the thickness sander. Be careful not to sand through to the glitter.

■ Wet-sand and buff the strips to a gloss. This binding bends easily with a bit of heat. (I use a hot water bath rather than direct heat—simmering the hot water).

Deep shelves provide a safe place for repairs between work sessions.

Luthier's Blue Book
Prices & Rates

Complete Setup:

Set nut action, set soundpost, fit pegs, fit new bridge, install fine tuners (when necessary), restring .... $60 + materials

Set nut action $10

Fit new ebony nut $30

Set or adjust soundpost .... $9 to $15

Install new soundpost and adjust

Violin & Viola $25

Cello $35

Bass $45

Install & fit new bridge

Violin & Viola .... $25 + bridge

Cello .... $35 + bridge

Bass .... $60 + bridge

Pegs:
Adjust or refit existing pegs

Violin & Viola .... $17.50 – $22.50

Install and fit new pegs

Violin & Viola .... $8.50 each + peg

Bush pegholes

Violin & Viola .... $20 per hole + peg

Fit new ebony saddle (Violin) $30

Install new tailgut (Violin) $15

Reglue fingerboard (Violin) $25

Resurface Fingerboard

Violin $35

Cello $50

Bass $70

Replace fingerboard (new bridge and nut may be required)

Violin .... $60 to $75 plus fingerboard

Reglue neck (requires refitting in some cases)

Violin .... $48 – $60

Cello .... $60 – $90

Bass .... $115 – $155
(Neck block repair is extra)

Repitch neck (Violin) .... $60 – $75

Repair broken heel in bass neck

3/4" maple spline inset ....
.... $120 plus neck reglue

Remove top and reglue

Violin .... $ 75 to $ 90 + repair

Cello .... $100 to $125 + repair

Bass .... $125 to $150 + repair

Bow repairs (violin)

Rehair with horsehair $40
(new wedge may be required)

Wedges .... $ 8.50 each

Replace tip .... $20 – $30

Replace slide .... $25 – $35

Re-grip .... $10 – $25

Heat-treat bow
(to straighten or re-camber) ... $15 – $25

Bending delicate wood marquetry and purfling with a modified bending iron

A highlight for me at last summer's (1997) ASIA convention in Burlington, Vermont, was playing the long-scale 00-45 style guitar which TJ Thompson had just completed for a lucky client. Afterward, TJ explained how he adapted our #689 bending iron for edge-bending the thin strips of wood used for the side purfling lines of a style-45 guitar:

TJ bolts a 3/4" thick aluminum "cap" to the end of his bending iron, with a spacer in between to create a small groove or channel around the perimeter. TJ experiments with each spacer's thickness, shape, and placement until the groove accepts the exact dimensions of whatever he's bending *after the metal expands and the wood swells.* Trapped in the groove, a purfling is less prone to deflect, fall apart, or lose shape during the bending operation.

"I use the cap for two things," says TJ. "To help bend delicate colored wood marquetry or herringbone, and for the tricky task of bending laminated wood purfling lines on edge to go around the sides of the guitar . At first I hand-shaped flat aluminum spacers — similar to the cap, but thinner and smaller—because I thought there wouldn't be enough heat transferred using just bent wire spacers. As it turned out, the wire spacers work just as well as solid ones. For example, 18 gauge wire is .046" in diameter, 20-gauge measures .032", and so forth.

"Set the bending iron on medium, and with colored marquetry or herringbone, lightly mist the strip with water; purfling lines you can just wipe with a damp rag. After you bend the piece, pull it from the groove and hold it in the formed shape until it cools."

TJ Thompson
Thompson Guitars, West Concord, MA

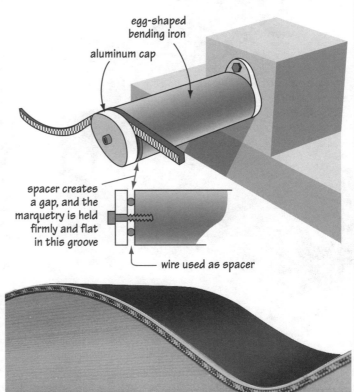

egg-shaped bending iron

aluminum cap

spacer creates a gap, and the marquetry is held firmly and flat in this groove

wire used as spacer

Northwoods Seminar 1998 Coming This Fall

The fourth biannual Northwoods Guitar Building & Repair Seminar will be held this September at Bryan Galloup's Guitar Hospital in Big Rapids, Michigan. For information on seminar topics, instructors, and exact dates, contact: Bryan or Susan Galloup at The Guitar Hospital, 10495 Northland Drive, Big Rapids, MI 49307, (616) 796-5611.

Jim Nunis

All fixed up...

Jim Nunis, 45, and his wife Inge live in Marietta, Georgia with a houseful of cats, dogs, and birds—and more than a few guitars. In the 1970s, Jim worked with Randy Wood and Danny Ferrington at Randy's Old Time Pickin' Parlor in Nashville, Tennessee. He later spent three years at Gruhn Guitars repairing all the electric guitars and the majority of the acoustics. Burned-out by the music scene, Jim quit guitar repair around 1979 to pursue a career in electrical products supply. A man who has worked on guitars for Steve Howe, Joe Perry, Eric Clapton, and Bruce Springsteen, Jim returned to building and repairing instruments again in 1991. He works part-time in his well-equipped home workshop. To date, Nunis has built perhaps 100 custom instruments in a variety of styles. We love the design of his electric mandolin, and we're impressed by his restoration of the Gibson ES-335 described here.

"Dan: Enclosed are before-and-after photos of the cherry-red 1967 ES-335TDC which we discussed. Because of severe water damage it needed a complete refinishing. It had rested on its treble side in a basement flooded 4" deep (up to the ƒ-hole). The guitar needed extensive reshaping and gluing of the treble side rim, top, and back, and regluing of the original binding. The maple plys of the treble side cutaway horn had disintegrated, so I patched in a veneer cap to return the horn's contoured shape, and saturated the area with superglue before sanding it smooth. Still, areas of the veneer were sanded-through into the cross-grain plys underneath. Hiding the blemish without painting the guitar opaque was going to be a trick, and I ended up using a variety of techniques.

"Using Zip Strip methylene-chloride stripper, I removed the finish carefully, avoiding the binding, and being especially careful of the neck. I didn't want to sand the neck or lose any of its size, because those later '60s necks are thin. After stripping, the body and neck retained their red color. Next, I cleaned the guitar with Dupont's Prep-Sol No. 3919-S, and Sherwin-William's Ultra-Clean. Both are silicone removers. This guitar must have been bathed regularly in silicone polish however, because even after my good cleaning there was no way to spray lacquer without serious silicone-caused fisheyes. I learned this by spraying a test patch of lacquer and watching it pool.

I cleaned off the test patch and sealed the whole instrument with two coats of fresh-mixed Behlen's Super-Blonde shellac. This acted as a barrier between the silicone and the lacquer. I was then able to do all the finish repairs without further trouble. It's best to let shellac coats sit overnight before topcoating with lacquer, especially if there's silicone underneath it.

"Next, I grained the area with a small brush, using artist's acrylic watercolors. I applied mostly pink and red tones to match the lighter background color of the wood, the washed-out cherry look of the stain remaining in the wood, and some of the darker grain lines. I used Pyrrole Red, Mars Yellow, CP Cadmium Red-Dark, Raw Sienna, and Burnt Umber—these colors were mixed with Titanium White and Naples Yellow.

"Then I got the idea to fog the area with a light mist coat of opaque red lacquer. I'd never tried this before, but it made all the difference. It was an automotive lacquer which Sherwin Williams custom-mixed to a cherry-red. I thinned it way down and fogged only the patched area, and it started to blend with the surrounding wood. Because of its thin vis

and just as good as old!

cosity, the red is more *translucent* than opaque. You can still see the wood and my graining work if you look closely.

"I mixed two different red ColorTone alcohol-soluble stains—Red and Cherry Red—into clear lacquer to produce transparent red lacquer "toners." Each was mixed in its own jar of clear lacquer, and they were not mixed together. I tested the strengths of the reds on scrap wood, and sprayed these alternately in light coats over the patch, feathering the edges. After about six light coats the patch looked almost right, and I sprayed a red toner coat over the entire instrument—lightly over the patch since it already had color—before starting with clear coats.

"Neither red looked right alone, so next I combined them to make a 50/50 mix of the two red alcohol stains, added to clear lacquer in a ratio of 1 part color to 5 parts lacquer. I used this for one uniform coat, let it dry, and followed with second and third toner coats of *different* colors. The second coat was clear lacquer with *orange* added, the third was clear lacquer with *amber* added. The orange gave it that special tint of the cherry ES-series semihollow bodies, and the amber replaced the yellowed vintage look and toned the binding. When these coats had dried to the touch, I scraped the color from

the binding while the finish was still soft enough to make this easy.

"I then sprayed four coats of clear lacquer (that's seven coats of finish so far, counting the three toner coats), let them dry overnight, and level-sanded them thoroughly the next day with 320-grit Fre-Cut sandpaper. Then I sprayed four more coats, sanding between coats two and three. I level-sanded the last coat with 400-grit Fre-Cut, and sprayed a last finish coat of six parts lacquer to four parts thinner to end the process.

"After the guitar cured for two weeks, I wet-sanded it with 600 thru 2000-grit wet-or-dry sandpaper and buffed it. I used my variable-speed Makita electronic sander/polisher (Model #9207PC) set at 1800 rpm, and Mirror Glaze #2, followed by #9. I use this same tool by the way, in the sanding mode with a 24-grit 6" sanding disc, to shape the mandolin's contours.

Then I aged the finish, using the techniques I learned from your video 'Repairing and Duplicating Vintage Finishes' (I really enjoyed this videotape, Dan, and learned a lot). After some appropriate dents, dings, and lacquer-checking, the 335 is now as "good as old." Thanks again for your help!

Jim Nunis
Guitar Concepts
Marietta GA

TradeSecrets!

Tool guru screws up his own workbench!

From Frank Ford of Gryphon Stringed Instruments comes this Trade Secret:

"Years ago, my local tool guru and guitarmaker Brian Burns talked me into switching from a maple-topped workbench to a bench of edge-laminated fir 2x4s. 'With a softwood top you're not going to waste time thinking about protecting the finish on your workbench,' he said, 'and you'll be free to beat it up and screw things to it.' Brian was really on target with that one. I get more use out of my softwood bench than I ever did with the maple one, and I'm not afraid to screw things to it—like my new bench clamps, which I use to squeeze loose bulging sides into place for gluing.

"It seems to be a peculiarly Gibson disease to have the sides loose from the linings while the top or back is still glued solidly. Since I've been using these bench clamps, I have not encountered a Gibson whose sides I couldn't squeeze back into shape. For example, the instrument in this photo is a Gibson L-5 from about 1930. It's in wonderful condition except for the small sections of sides that have come loose from the linings.

"After years of balancing bar clamps across the backs of guitars, I got tired of turning some of them into kinetic sculptures, if you know what I mean. I found a way to clamp the sides of virtually any instrument very securely, with a minimum of effort and risk. I made a bunch of identical angle brackets of 1/2" thick aluminum plate. They're about 6" high with a 4" leg. I drew a template, traced it onto the aluminum, and cut the pieces out on my wood-cutting band saw. After drilling and tapping

1/4-20 holes near the top, I drilled and countersunk holes diagonally into the inside corner so I could screw them to the bench. These brackets are incredibly fast and easy to use. Here's how they work:

"First, I suspend the guitar parallel to the bench so the areas I want to clamp line up with the height of the threaded holes in my brackets. Normally I use the famous 'ultimate guitar repair vise,' but sometimes I just set the guitar on riser-blocks. Then, with a Makita portable drill, a Phillips driver bit, and deck screws, I mount four to six brackets around the instrument about an inch out from the sides. After threading 1/4-20 hex-head bolts into the tapped holes and placing 1/2"-thick padded cauls between the end of the screws and the sides of the guitar, the guitar is held rigidly in place.

"Next, it's a relatively simple matter to add more angle brackets, screws and cauls where needed, to press whatever unruly sections of the sides are

sticking out from the lining, top, back, etc. I sometimes add flexible strips of wood or steel to spread the load and make the sides go where I want 'em.

"Here, in the case of the old L-5, I was able to work glue in from the inside using a thin section of palette knife soldered to a long bent 1/8" steel rod. I used hide glue for this job, so it was a bit of a hustle to get it clamped in time before the glue cooled. To give myself the extra time, I used a heat lamp to keep the section of the side quite warm while I worked.

"It was a fair pain in the rear to make all those parts, but if you've ever tried to squeeze the sides of an old Gibson back in shape, you know what a trial that can be! I swear the new clamps paid for themselves on the very first job! It was a Gibson style A mandolin from about 1915. It was in nearly perfect condition, except that the sides were so bulged out all around that previously I would've thought the only solution would be shortening the sides at the

end block. With the bench clamps, I was able to reglue the entire back and reshape the body all in one operation, using hot hide glue. I've seen the instrument recently, and it still looks like the back had never been loose! Even if I add all the time it took to make the brackets, I think I still made out well on this one job alone.

"The real advantage of this system is its versatility. Size is limited only by the bench top. I keep a box of 1/8" x 2" dowels handy when I'm breaking down the set-up. As I power out the screws from the bench top, I dip a dowel in Titebond and hammer it into the screw hole. After I get all the holes filled with dowels, I snick them off with a sharp chisel right away—no need to wait for glue to dry. My bench is repaired and ready. I'll just belt-sand or plane it next year and re-coat with some cheap epoxy. Maybe."

Frank Ford
Gryphon Stringed Instruments
Palo Alto, California

"GLUE RIG FROM OUTTASPACE"

Fred Burts of OuttaSpace Guitars in Appleton, WI writes:

Dear Stew-Mac Trade Secrets:

Here's a drawing of my "top assembly board." It's made from 5/8" plywood, one face of which is "veneered" with a layer of 12-gauge mild steel bonded with carpet tape. The maple side rails support the shims and wedges I use when joining tops (**ILLUS**). All the surfaces are finished with a light coat of lacquer.

With the steel side up, I clamp the braces in place by using speaker magnets as the clamps (they suck right down to the steel). I prefer the smooth wood side for joining tops, as in the drawing.

Fred Burts
Outtaspace Guitars, Appleton, WI

wood side up (with waxed paper cover): good for gluing tops

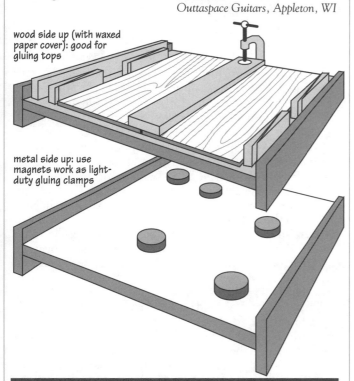

metal side up: use magnets work as light-duty gluing clamps

Quick way to position an acoustic's bridge

"As a novice luthier, I've had a hard time locating the bridge placement on an acoustic guitar. I may be reinventing the wheel, but here's a trick that works for me:

"Make a wire hook and fasten your #189 335-style tailpiece onto the strap button as shown. Attach the outside E-strings, and move the bridge around until the harmonic at the 12th fret matches the fretted string at that position. This then is the correct saddle position in relation to the nut (providing that you don't reshape either the saddle or the nut).

"Of course, you still have to measure to make sure the bridge is centered on the sound board."

Walter Mitchell, Jr., Dunwoody, Georgia

Jeff Hostetter and Amy Hopkins are featured on page 103. Here are two more hot tips from their shop . . .

Tip No. 1: When filling nut slots with super glue and bone dust (or whatever concoction you deem appropriate) taping the nut sides can become messy, especially if some of the glue leaches its ugly little way along the underside of the tape. This method seems to work well for us:

First, put your dust into the slot and gently clean the overspill. then twist up a piece of paper towel to a point and touch the point to the side of the nut slot opposite where your pipette applicator is—the glue fills the slot, and excess is absorbed.

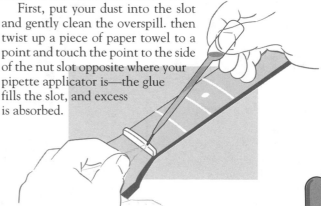

Tip No. 2: To cure the dreaded rising tongue syndrome (the fingerboard kicking up on the high end) on an archtop guitar such as the Gibson L-5C that we had in, we came up with this method:

A neckset was ruled out as the neck pitch was not that bad. In order to preserve the frets and fingerboard in their original condition, we cut out wood from under the fingerboard. We then put pressure on the fingerboard and pulled sandpaper through until it lay straight. We reglued the fingerboard, touched up the edges with colored epoxy, performed a quickie on the frets, and yahoo! Oh, by the way, the saw to use is a backsaw modified as in the small drawing at right: part of the saw's "spine" is removed to leave just the thin blade. This way, the saw can cut a slot deeper than the blade's width.

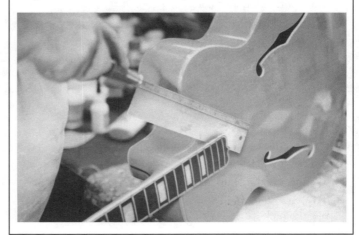

This phase-check bow tests pickups… no strings attached!

Walter Kraushaar sends us this handy idea from his shop in Germany:

"Hi! For happier days and more enthusiasm in guitar repair, we have a small idea to make pickup replacement more pleasant.

"The job at hand: install a new pickup in a Strat.
- De-string, and remove pickguard.
- Wire in the replacement.
- Reinstall the pickguard
- Restring and play… the pickups are out of phase!

"We feel like throwing things, right? With this "check-bow," you can test the phasing of your new pickup configuration without re-stringing, and so save time.

"Make a simple bow out of any piece of wood, install a tuning key, put a 17" string on it and tune it up. Don't shoot arrows with it–that hurts! Simply hold the string over the pickups, and pluck it to test the phasing. It works!"

*Walter Kraushaar,
K-Gitarren & Bass Service
Aachen, Germany*

Thanks Walter! Mike Lindskold, who edits our 'Wiring 101' column, suggests the following other uses for your bow:
- To find out whether the tone controls function correctly—checking their sweep as well as which frequencies they're affecting.
- To help determine what value capacitor to use on a tone control.
- To test a contol's effect on the sound.
- To see if the pickup selector is working correctly, and in the direction you want it to.
- To find a bad pickup, or troubleshoot a wiring problem.
- To give a rough indication of pickup output and whether or not the pickups are working well together.

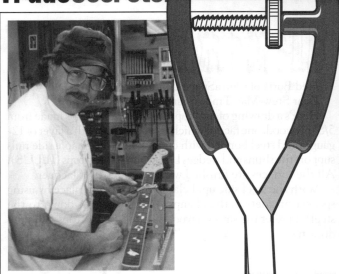

Rave-On Guitar Repair Tip

Michael Lemieux, his wife Linda, and their teenage sons Mikey and Jason live a half-mile from Canada, where they weathered the devastating ice storm of 1998 (check out Michael's nighttime photo of icicle-bound power lines, below). An outdoor lover who works for the Parks & Recreation Department, 44-year-old Lemieux operates "Rave-On Guitar Repair." He repairs guitars part-time in his full workshop at home, and once a week at Bob's Music in nearby Plattsburg, New York. Michael dropped cabinetmaking for luthiery after getting the Stew-Mac video "How To Make A Solidbody Guitar" in the early 1990s. He writes:

"Here's a picture of your #4495 fret tang crimping pliers after I modified them to give consistent crimping pressure over the entire length of the fret tang. On the existing pliers there's no way to keep the pressure from varying; my modification, however, gives you 100% control.

"First, I took a 3/8" solid brass rod and drilled and tapped it with a fine thread to accept your part #3960 post/thumbwheel set. I stripped off the protective rubber coating on the tool's handle, brazed on the brass rod, wire-brushed and re-dipped the handle, and finally inserted the post/thumbwheel set for adjustment. Once the post height is set where you want it, tighten the thumbwheel against the brass rod to lock it in place. This modification makes a world of difference when it comes to precision."

Michael Lemieux, "Rave-On Guitar Repair," Rouses Point, NY

Dave Hussong (left), Mark Kaiser (right), and Dane Billings (below).

1950s L-4 is reborn with a jazzy cutaway and a hopped-up pickup!

"Fret Repair By Mark Kaiser" is a far busier guitar repair shop than I expected to find in the small town of Franklin, Ohio, south of Dayton and north of Cincinnati. Kaiser's shop is located on the second floor of a restored 1880s bank building. Several other music-related businesses are also in the building, including: Steve Falearos' Babblefish Recording Studio, and Dane Billing's Active Electronics, a complete pro-audio service. Last but not least, on the first floor is the building's nucleus, the world famous Fretware Guitars, an awesome vintage guitar store owned by reknowned vintage guitar expert, columnist, and blues guitarist, Dave Hussong.

I was in Franklin to visit the "new" Fretware Guitars (it had been open for a year and a half), and to check out a collection of 200 vintage guitars which Hussong and several business associates had just purchased. The guitars ranged in diversity from a turn-of-the century Gibson Style O and a 1924 Lloyd Loar L-5, to a Lake Placid Blue Strat and a *blonde* 1958 Gibson ES-345. Dave offered to let me photograph anything we needed for the color section of Stew-Mac's upcoming finishing book. Finding a great repair shop upstairs was an unexpected bonus!
—Dan Erlewine

Dave Hussong and Mark Kaiser have had a working relationship for years. "I started utilizing Mark's talents when he was just out of high school," says Dave. "His repairs were done by the book even then, but now he's able to incorporate the antique aesthetic as well. If a repair job called for a 'relic'-looking finish, hell, we were doing that 15 years ago."

Mark Kaiser, 36, has been repairing guitars since 1980, after studying with Bruce Scotten and Mike Lennon at the Apprentice Shop, in Springhill, Tennessee (story, page 115). "The Apprentice Shop prepared me well for working in the business, and to this day I still do everything as they showed me. I was fortunate to work for Mike Lennon in 1984 and get a feel for how a professional guitar repair business really runs. When Dave Hussong got the idea of turning this old bank into a music complex in late '96 and invited me in, I was ready to hang out my own shingle."

Mark's guitar shop and Dane Billing's electronics shop are separate but complementary businesses that share a common entrance and customer greeting area. When customers enter, an

L-shaped display counter keeps them from walking directly into either of the shop areas. With strings on the wall and parts in the counter, the customer area has a music store feel. Mark can see the counter through the open doorway by his workbench. Even if he's in the middle of a glue job he can call out a welcome and make light conversation until he's able to set the work aside.

Customers can flop their guitar cases right up on the large counter to let Mark inspect their guitars. The counter makes for an important division between Mark, Dane, and the customers. It establishes a professional feel which helps them take in repairs quickly, necessary in a one-man shop. One man and one woman shop, that is. Mark's wife and partner Huet Tshin (pronounced "set chin") takes care of the books and does much of the prep work (she's a good fret puller). By the time this story's in print, she will be a new mother as well!

On the day I visited, Mark was preparing to bind a cutaway he'd installed in a 1950s Gibson L-4 non-cutaway archtop. Mark's customer felt the well-used, scratched and dented guitar wasn't worth much on the vintage market, so he wanted it converted to an L-4C, and equipped with a Charlie Christian pickup. The really unusual thing about the conversion was

the look-alike pickup that Mark *made* from a Gibson P100! (In the photo above, compare the original C.C. pickup with Mark's customized P100 with its slide-on false front.)

"The idea for the pickup conversion came from the customer," says Mark. "He sent me a blueprint to follow and a real Charlie Christian pickup to take measurements from. The P100 has plenty of power and is the same basic size and shape of the old Charlie Christian single-coil. I made a wooden cover which slides over the pickup's top flatwork and gives the outward appearance of a Charlie Christian pickup. Here's how to do it:

- Install the six polepieces from the bottom so the filister-heads aren't in the way of the sliding cover. Grind the ends of the polepieces so they're flush with the top flatwork, too.

- Make a thin wooden cap notched to slide over the top plate. I used maple, stained it black, and bound it with creme plastic to imitate the C.C. pickup (photo, above). The wood cover has a handmade steel "bar" polepiece inlaid through it and superglued into place. Once the pickup is screwed to the mounting block, the cap slides over the top. It looks like a real Charlie Christian, which does not

have top-accessible mounting screws.

- I wrapped a 1/2"-wide strip of adhesive-backed copper foil tape across the polepiece heads on the bottom, up the side, and across the top. Then I installed a strip of the same copper tape on the underside of the cover, against the steel bar polepiece. When the cap is slid onto the pickup it makes contact with the foil, touches the polepieces and senses the signal.

- Since I'd cut a hole in the

guitar for the cutaway, it was an easy task for me to install a clean, good-looking mahogany pickup-mounting block to the guitar's neck block.

- I filed the heads of the pickup's two oval-head mounting screws flat, and then countersunk the pickup's flatwork—right through the copper foil—so that the cover could slide on after the pickup was mounted.

- Admittedly, I grimaced while

cutting the pickup and cutaway holes in the top. The pain didn't last long, though, because the finished product is quite nice.

"In the end, the pickup was weaker than we'd hoped, so I called our local guitar electronics wizard, Jim Rolph, of JM Rolph Pickups in Highland Heights, Kentucky (see related story on page 118). Jim pointed out that this type of pickup should have a solid steel blade running through the coil. My fabricated steel blade laying on top of the coil form, lacked the mass for picking up the string's signal as well as the six polepiece heads of a P100—at least not coupled with the the Alnico-five magnets of a P100. He advised me to remove the Alnico magnets and substitute two *ceramic* magnets from a couple of cheap broken imported humbuckers—installed so they're resisting (opposing) each other from side to side. This gave back the output lost by the upside-down polepieces.

"Jim also pointed out something I wasn't aware of: Copper doesn't conduct magnetism, so the copper tape was probably weakening the signal. It did shield the pickup though, and the pickup sounded so good that I just left the tape on. Next time I probably won't bother with it though."

Mark Kaiser
Fret Repair
402 S. Main St., Suite 6
Franklin, Ohio 45005

(Mark shares his prices in our **Bluebook** *on the next page.)*

THE BLUEBOOK OF GUITAR REPAIR PRICES

Labor Rates (materials, parts, and strings are extra) **from Mark Kaiser's Fret Repair**

Restring
Includes buffing the frets, conditioning the fingerboard, tightening the tuners, oiling open-geared tuners, tightening loose parts, general cleaning, stretching and tuning the strings.

Bass 4 or 5-string	$ 8.00
6-string instruments (or banjo)	$ 10.00
Mandolin or classical guitar	$ 12.00
12-string guitar	$ 18.00
Floating tremolo w/locknut	$ 20.00
(Includes adjusting tremolo)	

Strap buttons (per button):
Install (used instrument)	$ 4.00
Install (new instrument)	$ 8.00

Adjustments
One adjustment only with original strings
Truss rod (easy access)	$ 2.00
(w/cover or difficult access)	$ 5.00
(requiring neck removal)	$10.00
Set intonation (per string)	$ 2.00
Lower nut (per slot)	$ 1.00
Fill nut w/bone insert & re-slot (per slot)	$ 8.00
Remove nut, shim & adjust	$ 15.00
Lower/raise saddle on acoustic	$ 10.00

Setup
Includes adjusting neck, nut, action, intonation, and restringing.
4 or 5 string bass	$ 20.00
Les Paul, Tele, or stop-bar guitar	$ 22.00
6-String acoustic or classical	$ 25.00
Strat-style w/vintage tremolo	$ 25.00
12-string acoustic	$ 35.00
Floating tremolo w/locknut	$ 40.00

Nut & saddle
(Add in restring service)
Plastic nut	$ 18.00
Strat-style 1/8-inch bone nut	$ 24.00
Gibson-style flat-bottom nut	$ 30.00
Martin-style angled-bottom nut	$ 40.00
12-string bone nut	$ 55.00
Bone saddle	$ 22.00

Headstock work
(Add restringing where applicable)
Install six plastic buttons on Kluson	$ 20.00
Ream peg holes for Grovers	$ 25.00
Dowel 3/8-inch holes for 1/4-inch posts (w/touchup)	$ 75-100.
Glue broken headstock & buff (without touchup)	$ 60.00
Add overlay(s) to broken headstock (with touchup)	$175-$250.00
Splice on new headstock with finish	$300-$400.00

Fret & Neck work
Minimum of three frets, add fret dress charge to single fret replacements.
Fret replacement (w/binding) per fret	$ 14.00
Fret replacement (w/o binding) per fret	$ 10.00
Complete refret (w/binding)	$225.00
Complete refret (w/o binding)	$175.00
Complete refret, maple fretboard (with sealer)	$175.00
(w/hi-gloss, color-match finish)	$225.00

Rebind and refret Gibson-style with touchup	$375.00
Partial fret dressing	$20-$ 40.00
Smooth sides of frets and buff	$15-$ 30.00
Complete fret dress, crown, buff, and set up	$65-$ 85.00
Pull fingerboard to replace broken truss rod	$200 -$400.00
Custom inlay work (per hour)	$ 40.00

Bridge work
Install Tune-O-Matic, Strat, or Tele bridge & setup	$ 35.00
Install floating tremolo w/routing & setup	$85-$175.00
Glue acoustic bridge without removing	$ 35.00
Pull bridge & reglue	$45-$85.00
Fill saddle slot, recut slot, fit saddle	$ 75.00
Install under saddle pickup with bone saddle	$ 60.00
Install preamp & pickup with bone saddle	$ 80.00
Handmade bridge with bone saddle	$100.00
Replace bridge plate, reglue/replace bridge	$125-$175.00

Electronics
Troubleshoot electronics	$ 15.00 & up
Install output jack (easy/difficult access)	$ 8-$20.00
Clean pots or switch (easy access/hollow body)	$8-$35.00
Replace 5-way Strat-style switch (pickguard mount)	$ 20.00
Replace pot or switch	$15-$30.00
Complete rewiring of a messy job (per hour)	$ 40.00
Install EMG pickup(s)	$40-$ 80.00
Install other pickup(s)	$20-$ 40.00
Shield pickup and control cavities	$40-$ 80.00
Route body for pickup and wiring	$45-$85.00

Neck resets
Harmony or Kay-style guitar with loose joint	$125.00
Martin-style flat top	$200.00
Archtops	$200-$300.00

Top & back repairs
Top replacement	$500 - $700.00
Back replacement	$300 -$500.00
Florentine cutaway	$600 -$800.00
Cracks, splices, broken braces, and patch work are to be estimated on hourly rate of	$ 40.00

Finishing (ready-to-finish)
Body (no sanding, no assembly)
Natural	$150.00
Sunburst	$180.00

Neck (no sanding, no assembly)
Natural	$ 50.00
Tint	$ 65.00

Assemble kit guitar
with setup	$80.00

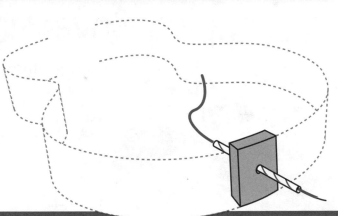

Hot tip for wiring acoustic pickups

Dear Dan: Here's an easy way to get an under the saddle transducer wire through the end block of an acoustic guitar for soldering connections on an endpin jack:

Stick a straw (or similar tube) through the end block from the outside and with your free hand reach through the soundhole and thread the wire through the straw. Also, with the newer jacks that tighten from the outside, this straw-trick also makes for a handy way to premeasure and trim the wire that otherwise might end up flopping around inside the guitar.

Roger LeBlanc
Roger's Guitar Shop
3659 Hwy 90
Pace, FL 32571
850-994-4724

Great Northwoods Building & Repair Seminar 1998

The fourth biannual Northwoods Guitar Building & Repair Seminar will be held Wednesday–Saturday, September 16–19, at Bryan Galloup's Guitar Hospital in Big Rapids, Michigan. Northwoods is a small seminar, with a limit of 30 participants, so sign up soon! For information on attending contact: Bryan or Susan Galloup at The Guitar Hospital, 10495 Northland Drive, Big Rapids, MI 49307, phone (616) 796-5611.

Tentatively, but mostly confirmed, this year's instructors are the following top professionals from our industry:
Joe Glaser–Glaser Instruments, Nashville, Tennessee
Mike Lennon–The Apprentice Shop, Nashville, TN (see pg. 115)
Fred Stuart–Fender Custom Shop, Corona, California
Phil Jones–Gibson Custom Shop, Nashville, Tennessee
Seymour Duncan–Seymour Duncan Pickups
Jim Rolph–JM Rolph Pickups, Highland Heights, KY (see pg. 118)
TJ Thompson–Thompson Guitars, Weston, Massachusetts
Tom Murphy–Tom Murphy Design, Marion, Illinois

Overlapping-Cove Peghead Repair Technique

Charlie Hoffman's repair shop

in Minneapolis, Minnesota has three full-time repairers with a combined 44 years of experience repairing in his shop. "It's the best crew I could ever hope to assemble," says the boss, 55-year old Charlie Hoffman, who after founding the shop in 1971 and repairing for many years, now devotes more of his time to building guitars. Hoffman's repair crew includes 20-year veteran Ron Tracy, 18-year-man Kevin Schwab, and the baby of the shop, Michele Beardsley (she has "only" worked there six years). They all send their greetings, along with Charlie's great way of repairing a "short break headstock:"

❶ This sort of break is across the grain and offers little or no gluing surface.

❷ Carefully align the two parts and glue them well enough to withstand the stress of the ensuing repair.

❸ On the idler pulley of a 6" x 48" stationary belt-sander cut (sand) a large cove in the neck. *Hold the neck firmly, and make the cut in a single pass so that the resulting cove is one simple curve!*

❹ Shape a curved insert which matches the wood type and grain orientation, and extends beyond the neck's contours for shaping later. (A bright light held behind the joint will help you see any gaps during fitting, and a male template to match the sanding drum profile will help. You can get a perfect fit if you're willing to take the time).

❺ Glue the fill in place with Titebond, or the glue of your choice.

❻ When the glue's dry, rough-shape the fill, and repeat the process on the other side—this results in an overlapping joint, which usually (hopefully) almost completely replaces the damaged wood.

❼ Final-shape, sand, and smooth the area, and go about the lacquer touchup.

"Hey Dan, come see us sometime!"

*Charlie Hoffman and the crew at
Hoffman Guitars
2219 East Franklin Ave.
Minneapolis, Minnesota 55404
(612)338-1079
www.hoffmanguitars.com*

Thanks, Charlie! We'll come to visit!

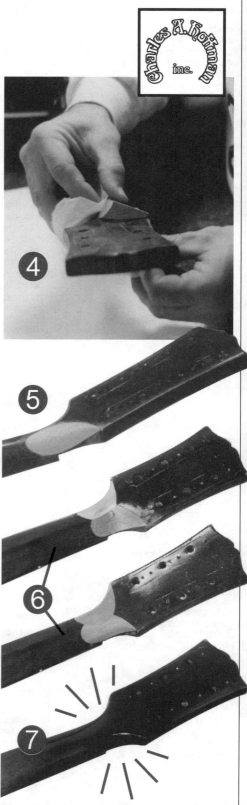

Masters at work in the Apprentice Shop

Mike Lennon

Mark Piper

Mike Lennon has kept busy in the almost quarter century since 1974; that was the year he and his friend Bruce Scotten graduated from the Roberto-Venn School of Luthiery in Phoenix, Arizona (Bruce was Roberto-Venn's first student). Lennon and Scotten both taught for the Roberto-Venn school before opening their own repair and building school, the Apprentice Shop, which operated for sixteen years in Springhill, Tennessee. During ten of those years the Apprentice Shop doubled as the guitar service department for Gibson USA in Nashville. As if that wasn't enough, they also built 500 Springhill Series flattop guitars for the Fender Guitar Company between 1992 and 1995. Somehow Lennon even managed to find the time to work at Gruhn Guitars in 1978 with Stephen Gilchrist, Matthew Klein, John Greven, Marty Lanham, and Phil Jones.

In 1995, Fender dropped the Springhill project in favor of buying the Guild Guitar Company, and Bruce Scotten retired from the guitar-making business because of severe allergies to wood dust. Mike took advantage of his greatest strength—repairing guitars—and now he's the owner of the Apprentice Shop, which he operates in a whopping 3600 square foot building, with his friend and shop-mate Mark Piper.

"In this business, it seems you repair by default, regardless of what your original intention was," says Lennon. "By 1986 I'd gotten so busy with repairs—the Gibson contract was enormous—that Bruce was doing most of the teaching anyway. He excelled at it, especially teaching the basics of acoustic guitar construction. He continued to do the majority of the teaching until we closed the school in '92 for the Fender project. When that project ceased in '95, and Bruce retired, it would've been hard to re-open the school without him, and I'm happiest repairing.

"We're not the service center for Gibson anymore, since Wayne Green and Roger Fritz set up Gibson's in-house warranty repair center in '95. But we still do a good deal of non-warranty repairs for Gibson, because we specialize in it and we know how to do things the Gibson way. It's convenient for them because we're close by, and we're good friends with everybody there. At times it feels almost like we work for Gibson."

Locating a replacement bridge Apprentice Shop style:

Veteran repairman Mark Piper has worked at the Apprentice Shop for twelve years. After graduating from the school in 1979, Mark spent six years at Swift Music Repair in Kansas City, Missouri until Mike Lennon offered him a repair position in 1985. It was Piper, along with repairman Mike Dowling (no longer with the shop), who kept the repair shop running during the Springhill project. Piper and Dowling also co-invented the Saddlematic (shown on the facing page). This adustable tool quickly and accurately determines the correct location for cutting a saddle slot in a newly-attached bridge blank, positioning a new bridge with a pre-cut saddle slot, and checking the saddle accuracy of an attached bridge.

"Mike Dowling first recognized the need for a Saddlematic-type tool," says Piper, "after becoming frustrated enough with saddle placement to inspire the tool we co-designed.

"When we make a replacement bridge," continues Piper, "it's complete, but without the saddle. The pin holes are drilled, the outline's done, usually slightly oversize, and the top is correctly radiused and sanded. We position the new bridge using the outer pin holes for alignment, and clamp it firmly. Next, we use the Saddlematic to make two pin-point impressions in the bridge top, at the treble and bass ends, centered exactly where the new saddle slot will be routed.

"Those two marks are used to center a small drillbit to drill down through the bridge, the spruce top, and into the bridge

pad. The drill-bit does not exit the pad, to avoid tear-out and a needlessly sloppy look. Then we use short scraps of the same .092" diameter steel dowel used for the Saddlematic pointers to pin the bridge in place during gluing. When the glue's dry, we pull the pins out and align our saddle slotting jig so the cutter cuts directly through the center of the two holes. We use either a .090" or a .125" four-flute spiral, reverse-cut, solid-carbide bit for routing most saddle slots, powered by a Ryobi trim router with a modified base to fit our saddle-slotting jig."

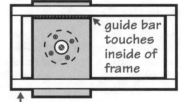

lexan base with router attached

guide bar touches inside of frame

the saddle jig is a frame placed over the bridge to guide the router in cutting the saddle slot (shown here from below)

Another Saddlematic enthusiast is Trade Secrets editor Dan Erlewine. "I love the Saddlematic," says Dan, "and have several. One is always ready to use, while the others are usually set to the exact saddle placement of a bridge repair that's either part of a bigger job, or one that I might not get to for a while once it's removed. When possible, I check the intonation of a bridge about to be removed and set the Saddlematic to it. Later, whether I choose to use that placement,

Using the twelfth fret for reference, the Saddlematic's marking pins are adjusted to record the positions of the treble and bass side of the saddle. Once set for a particular guitar, the tool holds that measurement for quick reference.

or move the saddle sharp or flat, the Saddlematic gives me a reference for locating the saddle faster and more accurately. There have been times when I could've used half dozen of them.

"Mike Lennon used the Saddlematic to help with the layout of a 24-3/4" scale neck he was custom-building for a Stratocaster. First he rested the roughed-in maple neck blank in the Strat's neck pocket. Next he set the Saddlematic to the 24-3/4" scale, and locating from the bridge saddles, he could see exactly where the twelfth fret (and fretboard) needed to be placed on the neck blank—thus indicating nut slot placement and peghead location quickly, easily, and without complicated drawings and measurements."

The Apprentice Shop is well known in vintage circles for accomplishing nearly impossible repairs. Mike's refurbishing of his 1955 Gibson Super 400 was one of the most impressive jobs we've seen. Starting with a back and neck only, he hand-formed the sides, graduated a rough machine-carved Gibson top,

assembled the instrument, and finished it to match his other Super 400 (both are in the photo on the opposite page). "We're sort of the end of the funnel," he says. "We do so much that other shops either can't or won't, that I guess word has gotten around. However, on a big rebuild like the Super 400, we're very expensive and slow because those jobs have to fit around our everyday repair schedule. Repairs like that get done when they're done—it may be a year or more—and we tell the customer upfront so they won't pressure us."

Mark Piper handles most of the shop's heavy finishing workload—which by his estimate is rapidly approaching 7,000 guitars! "There were times," said Mark, "when we couldn't have hung another guitar in the booth if we'd had to. I once counted 89 guitars in there—that was the record. Because of the volume we do, we finish differently than a lot of other shops. For example, we don't thin our lacquer and we don't sand between coats. We've

been using McFadden's ready-to-spray guitar lacquer since 1991, and our typical spray schedule is quite simple. It takes three days to complete the cycle:

Day 1: Spray two double-coats; one in the morning and one in the afternoon.

Day 2: Spray two double-coats just like day one.

Day 3: Spray two double coats.

Days 4 and 5: Let the guitar hang for two days, then level sand the finish with 240-grit no-load paper. Then spray a "flashcoat" to level out the 240-grit sanding scratches.

"The flashcoat step comes from Gibson," says Lennon. "It's a last coat to level out any final sanding scratches. At first I took my cues from the factory; it seemed like the smart thing to do. Consequently, I learned to adapt production methods to our small shop. The flashcoat eliminates the tedious wet-sanding stage before buffing.

"A traditional flashcoat is well-thinned—as much as three or four parts thinner to one part lacquer—but not ours. Since ready-to-spray guitar lacquer is

already thinned, we only cut the flashcoat 1:1, and sometimes we don't thin it at all. We'll usually add a little retarder, and sometimes we add some fisheye killer to enhance the gloss and improve the flowout.

"After the flashcoat, we let the guitar hang for at least three days—even though three months would be better! In other words, as long as we can. Whenever we really do have the option of letting the guitar dry for three months, we'll take it. Once the flashcoat has really cured, we go right to the buffer, without wet-sanding."

"We do some minor sanding around key areas such as the end of the fingerboard on archtops, or in mandolin scrolls. We'll use the white wheel only in those areas—never the red wheel. We're using white Menzerna 116 (Glanzwax) for the polish wax, and their red 113 GZW for the pre-polish, or "cut" wax. Did you know that if you mix the bar compound with naphtha you can put it on a cloth and use it for hand-rubbing? This gives a similar effect to the bar compound in hard-to-reach areas."

Mike Lennon
The Apprentice Shop
Springhill, Tennessee

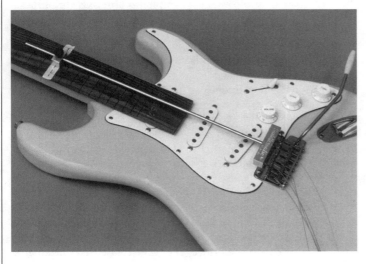

Blues Lovers Design Stellar Tool

Don MacRostie and I love the old country blues, and we enjoy spending time with the great blues singer and guitarist Paul Geremia when he plays in our town. We also enjoy helping Paul with his guitar repair projects. Sometimes he uses our shops and tools to do his own work in (Paul's no slouch when it comes to guitar repair), and sometimes we help him with the difficult stuff. For example, I installed a handmade neck on Paul's Stella 12-string in 1995. Later, when Paul got *two more* Stella bodies, I couldn't face whittling out two more neck dovetails. Don jigged-up to make *several* more necks, machining the joints on a simple router table. As it happened,

the project inspired our new neck joint routing templates. So thanks, Paul!

At left, Paul Geremia routs a slot for installing a 3/8" x 3/8" graphite reinforcing rod into the mahogany replacement neck. Coupled with an ebony truss rod, the neck has remained straight as an arrow for three years.

Don's simple plywood fixture held the neck firmly. The jig uses simple wooden shims for controlling the neck angle.

The router bit follows the template.

Later on, we used this same fixture, with the Stella's *body* clamped to the plywood upright, and used the router to clean out the mortise joint in the neck block. Next we filled it with wood, and re-routed it to accept the new dovetail, using our matched template set. The new neck fit the old body perfectly!

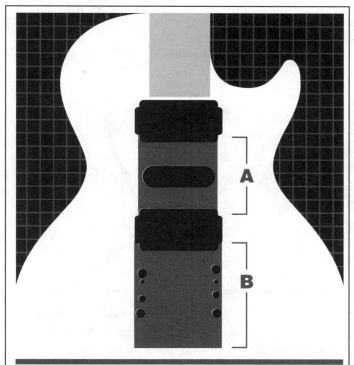

The Apprentice's Sorcery

Here's how Mike Lennon of The Apprentice Shop, Springhill, Tennessee, magically restored a 1954 gold top Les Paul to original condition. The guitar's face had been riddled with bridge and tailpiece holes, had a non-standard pickup routing between the two original pickups–plus the usual P90-to-humbucker conversion. "This would only work under a gold top or other opaque-finished guitar, of course," said Mike. "We restored it to original specs, except for leaving it with humbucking pickups. I've also used the same technique to undo Kahler tremolo installations on Les Pauls."

■ Plug all unwanted pickup cavity, stud, and bridge holes first. If you use dowels to plug round holes, be alert later when re-drilling, so the drill bit doesn't wander when you hit endgrain.

■ With a router and chisel, clean out the shaded area (A) to a 1/8-inch depth.

■ Make a piece of maple 2-7/8" X 2-1/4" X 1/8", to fit (A) with a slight overlap into the pickup cavities–which can be routed flush later. Soft western maple is best for fills because it doesn't show a shrunken glue line as much as hard maple.

■ Follow the same step with the (B) area using a piece of maple 12" X 4" X 1/8".

■ When the glue has dried at least 24 hours, trim the maple fills to match the top contours.

■ Lay out and redrill the appropriate holes.

■ To eliminate telltale shrink marks around the inlaid maple, seal the entire top with EverCoat's FeatherFill, a polyester sealer which is akin to a sprayable liquid Bondo. We sand the FeatherFill back 1/8" from the binding, so that its grey color doesn't show when we scrape the gold from the binding.

Mike Lennon, The Apprentice Shop, Springhill, Tennessee

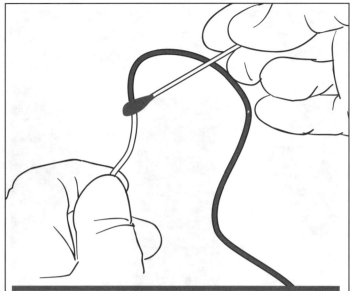

For wire of any color, start with white…

Jim Rolph, 49, owns and operates J. M. Rolph Pickups in Highland Heights, Kentucky, near Cincinnatti. This area is known for good pickup makers and good pickers, like Seymour Duncan, Lonnie Mack and Scotty Anderson. A great player himself, Jim's an old friend of Scotty's, and together the two have spent many hours putting the Telecaster electric guitar through its paces. When Mark Kaiser's shop-built Charlie Christian pickup lacked volume (see related story on page 111), he called Jim Rolph for advice.

"I've been rewinding pickups since 1977, and before that I was in the auto body business," says Jim. "A young bodyman always tries to outpaint the factory, but the work stands out like a sore thumb. I soon learned that the pros left cars looking untouched. Later I applied the same ideals to pickup rewinding, so my rewinds wouldn't *look* like they're rewound. I take "before" photos with a digital camera, enlarge the image later in color on the computer, and use it as a reference when I antique my work. Here are a couple of tricks I use for antiquing pickups:

Jim Rolph at work stamping out pickup flatwork–he has his own punch press!

"Have you ever worked on a guitar or amp that used colored wire instead of black or white? For example, mid-'60s Fender Teles used blue and yellow wire, and amplifiers use many shades of brown. We match vintage wire by starting with white and coloring it ourselves. First we strip the wax coating from the wire with a wax and grease remover such as 3M's 0915 or Prep-Sol™. Then we color the cloth insulation with alcohol stain. Once we've colored a wire we rewax the cloth by dipping it into the same wax solution that we use for potting pickups.

"Want to know a good way to make white cloth insulated wire look old and dirty? Run it through the charcoal ash which piles up in the barbecue. Or you can use brand new charcoal—just break it up into powder.

Jim Rolph, J. M. Rolph Pickups, Highland Heights, KY

This saxy dresser's got a really groovy pad!

Here's a letter from Peter Schmid of Suburban Guitar in Pendelton, New York. He uses a leather sax pad for the final buff of a fret dressing! I tried it, and it works great!
—*Dan*

Dear Dan: Jewelers use leather pads to polish metal, so why shouldn't we? We mount the enclosed sax pad on the same mandrel that comes with Dremel's felt polishing pads, and use it to polish frets. The pads are long-lasting, and cost only twenty cents each. If you don't get it centered just right, simply run the edge against some 60-grit sandpaper to true it up. We use a stick metal polish like jeweler's rouge, reapplied every seven to ten frets. This gets them smooth and shiny.

Peter P. Schmid
Suburban Guitar
Pendeleton, New York

YOU'LL FIND EXTRA TRADE SECRETS THROUGHOUT THE CATALOG!

TradeSecrets!
Hot tips & inside scoops. Editor: Dan Erlewine

VOLUME 35

father and son guitar-making team

Harry and Jim build batches of six in their workshop in Pennsylvania. The shop building has three bays with large roll-up doors.

Dynamic duo: this father-son team's a good combination

Jaros Guitars is the father-and-son team of Harry and Jim Jaros of Rochester, Pennsylvania. When the senior Jaros retired from his job as a machine repairman for Westinghouse in 1987, he was finally able to give full attention to his lifelong avocation of woodworking. "I've been playing around with wood since I was a child," says the 74-year old craftsman (at right, above). "I took industrial arts in junior high school and was hooked from then on. I served in the Air Force through World War II. Soon after getting out in 1948, I went to work for Westinghouse, starting out in their box factory making crates. I was about 24 years old. Like Jim with the guitars, I was always making something in my spare time, too. Nothing big, but I always built my own stuff. I built kitchen cabinets as a side job for a number of years, but eventually the pre-fab stuff became too much competition, so I quit."

We asked Mary Jaros how her husband liked this new kind of woodworking compared to the cabinet work he'd been doing for years: "I'd say he loves it," said Mary, "he really enjoys it. Oh, sometimes, they have to hurry too much and it sort of takes a little of the fun out of it for him, but it comes with the job, I guess. He gets over it, because people like their guitars so much."

Harry was brought out of his "retirement" in the winter of 1995. At his son Jim's urging, he agreed to give guitarmaking a try-if Jim would join him and develop his woodworking skills, too. Soon the two men were producing a veritable line of professional-quality guitars as fast as they could find enough curly and spalted maple for the highly-figured tops.

"Actually," said Jim, "Dad had wanted a project we could work on together, and since I'm a guitar player, it seemed that building a guitar was a natural. Dad never makes just one of anything, though, so we built four guitars right from the start. Thanks to him, even those first guitars were good. Only a year later, the summer of '96, we were displaying at our first

NAMM (National Association of Musical Merchants) show in Nashville, Tennessee. That's where we met Pam Webster and a bunch of the Stew-Mac crew (Pam's a member of the Stew-Mac purchasing department). We've also gone to a number of vintage shows, such as Arlington, the Fall Philadelphia show, and the Columbus Guitar Show. Now I wish I'd done more woodworking as a kid, because although I grew up around a woodshop, I'll never be as good as my dad. He knows things I never will."

By day, 38-year old Jim Jaros is the group leader and shipping receiver for a distribution warehouse of the Okonite Company, one of America's biggest manufacturers of high voltage electrical cable. "It's a good working environment," he says, "because my boss is a musician, too. Most everybody down there's a musician, in fact. Guitar building is a weekend thing, however, and usually a night or two during the week. I played in a band for years, travelling the tri-state area three nights a week or more, but I quit playing to build. My experience as a guitarist helps me though, because I have definite opinions on guitars and I know how they should play and sound."

Jim Jaros visiting at Stewart-MacDonald: that's Mike Linksold on the left, then Jim, Pam Webster, and Cathleen Matters

The Jaros Guitar "factory" is a home-based, part-time operation located in the beautiful Pennsylvania countryside. Jim, his wife Patty, and their sons Jason (14), and Taylor (8), live only 100 yards from Jim's folks, Harry and Mary (and coinci-

dentally, Harry's large well-equipped wood shop). The shop is a 30' x 40' pole-barn with 12' ceilings and three work bay. Each bay has its own sliding overhead door. Harry removed the center window of the middle bay and replaced it with a removable acrylic window pane. When it's spraying time, he replaces the acrylic with a "spray-fan insert" and lets Jim have at it with the spray gun. The area around the "spray booth" is protected from overspray with large, temporary sheets of cardboard (photo, right).

With all the power tools on wheels, there's always plenty of room to make lots of sawdust, and to spread out a batch of guitars during construction (see photo on preceding page). They build batches of six guitars at a time.

"Like a few other makers, our guitars are similar in style to the '59 Gibson Les Paul Junior. The '59 Junior has always been my favorite body shape, but since I don't like the weak neck joint, our necks are glued in-way in. The neck blank sits in a sloped channel routed into the body which determines the neck angle. The neck blank runs two inches past the tailpiece, and is glued in before the top goes on."

Harry and Jim each have their own specialties: Harry's the production foreman, jig maker, and whitewood builder; Jim runs the fretting, finishing, and set-up departments.

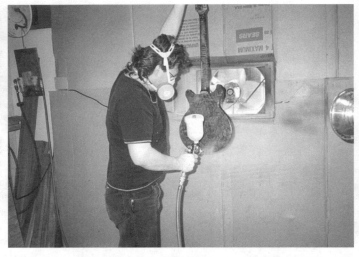

This craftsman's deep into body-building at age 74!

Harry Jaros was glad to share these tips on body building:

"The bodies are 1-7/8" thick (a 1-1/8" core of mahogany is sandwiched between a 1/4" maple back and 1/2" maple top. Hollow chambers in the mahogany keep the weight down, and help to produce the sound we like. Most of our gluing is done with Weldwood's Resourcinal glue-the powdered type that you mix with water. It dries hard and strong. Our body building process goes like this . . .

■ First I "rough-glue" the mahogany body blanks together with pipe clamps. After the glue's dry, I plane the blanks to size.

■ Next I use our shop-made "veneer press" which makes gluing on the back and later the top, easy. I made five presses, but should've made six, since we seem to be building in batches of

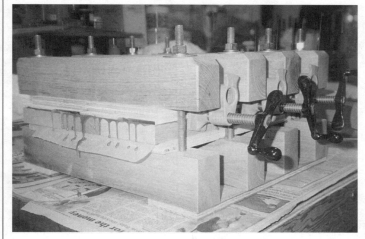

six. Between the rails of the press I use three pipe clamps to tighten the center seam while applying even downward pressure on the eight bolts with a wrench-performing two gluing operations simultaneously (photo above).

- Once the back's on, I bandsaw the body close to shape. I then remove any sawmarks and final-shape it on the router table, using a long flush-cutting router bit. I follow an acrylic template which is double-stick taped to the back.

- Next I use an oscillating spindle sander to clean up any chattermarks left by the router, and the sides are done.

- I rout the neck cavity into the body using a top-mounted router template screwed to the mahogany. The screw holes are hidden later by the maple top cap. The template runs on a slope, which sets the neck angle, and the routed area runs a good two inches past the tailpiece-it's almost like a neck-through-body.

- Once the neck blank's glued in, I rough away the the excess neck blank above the body with the radial-arm saw. Then I final-trim it flush to the mahogany, using yet another router template to support the router up off the work. This template also screws to the body, using the same holes made in the previous operation.

- Jim bandsaws the necks to the rough profile, and then shapes them all by hand-he returns the necks to me shaped, sanded, and fretted. I use the press to glue them in (photo below).

- Next, the maple top goes on-also glued in the press.

"A gluing press is well worth the time spent making it if you plan to build many guitars. Here's how to make one like ours:

- Cut 8 "rails" of oak or maple 2" wide x 3" tall x 19" long. Drill two holes in each rail, centered end-to-end and 15" apart (measure 2" in from each end).

- For the bottom four rails, drill 1/2" or slightly smaller holes so the carriage bolts fit snugly. Counterbore the bottom rail holes so the heads of the bolts are recessed below the surface. Also, square out the entrance of the hole to fit the square area of the carriage bolt shank.

- Drive the 1/2" x 10" carriage bolts into the bottom rails, then space the four rails evenly onto the two pieces of 3/4" x 4" plywood which serve as the base of the press. Make sure that all is square, then screw the base to the rails with the wood screws of your choice.

- Drill the holes in the top four rails slightly oversize (about 9/16"), so they'll slide on and off the carriage bolts quickly and easily.

When you glue up, use a 14" x 16-1/2" x 3/4" plywood caul on the bottom and two 7" x 16-1/2" x 3/4" cauls on top (one on each side of the center glue line). Put wax paper between the cauls and the pieces being glued.

We're both down in the basement, fretting...

"Like you Dan, my small shop's in the basement," says Jim Jaros, "It's the perfect size though, for fretting, inlaying, wiring, and doing set-ups away from the hustle, bustle, and sawdust of Dad's shop. Also like you, I'm a big believer in the neck jig. Dad built a workbench neck jig from the Stew-Mac plans, and I think the fact that we jig and level every neck blank before we fret it sets our guitars apart from many others in the playability department. [the Jaros' guitars play exceptionally well.-Editor] I've got neck-jigging down to a science now, and know just how much tension to put on our necks to

get perfect, low-action fret jobs every time. It's really easy to jig an unfinished neck blank-as opposed to you repair guys who have to be careful of the body and the finish (we're not doing repair work at this time, although we have in the past).

"I'm compression-fretting with your #4478 fret press and #4479 neck support caul. That fret press system has really improved my fret jobs. My favorite fretwire is Stew-Mac #149, and I use Franklin's liquid hide glue, heated so that it'll flow through a hypodermic needle, as additional assurance that they'll stay in. I run a bead of glue in the fret slots, twelve at a time, tap in the overbent frets on each end, and slide the blank through the fret press to seat them. It takes me 20 minutes to jig and level a fretboard, and 10 minutes to do the actual fretting. The fret jobs are so uniform that very little dressing is needed afterward."

Randy Allen's quick plastic sanding blocks

Here's a note from our friend Randy Allen, a bluegrass-loving builder of steel-string guitars, mandolins, and resophonic guitars in Colfax, California.

Dear Stewart MacDonald:

I'm glad to see you're carrying Weld-On glue. Seemingly the only glue that works with Boltaron binding material, Weld-On does less damage to ivoroid as well.

Weld-On is good for temporarily gluing pearl to wood (so you can scribe around the inlay) because it dries faster than Duco cement, and it allows the pearl to be removed easily with a twisting motion. Thus,the piece is far less likely to break. This saves me many hours of unnecessary repairs that come from picking the instrument up in a moment of frustration and throwing it out the window.

This adhesive works equally well applying Boltaron, ivoroid, and tortoise bindings to fingerboards. I bind the fingerboards on most of my models before fretting them-a job made easy thanks to your fret tang nipper. It's one of my very favorite tools in the shop. Weld On glue, by the way, is easily removed from the fret slots after the binding has dried, and before fretting begins. It gets very hard as it sets over time, however. For example, I left two tablespoons of Weld-On inside my favorite glue bottle (an empty Duco bottle with a Hot Stuff applicator tip) for four months. If someone had videotaped me trying to get the hardened glue out of there you'd have a big laugh. I finally destroyed the bottle trying to get it cleaned out so I could re-use it. The glue was noticeably harder, something like a super ball, and it could not be torn or broken apart. Don't leave this glue in your favorite glue bottle for too long or you may have another frustrating moment in your shop.

I thought Trade Secrets readers might be interested in my easy-to-make curved sanding blocks. These handy tools can be made from scrap ABS black plastic pipe. I use them primarily for finish sanding on the inside curve at the waist area of the body. I've also found them to be useful for sanding the inside curve on cutaways.

To make the tool you will need two pieces of scrap ABS pipe approximately 6" long. Rip one of the pieces lengthwise as in the drawing. Leave just over half of the diameter. This is easiest with a bandsaw, but you can saw ABS pipe with a carpenter's handsaw. Whichever method you choose, be very careful when ripping ABS pipe, and keep your hands clear of the saw blade.

To use the sanding block, take 1/4 sheet of sandpaper and wrap it around the ripped piece of pipe with the paper folded over the ripped edges. Then clip it over the unripped pipe and you now have a quick-change curved sanding block. By using pipe of various diameters you can have a curved sanding block for just about any situation.

Randy Allen
Allen Guitars - Mandolins- Resophonic
Colfax California
"Building Tomorrow's Collectible Guitars Today"

Here's a photo of Randy — still having glue trouble. This time, he's got a couple of guitars stuck to his shirt!

Reinforcing a nasty peghead break instead of replacing the neck

When neck replacement is not an option for repairing a badly-broken peghead, a lasting repair can be made by removing wood from the back of the peghead and laminating a hardwood "back-strap" in its place-not only covering the break, but extending beyond it onto the neck. Here's one way to do it...

After first gluing the break, remove wood from the rear of the peghead, accurately, on a homemade "drum sander" thicknesser consisting of a height-adjustable hinged table or "platen" mounted under the un-crowned drive drum of a belt-sander.

Using a coarse (50 to 80-grit) belt, feed into the drum with the belt moving towards the work (and with heavy instruments recruit someone to help support the weight)! Sand until well past the break line and when you stop feeding, pull the piece out instantly to avoid sanding a dip. I normally remove as much as .090" to .125" (at .030" per pass), and finish up by hand with a scraper.

To match the curve left by the sanding drum, you must pre-bend the laminate (usually maple or ebony) on a heated bending iron-wetting the wood occasionally during the process. Sometimes I'll clamp the bent laminate into a male/female bending form to hold it's shape while it dries overnight.

(See photos on facing page.)

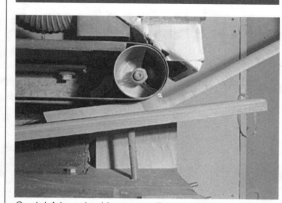

Crude! A board, a hinge, an adjustment screw, a sander.

These quick-made gluing cauls have wax paper double-stick-taped to their faces.

I use a space heater to heat the work (and immediate area) to 105°-giving me time to glue up with fresh, hot, hide glue.

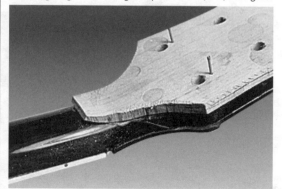

Often I remove the peghead overlay (or a thickness of the peghead face if there is no overlay) and laminate it too—creating a "peghead sandwich." The pre-bent laminate was aligned by small nails-the nail holes will be hidden by the tuners.

Irving Sloane dies at age 73

Irving Sloane, the mentor to hundreds of guitar builders and repairmen, passed away on June 21. He was 73.

Irving's books *Classic Guitar Construction* (1975), *Guitar Repair* (1973), *Steel String Guitar Construction* (1975), and *Making Musical Instruments* (1978) started many of us on a career path into luthiery.

Irving was more than an author. He was a graphic artist in New York, a jewelry designer in Brussels, and he never stopped working on guitars. After writing Classic Guitar Construction, Irving saw the need for quality tools designed specifically for guitars. His finger and palm planes, bridge clamp, fret rule, bending iron, thickness caliper, soundhole/purfling cutter, crack repair knife, and splint shaping jig are classic tools used in the world's best repair shops.

In 1987 Irving patented a new design for classical guitar tuning machines, to eliminate gear backlash. He designed the machines to look and work better than any others. Irving always combined the technical with the artistic side, to produce tools that worked as good as they looked.

We deeply regret the loss of a true inspiration in the field of luthiery. We will continue to offer Irving's tools and guitar tuning machines, so that future generations of luthiers can benefit from the lifelong work of Irving Sloane.

These neck removal & trimming jigs are big time savers

Rick Turner has been designing, building, and repairing guitars and guitar electronics—or writing about it—for as long as most of us have been on earth, it seems. In his most recent venture, "Rick Turner Guitars," Rick's been joined by his friend Steve Crisp, a renowned repairman from Austin, Texas.

"Crispy was faced with the usual problem of the repair biz," says Rick. "The better you get, the more you find yourself on the phone, with less time for actually doing the work. Steve just felt like it was time for a change, and it was lucky for me that he joined us. There are four of us, including myself, Crispy, Steve Lankford, and Mike Cornwall.

"As builders, most of us are into small one or two person shops, with a limited production of perhaps two to four instruments per month. We're trying to make the jump to at least 25 pieces per month, where certain economies of scale kick in and the finances start to work selling through music stores. The area in between—building six to twenty instruments a month—is a very difficult place to be. You have to be jigged up enough to do consistent work, but you can't really buy enough parts to price instruments competitively.

"*Finally* I've made an instrument that's well received, and pretty quick to put together. It's a cross between a Ramirez, a Tele, and a 335, if you can imagine such a beast. We're trying to build 30 a month, and if sales hold as good as they've been, we're headed toward 50 or 60 a month in the next couple of years. That size company seems very comfortable to us.

"Though we're really not doing much repair work these days, Steve and I thought you might like to see a couple of jigs which make short and accurate work of neck resets around our shop:

"The removal jig pops the neck out very easily (once the steam has done its work, of course) and it accepts virtually any size guitar. I did the basic design, and when Steve built it he added some nice tricks such as the adjustable shoulder holders. It uses the same lead screw that Charles Fox uses in his side bender—a Jorgenson screw, used in veneer presses, that's available in a number of woodworking catalogs.

"The trimming jig is Crispy's design, and uses a small offset-base laminate router to rout the outer rim of the new neck angle into the cheeks of the heel. We finish off with the Dremel and/or hand chisels. The neck bolts flat against the upright table, and the hinged acrylic trimming table adjusts for the neck angle by means of the slotted "chest lid supports" sold in furniture supply catalogs. They're also used for drop leaf desks and tables.

"In use, the offset trimmer gets in just far enough up under the fingerboard to feather out the cut to the necessary zero point. The results are as near perfect as you could hope for, and *quick*. Total time on Andy Summers' 1958 D-28 (pictured) was about 2-1/4 hours, including a light fret milling. At $225 for the job, it's a money maker using these jigs, and we make up for at least a few of the many jobs on which we made $5.00 per hour!

Rick Turner and Steve Crisp
Rick Turner Guitars
330 'B' Ingalls St.
Santa Cruz, CA 95060
408 460 9144
FAX: 408 460 9146

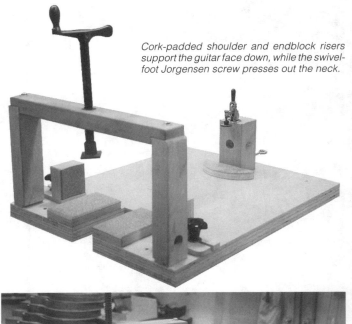

Cork-padded shoulder and endblock risers support the guitar face down, while the swivel-foot Jorgensen screw presses out the neck.

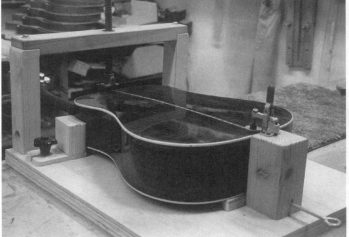

The endblock stop has a clearance hole to accept a guitar endpin strap button, and uses a toggleclamp to hold the guitar firmly.

The 3/4" acrylic table is hinged and adjustable on slotted chest lid supports.

Jig makes Dremel routing easy

To make routing the cavities for his "Aztec Stairstep" pearl fretboard inlays easier and more accurate, Jim Jaros (see the main story in *Trade Secrets* in the middle of this catalog) devised a nifty support platform for his Dremel router…

"Since all our fretboards have the same taper, or profile, from end to end," says Jim, "this simple wedge holds the fretboard firm and makes the perfect platform for the Dremel base. It's never unsupported as I move from the treble-side to the bass-side while routing. It's far better than trying to rout with the Dremel resting on the fretboard's 12" radius, which makes accurate routing difficult. For those who work on fretboards of different shapes and sizes, one side of this jig could easily be made adjustable to accept different fretboard profiles."

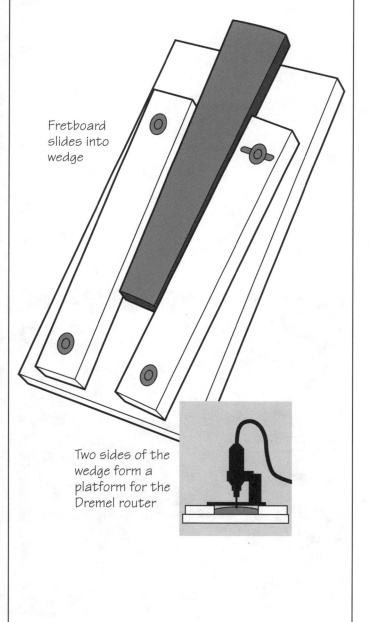

Fretboard slides into wedge

Two sides of the wedge form a platform for the Dremel router

Gourmet Guitars

Hi Gang! Thought I'd share a recent job with Trade Secrets. We took in a Danelectro-made Silvertone guitar with a cracked lipstick tube pickup that had a sizable gap. I called everywhere but no replacement was available for the original. [*I guess Bob didn't call us at Stewart-MacDonald! check out our replacement Lipstick pickup. Of course fixing the broken one, as you guys did, is always the best solution whenever possible. Thanks for the tip! –Dan*]

I spoke to Lindy Fralin, who said he has seen this more often than you'd think. Lindy suggested bending the original back into shape and soldering it. Bill Loveless, an excellent local luthier, and I thought about it and came up with the idea of using a small hose clamp from the local auto supply to hold the crack together while we soldered it.

We wrapped masking tape around the lipstick tube to prevent scratches, held the tube in a small vise by the hose clamp screw, and ran a small line of solder down the crack from the inside. After using a small rat-tail file to remove the excess solder, we took off the hose clamp and the tape. "Presto"-we really had to look hard for the crack. It worked great!

Thank you for all of the tips. I really enjoy them!
Sincerely,
Bob Shade, Gourmet Guitars, Greenbelt, MD

Close-up of cracked tube (crack on far side)

Cracked tube with tape and hose clamp

Repaired tube

Back on without a trace!

Laying out the end-to-end shape of an acoustic guitar side

Repairman Flip Scipio of Staten Island, New York is also a good artist. I asked Flip how he'd go about laying out and drawing the somewhat tricky curved profile of the side of an acoustic guitar. This was his answer…

Dan: So-you'd like to make a paper side profile for your guitar-to-be. Use this geometric trick. It's a really nice way of designing your own curve without constantly having to build elaborate jigs, and it allows you to shift the apex of the back's curve effortlessly.

On a large sheet of graph paper, draw one half of your guitar shape. With a pair of dividers set at one inch, mark off the perimeter and number each mark. This will give you a reasonable estimate of how long the side really is, and the numbers you'll transfer to a second drawing.

This second drawing should be exactly underneath the first drawing: a full-scale horizontal side view of the profile (arch, or 'taper,') from neck block to end block as you would like to see it. Mark out the height of the heel and the end block first, and then connect them with a curve that you design.

Next pull lines from the numbered markings on the first drawing to the second, side drawing below; these lines must be perpendicular to the top line of the lower drawing. This will tell you how high the sides are at one inch intervals.

Finally, make a third full length drawing of the side (28" in this case), layout 1" intervals, and transfer the height measurements to the appropriate numbers. Mark out the neck block and end block height, connect the dots, and voilá: one reasonably accurate side profile!

You can then cut the piece of paper out, Elmer's glue it to your wood, and saw on the dotted line.

Flip Scipio
Scipio Guitars, Staten Island, New York

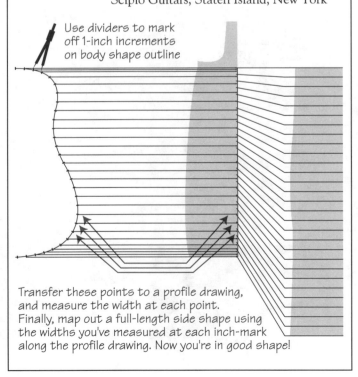

Use dividers to mark off 1-inch increments on body shape outline

Transfer these points to a profile drawing, and measure the width at each point.
Finally, map out a full-length side shape using the widths you've measured at each inch-mark along the profile drawing. Now you're in good shape!

Swiss Precision

Dear Stewart-MacDonald:
The bodies of my solidbody electric guitars are unbound, with both the top and back rounding gradually to the edges. I discovered a new trick for getting the round shape uniform around the entire perimeter:

■ Cut the shape of the guitar body from a piece of wood which has been thicknessed very closely to your final specifications. Leave any extra amount you like for final-sanding after the rough-in work is finished. Rout for the neck, pickups, and controls as necessary.

■ Rout a "binding channel" on the back and top with a .090" router bit, set to the height you need for your curves (ILLUS).

■ With a file, rotary sander, and other tools of your choice bring back the wood of the top or back to the bottom of the binding channel.

■ Result: you've got a perfect arch on the body!

Patrick Hufschmid
Guitare Reparations
Aigle, Switzerland

Patrick: Thanks for the good idea!
–Dan

Lone Star luthiery: Hot tips from Texas

Dan Erlewine and Jay Hostetler report from the Texas Guitar Show

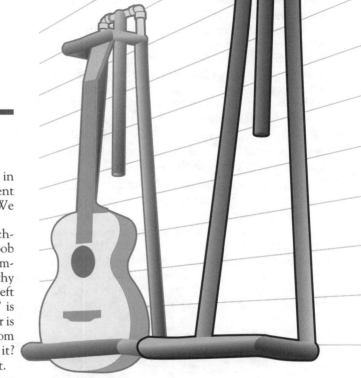

Collings Guitars is racking up a perfect reputation

After displaying at the Arlington, Texas Guitar Show in October, Jay Hostetler and I drove south to Austin and spent several days visiting the area's guitar builders and repairmen. We started at the Collings Guitar Company.

Bill Collings

Bill Collings openly shares his techniques with other builders (he and Bob Taylor consult each other often). Seemingly, Bill has few secrets. After a lengthy visit at the Collings factory, Jay and I left with the feeling that the only "secret" is simply that every part of a Collings guitar is made and assembled perfectly, with no room for improvement. Sounds easy, doesn't it? Here are some highlights from that visit.

I'm always gratified when I see other shops using a neck-jig to ensure perfect fretwork, because I'm such a believer in the neck-jig. It came as no surprise that Bill Collings jigs each guitar before and after fretting; first to level the fretboard perfectly, afterward to level the tops before final dressing.

These inexpensive PVC guitar racks are easy to build, and hold instruments of different sizes safely and securely.

Secure storage with wall-hung racks

Storage is always a problem in any shop, especially when a newly lacquered instrument is in clamps waiting for neck-sets or bridge-glues to dry. The walls of the Collings set-up room are lined with two dozen of the safest storage racks we've seen (illustrated at right). Mounted up and out of the way, these clever wall racks are inexpensive and easy to make from 3/4" schedule 80 PVC plumbing pipe connected with 3 "T" and 8 "L" (90°) fittings, using PVC glue. The racks are then wrapped in foam pipe insulation, which is slit, popped onto the pipe, and taped in place. The vertical center piece protects the peghead as the guitar is slid up into the rack before being lowered into position. These racks are as good-looking as they are practical.

Dan Erlewine

Steve Wise levels frets on a Collings guitar near completion.

DINGWALL DESIGNER GUITARS

Dingwall Guitars rises from the ashes

A disastrous fire in 1996 required 16 months of rebuilding before Dingwall Designer Guitars was running again in Saskatoon, Saskatchewan, Canada. "We have fewer models now," says owner Sheldon Dingwall, "and we're only making basses, which is what we're known for. All our new tooling was drawn on laser CAD and then built from steel on CNC machines to help us hold close tolerances on manual machines. More important though, if there's ever another fire I can go right out and replace the tooling immediately. Thought your readers with disk sanders might appreciate a simple and accurate way to thickness nuts and saddles:

■ Square-up the table and miter-gauge of the disk sander. The gap between table the and the sanding disk shouldn't be more than half the thickness of the saddle blank.

■ True one edge of a scrap block of wood or MDF board ("Face A"). Holding Face A against the miter-gauge, true Face B against the running disk.

■ Sand one side of the saddle flat then place it on the table between the MDF and disk. Slide the MDF toward the disk while holding it tight to the miter gauge. Use the trued face of the MDF to apply light pressure to the saddle. The saddle faces will then be dimensioned perfectly parallel to each other. Mic the piece often as material is removed.

Saddle (white) →

B

A

Miter Gauge

"After having the headstocks of several maple necks blow off on a router because of glue line failure (it's frightening), we ran some tests that showed as much as 60% glue line failure! Following the Franklin glue company's advice on surface preparation – and our own experiments – brought few improvements. Then an employee, Linda Breton, came up with the idea of raising the grain with water prior to gluing. Using this technique, our tests on maple showed less than 2% failure at the glue line. We raise the grain just as you might before finishing, but we don't sand it. We let it dry, then glue up the pieces. The opened pores accept more glue and the joint is far superior."

Sheldon Dingwall
Dingwall Designer Guitars Saskatoon, Saskatchewan, Canada

Sheldon Dingwall

Sheldon and head of production Brian Kinash with a Voodoo bass.

Brian Kinash using the portable sanding box. It hooks up to a dust collector with high-efficiency bags. The work surface uses 5/8" dowels covered with foam pipe insulation.

Laser-cut steel body templates and drill guides are color-coded by model and stored in production sequence.

Indexing Jig For Tuner Bushings

A friend's early 60s Tele had been poorly retrofitted with Grover tuners. He came to me wanting the Grovers removed and a set of Gotoh vintage-style tuners reinstalled in their place (they look like the old Kluson Deluxe). The tuner holes had been been poorly hand-reamed to a very unround 3/8". Normally our slightly oversize #3458 conversion bushings fill 3/8" Grover holes perfectly, and downsize them for the smaller-shafted tuners, but these holes were more oblong than round (see below). I wanted to clean them up by boring them with a 3/8" end mill, or by drilling them with a non-twist-point drill bit (a Forstner bit or a brad-point bit) just to kiss the sides of the hole. How would I know where to center the drill bit if the existing holes weren't round? And if I drilled off-center in any direction, the Kluson-style tuners would never go on, because their base plates are designed to touch each other.

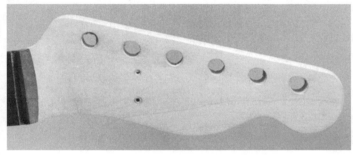

I was saved by the mounting-screw holes from the original tuners which, unfilled during the Grover conversion, remained untouched in the back of the peghead. I used them as a locating point to keep the drill bit on center with where the new tuner shafts were about to end up . It worked perfectly, and here's how:

- Measure the distance, between centers, of the mounting hole and the shaft. I measured 25/64" (**photo 1**).

- Lay out a straight line on a hardwood board and make two marks on that line 25/64" apart. One marks where the mounting screw goes, and the other marks the shaft hole to be re-drilled. Drill a small hole at mark 1 and press a steel "locating" pin into it that will snugly fit the tuner mounting holes in the rear of the peghead (**photo 2**).

- Measure the distance from the centers of the tuner mounting holes to the edge of the peghead (this will vary slightly between pegheads). Draw a second, parallel line at that distance from your first line (we'll call this "Line X"). Press a tuner mounting hole onto the locating pin, line the peghead edge up with Line X, and lay a wooden "fence" along the line and superglue it to the hardwood board. This makes a precise stop for the peghead edge to locate against while you're drilling (**photo 3**).

- With the peghead on a tuner mounting hole and up against the fence, drill a 3/8" hole clear through into the backer board. This makes a backer hole to ensure that you won't punch out wood from the rear of the peghead if you drill through. Drilling through isn't necessary, since you only need to drill for the depth of the conversion bushing (**photo 4**). Set the lower tuner hole for each key on the locating pin (peghead against the fence) and drill all six holes. When the keys are installed, the shafts will center to the new bushings and only a small amount of the hand-reamed holes will show when done!

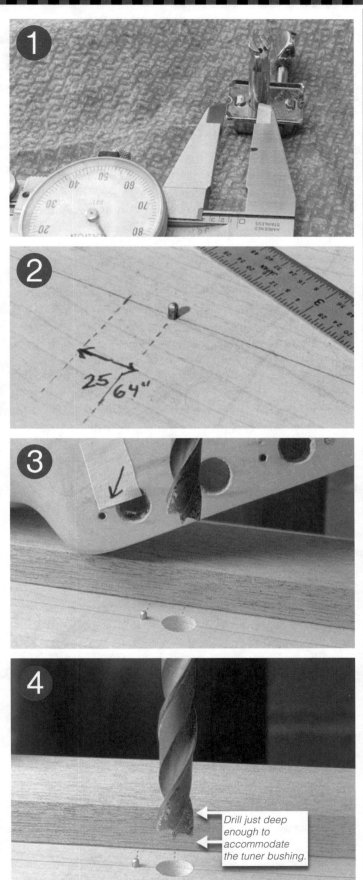

25/64"

Drill just deep enough to accommodate the tuner bushing.

Dan drops in on cousin Mark in Austin

In 1970 Mark Erlewine joined my fledgling guitar building and repair shop in Ann Arbor, Michigan. We became partners and dubbed the business Erlewine Instruments. In 1973 Mark followed the lure of the Old West and moved to Austin, Texas where he founded Erlewine Guitars. Soon I left Ann Arbor too, moving north to Big Rapids, Michigan in 1975 to open Dan Erlewine's Guitar Hospital. Mark and I still stay in touch, and keep each other up to date on the latest repair techniques.

Mark called soon after getting to Austin. He was excited about a new neck removal technique he'd just learned from Larry Jamison and Michael Stevens at Guitar Resurrection. This was the steam-through-fret slot-technique that leaves the fingerboard and neck intact, and which we all use today (see the neck removal tools on page 15). Back then, even the Martin Guitar Company didn't know this technique, and since most repairmen kept their trade secrets in those days, I was grateful to those Austin guys for sharing such a great idea. People in Texas are just friendly I guess, and confident in what they know.

Though perhaps best known for his Laser guitar (played by Johnny Winters) and his Chiquita Travel Guitar (a co-venture between Mark and Billy Gibbons), Mark also makes the Erlewine Automatic, a handsome guitar that was the first of the carved-top, glued-neck, Strat-inspired guitars.

"I built the first Automatic for Billy Gibbons-it was his 'Have Mercy' guitar. I still build a small number of Lasers and Automatics by hand each year, and the Chiquita's still travelling well, although she is getting on in age," quips Mark. Erlewine built the first Chiquita prototypes in 1978, before having them reproduced overseas, where they are still being made today. "Of course the mainstay of my business is repair work — and within that category, fretmills, nuts, and saddles are still the bread and butter."

Dan (left) with his cousin, Mark Erlewine of Erlewine Guitars in Austin.

A tool with a history of its own (below): Mark's buffer came from the old Kalamazoo Gibson plant. It has poured-bronze "Babbett" bearings and was powered with a flat leather belt. Mark had it converted to V-belt drive. Mark wraps the dust-collector hoods with the same foam pipe insulation that Collings Guitars uses for their wall racks (see story on page 47).

Mark in the front of his shop in Austin. Mark uses lighted, glass-fronted display cases to display sample Automatics, Chiquitas, and Lasers (also displayed is a gold record presented by Billy Gibbons for Mark's steel playing on the song "Leila" from ZZ-Top's "El Loco" album).

TradeSecrets!

At Precision Guitar Works: a custom-built carving machine and a quick tip for making side dots

You may know Tony Nobles as author of the "Guitar Shop" column in *Vintage Guitar* magazine. Tony also owns and operates Precision Guitarworks in Austin, Texas, where he repairs and builds guitars.

"I got my start at Erlewine Guitars, working five years with Mark before opening my own shop in 1995," says Tony. "Mark taught me most of what I know about building, repairing, and finishing guitars. Nobody does a better vintage Gibson sunburst than Mark." Recently, Tony built a giveaway guitar for *Vintage Guitar*, made from a #4913 Stew-Mac solidbody guitar kit and finished with Stew-Mac supplies.

"On this finish, the coloring was done with your new Color-Tone liquid stains, except for the black, which is opaque. I was out of black lacquer at the time, so I tried a glycol ether-based liquid lampblack. I poured it into clear lacquer hoping it would work and it did! Now, in Stew-Mac's new book *Guitar Finishing Step By Step*, I read that some glycol ethers are compatible with nitrocellulose lacquer, so I guess my instincts were right. That book's going to be a real help to guitar finishers."

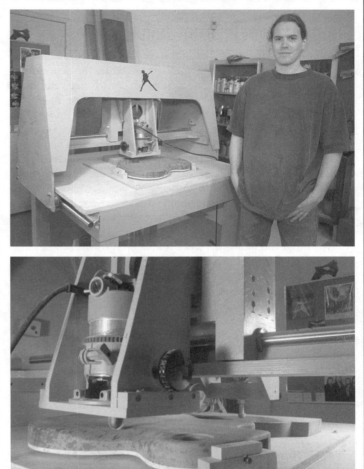

A retired machinist, Dave Pedersen designed and built Tony's wood-framed carving machine. The router carriage is controlled by a pattern-following stylus, and uses linear bearings to glide along polished rods on the X and Y axis. The router also moves up and down in similar fashion, and the cut is controlled by hand pressure from the operator.

Tony builds Gerald Weber's "Kendricks" guitars, including this single-cutaway carved-top version which resembles a cross between a Gibson Les Paul and a Guild Bluesbird, but smaller and lighter.

Tony uses a leather punch to make 3/32"-diameter fretboard "side dots" from Stew-Mac's #4411 tortoise-shell .060" binding.

Simple, clever tip from Julius Borges

Julius Borges operates SBS Guitars in Littleton, Massachusetts (SBS stands for Schoenberg/BorgeS). Julius builds the Schoenberg guitars for Eric Schoenberg, as well as his own Borges guitars in several models. He builds almost entirely with hot hide glue because "it makes a huge difference in tone," he says, "and we end up with a more clear-voiced guitar. You know, Titebond is vinyl, so you're putting vinyl between all of your pieces when you use it. An acoustic engineer will tell you that as soon as a soundwave hits a dissimilar material (which vinyl is to wood more than hide glue is) that part of the soundwave deflects. So you don't have to be a rocket scientist to figure what happens from there. Excepting a heel cap or headstock veneer, we glue everything structural with hot hide glue.

"We mix fresh glue each week and keep it in the refrigerator. We use Stew-Mac's glue pot with water in the second sleeve and suspend a honey jar in the water. Though we keep the cap on the jar, the glue still thickens during the day, so we add water in small amounts until it runs freely off the brush again. We throw out each day's leftover glue. If you think of hide glue like food-as something you plan to eat-you'll know when it's bad. If food gets smelly and slimy in the fridge you don't use it. It's the same with hide glue."

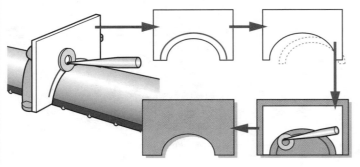

Hot Tip: Copying Neck Profiles

"Say you want to grab the neck profile at the 2nd fret. Take a piece of acrylic, rough out the basic neck shape with a bandsaw or coping saw, and mark a centerline on it. Next clamp a capo near the second fret, mask the neck's finish for protection, and prop the acrylic against the capo to keep it at 90°. Poke a metal scribe through a small washer, roll it around the neck shape, and scribe the shape onto the acrylic. Clean up to the scribe line. Lay the acrylic onto a second piece, and with the same washer, scribe inside the first piece onto the new piece. You'll have the exact profile of the neck."

Julius Borges
SBS Guitars, Littleton, MA

Thanks, Julius! Don MacRostie uses our 'Hold Heet' glue pot without water (see Trade Secrets Vol. 32 in the winter 1998 Stew-Mac catalog). He made a wooden lid with a tapered hole in the center in which he suspends an 8 ounce Cheeze Whiz jar filled with glue (Don likes this jar because it's tapered, and has a locking "bayonet" lid). A thermometer placed through the lid reads 160° because the chamber is closed by the lid, but the glue reads 145°. Don also uses a tin can as a cover to keep the heat from dissipating through the top of the Cheeze-Whiz jar.

Shop Tips from Tracy Longo

Dan and gang:
Here are a few tips and ideas for you. The first is simple but nice...

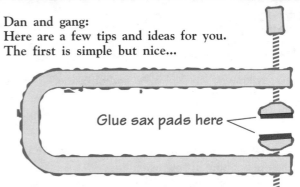

Glue sax pads here ←

Leather saxophone pads are perfect for the round jaws of your Waverly bridge clamps. Just superglue them on and you'll clamp more surfaces better without marring them.

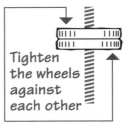

Tighten the wheels against each other

When installing or removing the threaded posts for Gibson Tune-O-Matic bridges, thread two scrap thumbwheels onto the post and tighten them against each other. Then grab them both with vise-grips or pliers and back the post out.

I got this idea from Two-Tech's bridge. I even thought of patenting it, but I never will. First, I just did it to the A-string alone, and the difference was so great that I did an entire set of saddles. Now I do the mod often (but not on vintage saddles). After removing Gibson Tune-O-Matic saddle inserts from the bridge body, drill two holes in the insert, one on each side of the string path. Use a 3/32" drill bit, or as large as you feel comfortable using without weakening the support under the string. Drill at an angle, from the saddle's beveled side, to keep the hollow areas closer to the string. The result is enhanced sustain, more volume, and increased string life. Don't ask me why the strings last longer, but they do. Try it!

Drill a hole on each side of the string

I use a Stew-Mac metal fret protector over bridge saddles that are glued in so I can shape the saddle without harming the bridge around it. (You'll need to enlarge the hole a little).

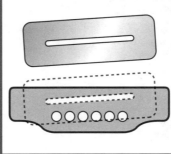

Tracy Longo's
Guitar Tech Corner
Ventura California

Modifying a drill bit for use with brass and plastic

Brass and plastic don't like the positive rake angle common to most twist drill bits. These materials can be drilled much more cleanly and accurately if you first modify the bit so that the tip of each flute has a 0° or neutral rake angle. This can be done simply and safely on a belt sander. Holding the bit at a downward angle with the flute tip in the same plane as the belt surface, remove only enough material to create a flat spot on each flute.

An improved countersink for pickguard screws can be made by modifying a 15/64" drill bit. Combine the same 0° rake angle described above with a reground point angle of 82°. You'll get a countersink that doesn't wander, and leaves a perfect countersunk hole for a #4 pickguard screw.

Sheldon Dingwall
Dingwall Designer Guitars

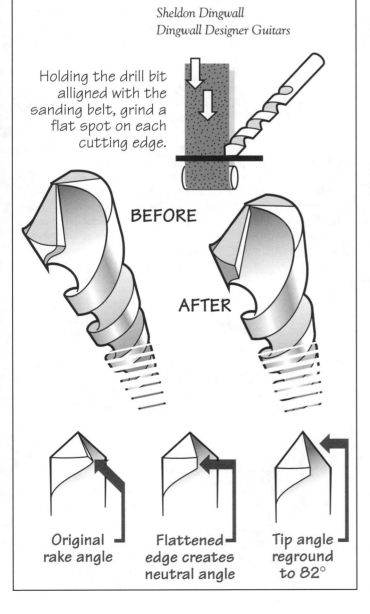

Holding the drill bit alligned with the sanding belt, grind a flat spot on each cutting edge.

BEFORE

AFTER

Original rake angle

Flattened edge creates neutral angle

Tip angle reground to 82°

Jamie Kinscherff

Jamie Kinscherff worked at Taylor guitars from 1978-1980 and again from 1987-1989. In 1990 Jamie opened his own shop, Kinscherff Guitars, in Austin, where today he produces 24 to 30 of his powerful-sounding flattop steel string guitars each year. Most of his guitars go out of state, the majority to his one big dealer, Traditional Music in Lucedia, California. "I share shop space with Bill Giebitz," says Jamie. "It works out great for both of us because we don't compete. I don't repair and Bill doesn't build. Bill uses my power tools when he needs to make some sawdust, and I use his brain when I'm stumped. He's very bright and an excellent problem solver."*

Jamie's thickness sander (below) was designed and built by Tom Ellis. It has an adjustable table which rides up and down on all-thread rods mounted at each corner. The rods are activated by toothed pulleys and a chain drive via a handscrew. Two spring-loaded rubber rollers act as hold-downs. Powered by a separate motor, they're also power feeds.

Kinscherff's heavy-duty back brace gluing jig uses spring-loaded steel bars to force the curved bottoms of the braces against the matching curve of the cork-padded forms. "I can glue all the braces at one time and have plenty of room to clean up squeeze-out without pulling any clamps off. And the press has a turntable on the bottom, which lets me twirl the piece to clean up quickly."

Left: Jamie Kinscherff with Jay Hostetler.

* Read about the Bill Giebitz neck jig on page 141.

Make your own decals for one-of-a-kind instruments...

"The decal I used for the guitar giveaway in the February 1999 issue of *Vintage Guitar* magazine was made at a Kinko's copy shop while I waited. They computer-scanned the "artwork," which was simply the logo torn from the magazine, and transferred it to the same clear Mylar® film used for overhead projectors. I had the logo printed in reverse, with the ink on the bottom, so I could steel-wool the decal to match the neck's matte finish. I've made decals before, and usually have the ink printed on top. That way I can lay the Mylar into the wet finish early in the finishing stage, without having to worry about the ink blurring from the solvent. Then I spray several light dry coats of lacquer over the ink. This locks in the ink, before building up successive coats of lacquer on and around the .004"- Mylar. Eventually the Mylar's outline disappears into the clear coats. Either way, bottom-printed or top-printed, be aware that the solvents in lacquer may soften the decal's ink. Another option is to have your decal printed on self-adhesive Mylar. Then you can lay the decal on top of the final rubbed-out finish."

Tony Nobles
Precision Guitarworks
Austin, Texas

Tony and Stew-Mac V.P. Jay Hostetler. Tony holds the Vintage Guitar magazine giveaway guitar.

A quick modification gives you X-ray vision when using this knob-puller

In Trade Secrets Volume 32 (see page 100) we described David Jones' router carriage and binding rout set-up, along with a "tail vise" he made from a Jorgenson screw clamp. David's back with another good idea:

"Dan: In the Stew-Mac catalog on page 30 the drawing of the #3515 Knob & Bushing Puller is cut away to illustrate how the tool works. You know, the tool works MUCH better if you actually do cut away the housing so that it looks like the drawing. I had to cut mine in order to remove a volume knob that was almost right on top of a bridge. As long as you don't cut away too much sidewall, the tool remains stable. Two main advantages of the modification are:

1 **You can make sure you've got the puller positioned correctly, and see what you're doing as the knob comes off,**

AND, the biggie:

2 **You no longer have to turn (and turn...) the wingnut until the extractor clears the bottom of the housing to get your knob back — a slow operation if you're removing a set of four Gibson-style volume and tone knobs.**

A slot 90 degrees wide by 2" tall has worked well for me, and has been plenty for any knob I've gone after. Hope to see you in Nashville at the '99 ASIA Symposium!"

Yer Pal,
David Jones from SC

Thanks, David! This is an indispensable tool, and how we got along without it I'll never know. Like you, I cut away the side of my knob puller the first time I used it, but I never realized a Trade Secret was staring me in the face until you reminded me. It's an easy modification that takes only minutes to do. My mod was quick and dirty: I drilled a series of holes in the side and sawed up to them with an X-Acto® saw. I never got around to filing the edges smooth, so mine looks a little rough!

– Dan

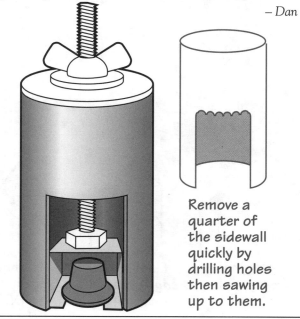

Remove a quarter of the sidewall quickly by drilling holes then sawing up to them.

The Inside Story on Superglue

Recently while refretting a Gibson Montana-made flattop and using a soldering gun to heat the frets before pulling them (to loosen any glue that may have been used in fretting), I was repulsed by the smoke and odor. It seemed more noxious than usual, and then I realized why: the frets were superglued in. I wondered: "Since superglue is a cyanoacrylate product, am I breathing heated cyanide fumes, or what?" Worried that I might get sick, I opened all the windows, turned on the fan, put on my spray respirator and finished removing the frets. I vowed to find out more about heated superglue fumes, and superglue fumes in general, because this wasn't the first time I'd experienced the smell. We'll all be removing more frets that were originally superglued — the first wave is just now coming through. Here's how the chemist who formulated our new superglue answered some of the more common questions we are asked about superglue. If you have a question, or a tip about instant adhesives, please send it to us!

Dan

Here's the word from the chemist: "Cyanide is used in the manufacturing process, but it's not present at all in the bottled glue. The fumes, heated or unheated, are somewhat noxious, as is any smoke you breathe, but less so than many other products used in woodshops, such as ones containing methylene chloride or toluene (paint stripper and lacquer products respectively). Superglue in uncured form is 80 to 85 percent pure ethyl-based monomer, but there are no solvents in it. The remaining 15 percent is a stabilizer, a polmerization inhibiter, and a thickening agent — none of which is particularly harmful. Superglue and its fumes are an irritant to the mucous membranes however, and when you heat superglue or put it on a hot surface the fumes are definitely unpleasant.

"The accelerator ('Blast'), which hastens the glue's curing time, is primarily heptane, a

Continued, next page

The inside story on superglue

relatively mild acetone-like solvent that flashes off quickly and leaves the curing agent behind. (The curing agent is a proprietary substance which is dissolved in the heptane carrier). I won't tell you what it is, only that it's no more toxic than the carrier itself. Accelerator is flammable, the fumes aren't good to breathe, and you should treat it with the same cautions and restrictions you would gasoline. Work in a well-ventilated area, handle it with nonporous protective gloves, wear eye protection, dispose of contaminated papers and rags outdoors, and keep it away from food, pets, children, and pregnant women."

Q How long does accelerator remain active in the area where it's sprayed?

A It's commonly said that accelerator retains its potency, or ability to harden superglue that comes in contact with it, for 45 minutes. However, it has the potential to remain potent for as long as three hours. I'd wait that long if you want a guarantee that glue applied in the same area won't accelerate.

Q Let's say I wish to use the #20 medium glue to make a clear fill in a 1/8" deep indentation — it might be wood or finish. I've been touching a little accelerator to the bottom of the hole to ensure that it dries on the bottom, and then repeating the process in layers until the hole is full. Sometimes a white or blue edge appears on the crater, and sometimes it doesn't. Sometimes the

whole mess gets frosty or frothy. What determines if this will happen or not? What causes the blue-white ring? Is that a blush?

A Superglues are moisture-curing adhesives that react to water or moisture present in the air, or in the pieces being glued. This is why superglue "kicks off" so fast in humid areas and during the summer, or why some days your drop fills are clear, and some days the white ring appears. You can make perfectly clear drop fills by using only superglue and letting it cure for 24 hours. All the superglues you're using will be hard as rock in 24 hours if the application isn't excessively thick.

Q Is there a shelf life for superglue?

A Both superglue and accelerator have a one-year shelf life after opening. Even then, the glue retains its strength, but is losing its quick-drying ability.

Q How long would you clamp projects with the different glues?

A It depends on the application. For thin glue joints the clamp time is going to be faster than fractures and areas where the glue is applied thick and used like an epoxy. For the average well-fit part expect the following set and clamp times: the #10 water-thin sets in three to five seconds but you may wish to clamp it for up to two minutes; the #20 medium sets in ten to twenty-five seconds, but you may need to clamp

Black superglue on ebony fretboard

it for up to three minutes; the #30 and #40 (gap-filling and gel respectively) set between thirty seconds and up to several minutes. All these glues don't get a true cure for twenty-four hours, and of course set and clamp times are substrate dependant. For example, on rubber, cyanoacrylates usually set in 1 to 2 seconds, which is much faster than for other substrates.

Q Is there any reason that the #40 gel type glue isn't as strong as the others?

A No reason. It's every bit as good. It just takes a little longer to cure. There are places and ways you can use gel superglue where you couldn't use the others, because it clings instead of flowing.

Q The black superglue is handy for working on ebony fretboards. Both the black and white superglues are ideal for touching up gaps and repairing black and white bindings. They can be used for finish touch-ups ("drop fills") on guitars with white or black finishes, and the white makes a great base for tinting with other colors. Does the glue lose strength or hardness because of the colorant added at the factory?

A No it doesn't. Not at all. ∎

Here white superglue has been mixed with a tiny bit of Honey Amber Color-Tone stain to produce an off-white for a binding repair.

Return! OF THE NECK JIG!

A short history by Dan Erlewine

I first began simulating string tension during fret work in the late 1960s. Trying to level fretboards accurately, especially on unruly necks, I weighted, clamped, spool-clamped, and wedged necks and bodies in a variety of ways before actually building a tool for the job in 1974. I dubbed it the "neck jig." My neck jig continued to evolve, and in 1985 I made a dozen full workbench models like the one pictured below and sold them to my

Above: the original jig (1974). Below: the second generation.

friends. When I moved to Ohio to work at Stew-Mac in 1986 the neck jig went with me and, redesigned, became the "Luthier's Workstation." One of my first projects at Stew-Mac was building several hundred of these tilt-table jigging workbenches which have graced

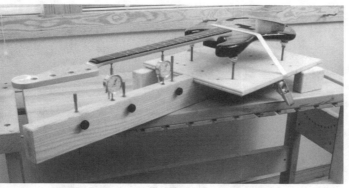

Top: the new Neck Jig sitting on top of my old neck jig with the top rotated upside down. The lower photo shows the jig clamped into the repair vise — which puts it in the playing position.

My first "production" neck jig.

Stew-Mac's second-generation production jig.

these pages more than once. There were two versions of Stew-Mac's Workstation.

We discontinued the Workstation in 1988. Though it was an excellent tool, it was expensive and a bit space consuming for some shops, and it was a shipper's nightmare. Since then we've often thought about making a compact, portable, inex-

pensive neck jig that would work as well or better than the original. Recently, Stew-Mac's Don MacRostie and Todd Sams designed and built the new table-top fretwork tool shown here. This new "Stew-Mac Neck Jig" reflects the influence of the neck jigs used by veteran repairmen Dan Kelchak, Bryan Galloup, Bill Giebitz (see page 141), and of course yours truly, whose demonstration of a dial-indicating neck jig at the 1995 GAL convention spawned our initial reasearch into this project.

The Stew-Mac Neck Jig does everything I need faster, easier, and better than the ones I've used for twenty-five years. This new tool is wonderful in its simplicity. I usually install the frets with the guitar supported in the jigged "playing" position, then level their tops, too. With the older models, I have to "unjig" the guitar for final dressing because it's too awkward to dress frets with the guitar clamped in the center of the worktable. This new tool is much more accessible; I can get right in close to the neck and dress the frets with-

out unjigging (above). The jig holds the guitar firmly and leaves the neck free!

The neck jig's size, light weight, and beam construction contribute to easy mounting in a variety of ways on tabletop, clamped in a vise, or clamped in a carpenter's "WorkMate" stand.

∎

TradeSecrets!

Take me back to Texas: Another hot tip from Collings Guitars

Our previous Trade Secrets (on page 127) offered a glimpse of the Collings Guitar factory in Austin, Texas, where the approach to guitar-making is based on long experience and great success. Here's another look: the drilling and routing templates Bill Collings uses for locating the bridge and stripping the finish prior to gluing on the bridge and the fingerboard extension (the neck bolts on, and the only glue is under the fingerboard extension). All the jigs and fixtures are computer-drawn and cut on a CNC machine from phenolic or steel for accuracy.

❶ This jig indexes off the fingerboard side of the nut slot, self-centers on the fretboard, and locates the bridge.

❷ Holes drilled through the two drill bushings align two of the bridge pin holes and also locate the jigs which follow (right).

❸ The next jig is a bridge-shaped tracing template.

❹ Dick Dubois traces around this jig with a sharp knife.

❺ This jig uses pins to locate it on the same two holes. A small router is used to remove the finish cleanly, without chemical stripper or heavy scraping.

❻ This jig is the routing template for the fingerboard extension.

❼ This is all the lacquer that gets routed away for the fingerboard glue joint. This makes neck removal easier should a neck reset ever be required.

❽ The bridge and neck are clamped at the same time.

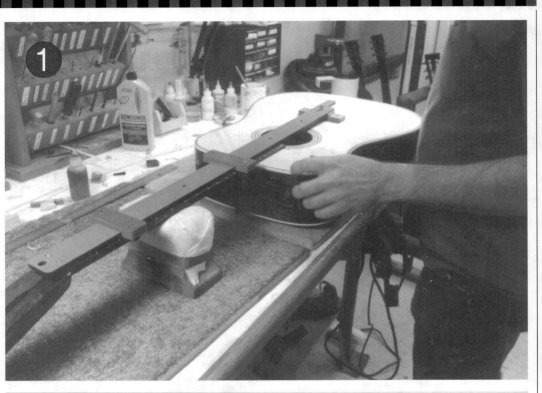

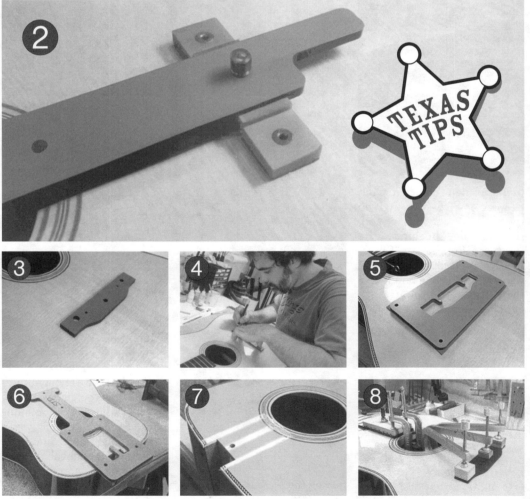

TEXAS TIPS

HOW TO GIVE A SNUG FIT TO EACH FRET

THE BARBS ON EACH SIDE OF THE FRET TANG ARE SLIGHTLY OFFSET... LEAVING NARROW GAPS

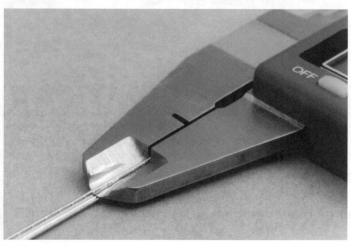

A fret tang should fit snugly in a fret slot. The actual size of the fret tang (not including the small diamond-shaped barbs) should match the slot — or be slightly bigger if you wish to straighten or stiffen a weak neck. Most fret slots are cut deeper than the tang, leaving some space at the bottom. This is even more reason why a snug fit in width is necessary for good "fret compression," and to produce a rigid neck for good tone. Since fretwire can vary as much as .004" or .005" from batch to batch, it's a good habit to check a fret's measurements, especially the tang, when you're choosing a fretwire for a given job.

Viewed from the bottom, the tang of most fretwire looks like the drawing above (with many variations, of course). The tang is formed with small raised diamond-shaped barbs which embed in the wood to hold the fret in place. The barbs are spaced evenly on each side, but slightly staggered on opposite sides, which leaves little room between them (about .023") for a caliper's jaws to fit, should one desire to measure the actual tang size.

Our new #3792 Luthier's Digital Caliper, like its dial caliper predecessor, has a slot in one jaw into which a fret tang will fit for easy crown height measurement. There's no way to measure the fret's tang with the same ease because of the barbs. It's easy to measure the outside dimension of the barbs, of course, but getting between them, or under them lengthwise, to measure the tang is nearly impossible with most fretwire.

Ground jaws compared to unground jaws: the ground jaws (top) measure .015", compared to the .025" of the unground jaws.

I couldn't resist buying the new caliper when I saw it was under $50. I'd also wanted a second pair so I could try grinding the jaws of my old calipers thinner to measure between the fret barbs accurately. My grinding was timid, and not too pretty, but it worked well enough that I ground the new pair, too.

■ I opened the jaws far apart and rested the jaw being ground on a block of ice to keep it cool.

■ Wearing eye protection, I used both a 3/8"-diameter brown stone and a 3/4"-diameter green stone wheel powered with a Dremel Moto Tool and ground each jaw separately. Later, I switched to my flexible shaft handpiece because it operates at a lower angle, flatter to the workpiece.

■ The jaws just barely fit between the barbs vertically (upper photo). However, they fit under the barbs comfortably (lower photo), and give the most accurate reading that way, if you have carefully deburred the end of the fret wire with a small file beforehand.

— Dan

NOTCHED STRAIGHTEDGES

Notched straightedges are important fretting and set-up tools that help evaluate the fretboard's end-to-end straightness (or lack of straightness) as no other tool can. Their notches allow them to rest directly on the wood of the fretboard rather than resting on the frets, which may be worn and uneven. (See our #3812 and #3813 notched straightedges on page 12).

For me, the most common use for a notched straightedge is to isolate the humps and valleys in a fretboard which are causing fret buzz. When I can truly see that the problem's in the wood, and not just badly seated frets, I can determine easily if it's a waste of time to level and dress out the problems in the frets, and better to just refret completely.

I rely so much on the notched straightedge that I've ground my own from our #3799 24" regular straightedge for scale lengths other than the two we offer. I now have quite a collection of notched straightedges for 36", 34", 30", 25-1/2", 25", 24-3/4", and 24-1/2" scale lengths.

I lay out the notches with a marker pen, then grind them slowly — cooling them often — using a reinforced abrasive cut-off wheel on the bench grinder. Then I clean up the roughed-in notches with a smaller abrasive wheel and grindstones mounted in my Dremel tool or a rotary handpiece.

Ideally, a badly upbowed fretboard can be straightened with the truss rod alone, or oversized tang frets can be used to help wedge the neck straight. When wood needs to be removed, however, you want to remove as little as possible, and from the right areas. If you average the problem areas from end to end, you'll remove the least amount of wood overall. This is why specialty fretting tools such as the neck jig (see page 49), accurate straightedges (both regular and notched), radius gauges and feeler gauges are important to keep us from blindly sanding away at the fretboard.

Sometimes a guitar's neck is so upbowed with excess relief that the notched straightedge contacts at each end and can't "read" the middle area. Or, it's hard to tell if the upper portion of the fretboard is rising up and causing string buzz. Other fretboards are so irregular and "lumpy" that the full length straightedge just can't get a good read. Because of this, I ground both of our notched straightedges in half at the ninth fret so that I could read each half of the neck separately. They come in handy all the time.

– Dan

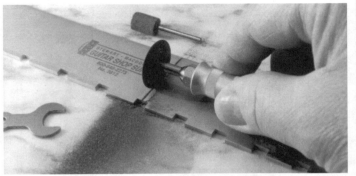

I ground the straightedges on a slab of marble which had been in the freezer overnight. The combination of cold marble, and a thin "wafer" abrasive cut-off wheel, kept heat build-up to a minimum. By using the Dremel rotary handpiece, I was able to hold the cut-off wheel at a right angle to the work.

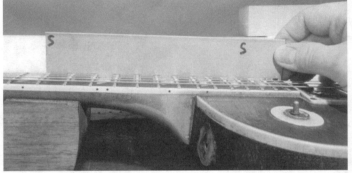

The short notched straightedge helped me find out why this Les Paul buzzed in the upper register. The fingerboard was loose, but I couldn't see it because of the built up dirt!

Notched straightedge collection.

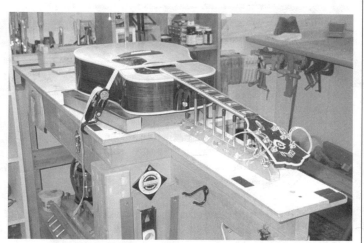

TEXAS TIPS

The Bill Giebitz neck jig

Bill Collings (see page 127) has influenced the majority of Austin's builders and repairmen, including Bill Giebitz, who worked in the Collings factory for a couple of years before opening his own repair shop. Like Collings, Giebitz is also a neck-jigger. Bill has a modern streamlined version of the "Luthier's Workstation" neck-jig fretting bench produced by Stew-Mac in the mid-1980s. Bill's bench doubles as both a fretting station and a neck resetting bench.

"I've taken a lot of your techniques Dan, and modified them to suit my style — like the 'fret tang sizer' you used in Stew-Mac's *Fretwork Step-By-Step* book. My tang sizer is simply two files ground to the appropriate shape and superglued to the jaw faces of a small machinist's vise (left — mounted to Bill's workbench leg under the Fret Bender). The tang sizer, and the Jaws fret press, have become two of my most valued fretting tools.

"When jigging, the guitar body must be held firmly on the bench. Instead of mechanical hold-downs, I use a single web clamp stretched over the waist," says Bill. "The clamp was made for truck beds, and I bought it in a hardware store automotive department. It has a wide flat hook on each end to grab the lip of the table top (this can be seen in the photo at upper right). A pair of long wood blocks surfaced with rubber hold the arched back up off the flat tabletop."

Bill uses the playing position to evaluate and jig problem fret jobs. The tilt feature is built into the bench (the top flips up 180° on hinges).

Bill's neck joint steamer (left) is an espresso maker that sits well below the tabletop. The steam hose runs up through a hole in the table. The hollow boxed-in chamber of the table houses a small fan, which draws steam and moisture away from the work area and out the end of the table.

At right, Bill demonstrates his neck-removal set-up to his assistant, 17-year-old Ringo Ramos. "Ringo had been repairing guitars for a year or so" said Bill. "She showed me work she'd done on her own guitar-a neck reset, refret, new bridge, and a complete refinish. It was really good work — I was so impressed that I hired her instantly!"

BENCH GRINDER SAFETY

A good friend of mine once bought an inexpensive bench grinder to use at his dad's cottage. When he turned it on, one of the grindstones flew apart, seriously injuring his face. If his father hadn't been there, (a world famous heart specialist who was able to stop the blood while driving his son 25 miles to the hospital) my friend would have bled to death in the garage. He was lucky.

I tell this story often because it scares me. I'd never considered a bench grinder to be particularly dangerous. Since then I've followed these bench grinder safety rules:

■ Wear eye protection whenever using bench grinders or hand-held grinders. A clear full-face shield is best.

■ Grinding stones can shatter if they're cracked, or loaded (glazed) from never being cleaned. Also, if one edge of a wheel sits submerged too long in cutting fluid (more likely in a metal shop), it can become bottom-heavy, causing it to run off balance and break apart.

■ Never run a grinding wheel faster than its rated RPM.

■ Work only on the wheel's front edge, never on the side!

■ Stand to the side when turning a grinder on and let it run for one full minute before using it. Avoid standing directly in the line of fire when using it if possible.

■ Do not run the grinder without the wheel guards and safety glass spark arrestor in place.

■ "Ring test" a grinding wheel for cracks by suspending it through the center hole on a stick, and tapping lightly with a blunt non-metallic object. A good wheel will ring! A dull sounding wheel may have a hidden crack. Discard it and buy a good "ringy" replacement. For most guitar shops, a 60-grit gray aluminum oxide wheel is a good all-around choice for grinding tool steel.

■ Clean built-up metal particles from a running wheel using a "star wheel" dresser. It removes a thin layer of stone and built-up metal while shaping and squaring the wheel's face (below). Caution: Stone dust fills the air when you are cleaning a wheel. Wear a respirator and work with good ventilation!

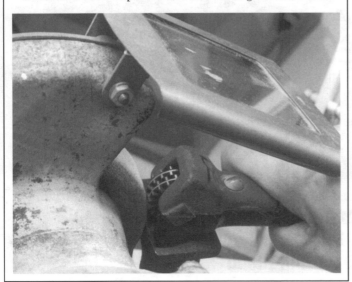

Setting brass inserts into a benchtop

Here's how to set a brass insert into a benchtop — or into the new Stew-Mac Neck Jig (see page 137). If you run into an odd-shaped guitar or other instrument, you may wish to add an insert or two to the neck jig board. The best way to install the inserts (extra inserts, and the threaded rod with swivel foot are available if you need them) is to make the simple tool shown here.

■ Use a 1-1/2" long allen cap screw with 5/16"-13 thread.

■ Install a 5/16" hex nut on the cap screw thread. The hex nut will keep the cap screw thread from bottoming out in the brass insert and making it impossible to loosen without loosening the insert with it (and you want the insert left behind, in the wood).

■ Use a large countersink to chamfer the 1/2" hole which is drilled in the plywood to accept the insert. (This keeps the plywood from lifting and splintering as the insert is driven in).

■ We power drive the inserts using the above "tool" in an electric drill, and a sawed-off allen key inserted in the cap screw head to drive it. We install the brass inserts slot-side-down for a nice clean look on the board's surface.

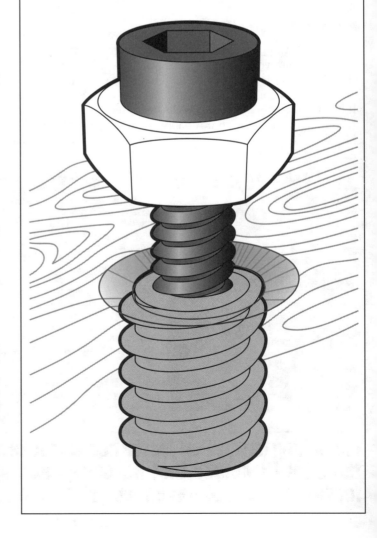

TradeSecrets!
Hot tips & inside scoops. Editor: Dan Erlewine

PEGLEG the One-Legged Workbench!

My most recent heartthrob is a height-adjustable column, bolted securely to the floor, with fixtures to hold guitars for repair work. I can walk entirely around this workstand and it suits me better than any bench I've owned (photo, right). Mounted on the head of the workstand's 360-degree rotating column is a tilting "cradle vise," with jaws that hold a jig or fixture. Stew-Mac's R&D shop made this stand from heavy plate steel, but it required tools and machining capabilities that most woodshops and guitar repair shops don't have, including a milling machine, cutting torch, welding equipment, metal lathe, and a skilled operator.

Immediately I wanted a second stand in my shop, but I needed an easier way to make it. I bought the "heavy-duty roller-support stand for jointers, planers, and tablesaws" pictured on page 155 in the 1999-2000 edition of the Sears Craftsman Power and Hand Tools catalog (item #21417, at $99.00 plus $30 U.S. freight). With minimal work and some hired welding, it's as good as our custom-made stand. Here's how to make it, without the luxury of the Stew-Mac R&D team...

The support stand fastens together, rather shakily, by means of Allen-head set screws. After much drilling, tapping, and experimenting to make it sturdier, I ended up having the outer column welded to the base (light area in the photo above), and the split-ring column clamp welded to the top of the outer column (photo 1, page 144). The welds made it solid and eliminated screws or bolts. Next time, I'll use the Allen set screws

(continued on page 144)

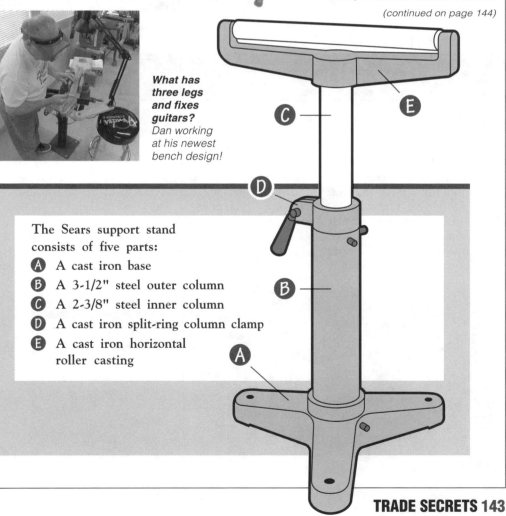

What has three legs and fixes guitars? *Dan working at his newest bench design!*

The Sears support stand consists of five parts:

- **A** A cast iron base
- **B** A 3-1/2" steel outer column
- **C** A 2-3/8" steel inner column
- **D** A cast iron split-ring column clamp
- **E** A cast iron horizontal roller casting

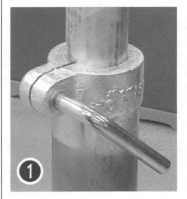

① Weld only 1/4 to 1/3 around the clamp — it must retain the freedom to close when tightened.

② A plumbing shop cut the pipe thread onto the top of this 2-3/8" column so a 5" cast iron plumbing flange fits onto it.

③ This angled wood block bolts to the flange and holds the "cradle vise," the heart of the workstand.

④ The triangular block is drilled and tapped for the 5/16-18 Allen cap screws which fasten it to the flange.

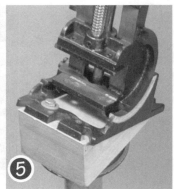

⑤ I drilled my own bolt holes in the vise casting, but it's overkill—don't bother.

⑥ Although the vise is calibrated to swivel 90 degrees, it travels an extra 15 degrees.

The one-legged workbench

only to align the parts and hold them during the welding. I'd also recommend using an experienced welder—a novice may tell you incorrectly that heavy cast iron and a relatively thin steel column can't be welded.

I stored the support's roller casting and roller in case I need it in the future. I took the inner 2-3/8" column to a plumbing shop, had a pipe thread cut on the end, and screwed a cast iron 5" plumbing flange onto it (photo 2). To the flange I fastened an angled wood block that holds the "cradle vise," the heart of the workstand (photo 3). The wood block measures 8-1/2" x 5-1/2" and is angled at 25 degrees. I drilled and tapped it for the 5/16-18 allen cap screws which

fasten it to the flange (photo 4).

The cradle vise is a #4000 "Super Tilt Vise," purchased for $39.95 from Kitts Industrial Tools, 22384 Grand River, Detroit, Michigan, 48219 (800-521-6579). The jaws are 4" wide, 1-1/2" deep, and open to 4". The vise simply bolts onto the block (photo 5). The vise is calibrated to swivel 90 degrees,

but it actually travels an extra 15° (photo 6). Therefore, when mounted on the 25-degree angle block, the vise can tilt 80° in one direction (into the playing position for neck jigging, which is about 80 degrees), return to level for working, and tilt 25° in the opposite direction to facilitate dressing the fret ends more easily (photos 7, 8, 9).

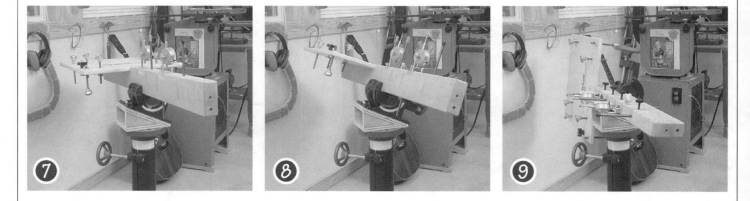

⑦ **⑧** **⑨**

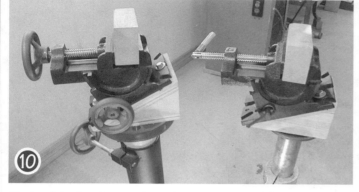

The handwheels make operation easier, and eliminating the length of the long clamp screw makes it more user friendly.

A ball bearing lets the inner column rotate 360 degrees smoothly.

Two holes are drilled and tapped through the vise jaws to accommodate cap screws which add extra grip in holding the wood beams of the workstand, jigs, and fixtures.

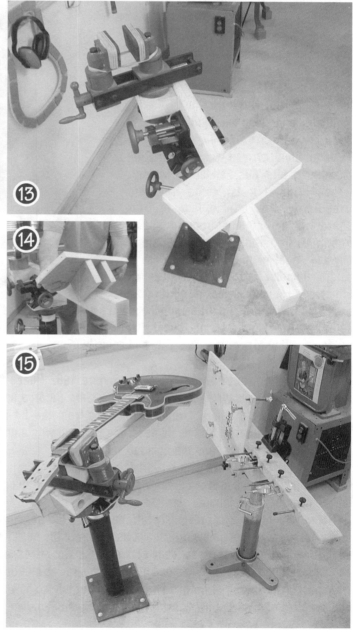

- I removed the two screws holding the rear jaw of the vise and drilled larger holes through both the vise and the rear jaw. These are clearance holes for 3/8-16 allen cap screws, (photo 12, above) which thread into holes tapped into the wood beams of the neck jig, the workstand, and other fixtures. The bolts combine with the vise jaw to hold the work firmly. I also added cast iron hand wheels to the vise and shortened the threaded shaft of the vise jaw clamping screw so when tilted it wouldn't hit me in the stomach (photo 10, top).

- The inner column has several 3/8-16 holes tapped into it to accept the 3/8" hex-head bolt which fastens a 1-1/4" diameter ball bearing to the column (photo 11). The bearing lets the inner column rotate 360 degrees smoothly, and the tapped holes are spaced several inches apart to adjust the column's height.

- The "workbench" is simply a 36" x 2" x 4" hardwood beam with a side block and vise mounted on it (photo 13). The vise is heavy, and is mounted close to the column for the best support. The angled table is the "benchtop."

- The "benchtop" is simply a three-piece wooden platform that slides along the beam to support the body of an instrument (photo 14).

- Now I have two of them (photo 15)!

Dan

FRETTING UNDER PRESSURE

In April, Bryan Galloup visited us here in Athens. Bryan runs Galloup Guitars, a combination repair shop and building/repair school in Big Rapids, Michigan (the Great Northwoods Seminar is held biannually at Bryan's shop). After touring Stew-Mac looking for new stuff, he visited my shop for a couple of days and played the guitar he'd just built. I finally put him to work and got some trade secrets in the bargain! One was a trick for modifying and using our #4483 fret arbor press...

When Bryan arrived I was just starting to refret a late-'60s Fender Telecaster. It had original frets, some fretboard irregularity, and a nice lacquer fretboard finish that must remain intact. I normally fret a bolt-on neck with either our Jaws tool or the fret arbor press (I seldom hammer frets into a bolt-on neck). Either way, I mount the neck on a surrogate body and use the neck jig, tilted into the playing position, to "read" the neck (see photo #9 on page 144) and determine what shape the fretboard is in. Then I adjust the truss rod to its optimum position. This Tele had some high and low spots, and a distinct rise at the last four frets.

If it's the first refret of a guitar made before 1982 (that's the year Fender quit installing frets sideways — see our *Fretwork Step By Step* book, or *Trade Secrets Volume One* for the story), I remove the neck from the jig to drive the frets out sideways (photo above). You could never tap frets out with a guitar in the neck jig. It requires too much force, and the jig's too sensitive.

Next, I install the frets with the arbor press, and then return to the neck jig for fret levelling. I expect to take out the dips, rises, and tilted-up end by levelling the fret tops instead of the fretboard.

Note: If the guitar was previously refretted, I pull the frets up and out with nippers in the normal way (not sideways), leave the guitar in the neck jig, and fret it with our #4380 Jaws portable fret press. Then I take out the dips, rises, and tilted-up fretboard end by levelling the fret tops instead of the fretboard, as mentioned above.

A quick pictorial run-down of an arbor press fret job is shown here — starting with a description of my arbor press setup, and how Bryan improved it...

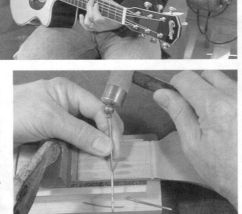

■ My arbor press has a thick slab of maple around the base, to match its height and extend the work area by 7-1/4" on each side of the press. A 1/4" wood "guide strip" runs the length of the slab to keep the sliding "neck table" on track. (*Bryan uses a rear fence instead of a raised center guide — simpler and quicker. I may switch to that setup*)

■ Bryan removed the upper hex-head lockscrew on the front of the press and installed a little "handwheel" to more easily lock the arbor shaft in place once the fret is pressed in (much like the quill lock on a drill press). This comes in handy when holding a fret that doesn't want to stay down while glue dries.

■ I installed our #4468 inspection mirror on the base of my press. It snakes around the arbor press...

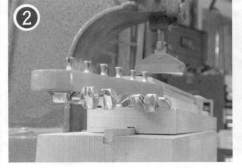

■ The neck table consists of our #4479 guitar neck support caul glued to a 23" x 3-1/2" x 1" maple board which is slotted on the bottom side to ride on the 1/4" guide strip.

■ At the heel end, four neck mounting screws are countersunk into the 1" thick table. They're sawed to length, leaving only 5/8" of exposed thread. The screws keep the neck from tilting as the frets are pressed in, and the sliding wedges adjust to support the heel at the same height as the cork-padded neck rest.

■ Clamp the arbor press table onto the work surface so that it doesn't move.

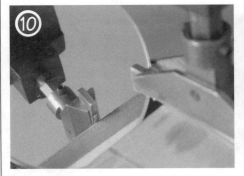

■ Bryan uses the shaft clamp to hold the fret down as he taps the fret from the side. This forces the barbs of the fret tang into new wood, as Leo Fender did by installing the frets sideways. This is a *guaranteed* method to keep a fret down in a difficult slot.

■ Unlike Bryan, I cut each fret's tang to exact length before installation using the Stew-Mac fret tang nipper. I let the fret crown overhang, but trim the tang just shorter than the end of the fret slot on each side. I do this to avoid filing onto wood or lacquer when cleaning up the fret ends. I can trim and bevel the overhang nicely and barely touch the wood or the finish

■ Unless a great amount of excess fret overhang is used, the fret press shoe hides the end of the fret from a hammer blow. For better control, I move the radius caul over a little in the "shoe," and use a nail-set to get a solid blow on the short overhang.

.■ ...and gives me a close-up view of the opposite side of the neck as I work. It's a great help!

■ After a maple neck's original frets are slid out sideways, refretting the clean slots is often easy. Sometimes the wood holds the frets tightly, sometimes not. With a sharp awl you can tap the fret out from the bass side to the treble, leaving a very clean slot.

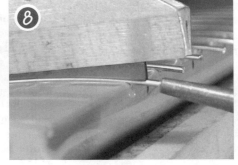

■ Clean and/or deepen the slot with a saw or knife. Here I'm using our #4851 fret slot cleaning tool.

FRETTING UNDER PRESSURE
Continued from pg. 147

⑬

■ Apply hide glue.

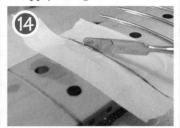

⑭

■ Work the glue into the slot and remove the excess with a rag dampened in hot water.

⑮

■ Press the fret in.

⑯

■ Lock the arbor press shaft when the fret isn't holding well.

⑰

■ Tap the fret sideways when necessary.

■ Let the hide glue dry overnight, clean up the fret overhang, then return the neck to the neck jig for fret levelling.

Al Rorick's Do-it-yourself Dobro!

Al Rorick runs Stew-Mac's production shop, and on most weekends he repairs guitars at Dan Erlewine's home shop. A former journeyman machinist, Al's a quick jig-maker and a good problem solver, and he's become an important member of the Stew-Mac R&D team.

Al loves traditional Delta blues and is a good slide guitar player. He builds a good slide guitar, too. Several years ago, Al made a number of small wood-bodied "Regional" guitars that were quite nice. "Regional was my combination of Regal and National," quips Al, "and I only sold them locally — another reason they were "Regional." Recently, having sold all my Regionals, I whipped up the little one shown here from a junked-out Harmony yard-sale "classical" guitar which had collapsed under steel strings. It was sort of a joke, but fun though — just a quick weekend project that produced a serious little guitar that plays and sounds great.

"The guitar's plywood top was caved in and loose from the sides. I flooded the loose seams with superglue from the inside and clamped it up. I knocked off the bridge with a hammer, then I cut the top circle with a Dremel tool on a radius swing arm pinned on center beneath where the bridge had been. Our #5152 1/16" spiral downcut bit made the cut in three passes. I measured the scale length (23") to locate the bridge saddle center, and did some quick calculations for the well depth."

■ The sound hole is plugged with a piece of the soundboard cut to exact size with a fly-cutter. The plug has a larger "flange" piece under it to create a good joint, and I superglued it in place.

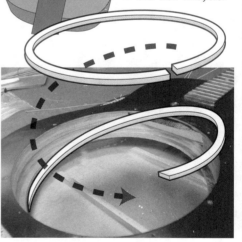

Left: *use a flycutter to create circular sound-hole "plug." Back this with a larger-diameter circle to create a flange.*

Below: *Split rings twist to thread into guitar body, building the "well" in layers.*

■ The "well" is laminated from three pieces of plywood: two layers 3/4" thick, and the bottom rim which is 1/4" Each piece has a cut in it so I could twist it through the hole like a spring. The top layer has a wider cut in it to clear the braces, which I left intact because the shoulder area was quite strong. I glued the pieces in, one at a time from the top down. It added strength to the lower bout.

■ I used a beat-up old National cone. I intend to replace it with our #1534 cone, although I may have to add 1/8" thickness to the rim to raise the cone, since they are slightly different in height. I could also make up the difference with the bridge.

■ The 1/8" masonite coverplate was cut out with the same swing arm/Dremel technique. In addition to the port holes in the plate, I drilled six small holes under the tailpiece to accommodate the string ball ends. This lets the tailpiece lay flat against the masonite for better downward pressure on the saddle. This guitar didn't have much of an optimum neck-set angle.

I finished the job with a couple of quick coats of Behlen black spray lacquer, and steel-wooled it to a flat sheen.

Adding a flute to our vintage-style bridge pins

I love our smooth unfluted vintage-style bridge pins, but there are times when I wish they were slightly fluted. These pins are slightly oversize; with a slight "kiss" of our bridge pin reamer they often fit nicely in the bridges of vintage instruments — guitars which have deep string slots where the pin is simply a safeguard to keep the string in place, and where new smaller pins are often too loose.

I usually don't cut the slots so deep in a new bridge, especially when the holes are close to the saddle. The slot should be appropriate for its string — perhaps 3/4 of the string winding rests in the slot and the string holds in place without the pin (but barely). I create appropriately-sized flutes in our vintage pins; a small flute on the treble E-string and flutes that graduate in size toward the bass E-string. Here's a bridge pin fluting tool that Al Rorick and I dreamed up. It's a block to hold the pin and a scraper to gouge out the flute:

- Drill a hole 5/16" from the edge of the flat side of a block of hard maple (a Stew-Mac radius block was perfect). Ream it with our #3229 bridge pin hole reamer, and saw a slot 9/32" deep on the block in line with the reamed hole. Glue a .020" strip of 5/16" binding material onto the block, 1" back from the front edge. Widen the front part of the slot with a Dremel bit to accept the width of the scraper.

- The scraper is a piece of 3/8" acrylic sheet, 8-5/8" x 1-3/4". I drilled a .116" hole (#32 bit) in the exact center, and tapped the hole with a machine screw having a thread outer diameter .013" larger than the hole (a machine screw will tap its own thread into acrylic if its O.D. is about .015" larger than the hole). Then I sharpened the tip of the machine screw into a rounded, flat-faced scraper (pictured). It works best for me when it extends 1/4" out from the acrylic sheet.

- The binding is a depth stop for the scraper plate and holds the plate at the same angle as the bridge pin taper. When you scrape, the blade rests on the bridge pin and the plate is free. The scraper follows the pin, cutting until the plate contacts the shim—at which point it cuts no deeper. You can deepen the cut by turning the screw 180°, reversing the plate end-for-end, and repeating the process.

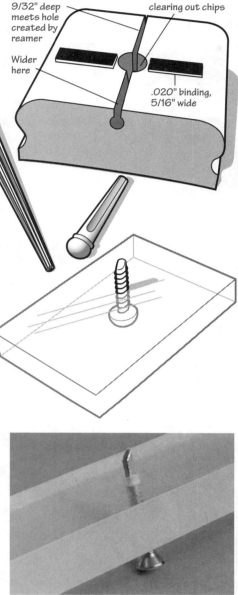

Bandsaw cut 9/32" deep meets hole created by reamer

Wider here

1/2" hole for clearing out chips

.020" binding, 5/16" wide

Extending through the acrylic by 1/4", the end of the machine screw has been filed into a beveled cutting edge (above). This scraper follows the slot in the block holding the bridge pin (below).

Brush-on Superglue

We now have a "brush-on" version of our #20 medium instant adhesive. It's formulated to dry slowly, flow out, and produce a smoother surface than faster-reacting versions. It comes in a special bottle; the applicator brush has polyethelene bristles that won't harden on contact with the glue. The bristles will harden, however, if used in our other instant adhesives.

Our brush-on glue has a higher ratio of stabilizer-to-activator. It doesn't react with air and moisture as quickly, so it cures more slowly. The bond is nearly as strong as our other instant adhesives.

I used our new brush-on glue to apply a quick finish to the bare heel of a Gibson SJ, which had ended up slightly long after a neck reset and major neck block surgery. The heel needed to be trimmed flush with the back. I got an instant finish like this…

- I colored the bare mahogany with a drop or two of our Color-Tone Medium Brown stain, mixed in acetone to dry quickly. I then brushed on a coat of the new adhesive. It goes on smoothly. You can flow out a heavy coat if you choose, or use several thin coats, sanded between coats.

- The bottle has an insert in the cap to remove excess glue and straighten the bristles as you pull the brush out.

- I sprayed accelerator on the first coat and sanded it immediately, then applied a second wet coat. The coat leveled well and dried quickly. The bristles, however, started to harden due to the accelerator, so I quickly washed them in acetone and combed them out with a razor blade.

- I rubbed out the finish within 15 minutes.

NOTE: We're often asked if instant adhesive can be stored in the refrigerator to extend its shelf-life. According to the manufacturer, refrigerating an unopened bottle will extend the glue life. However, if the bottle has been opened, don't refrigerate it—it will absorb more moisture, and harden more quickly than if you leave it at room temperature.

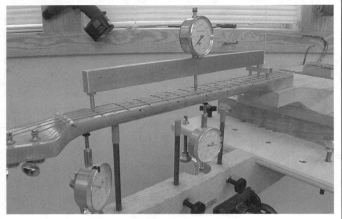

Using The Neck Relief Gauge

The neck relief gauge is a great measuring tool. It was inspired by a similar tool at Collings Guitars. We also saw it in use by several other Austin luthiers who'd worked for Bill Collings. The aluminum beam measures 14" x 1" x 1/2". We modified our tool by adding three holes on each end of the beam, 1-1/2" apart, to adapt the tool for guitars, mandolins, and "in-between" instruments. We also added an "outrigger" so the tool can stand without being hand-held. Though we made the gauge for checking neck relief, we discovered several other important uses for it…

■ First of all it's a great tool for checking and adjusting neck straightness and relief. It's a complimentary tool for the dial-indicator neckjig, giving proof-positive on both sides of the neck, as in the photo above, that the fretboard surface is where you want it.

■ The outrigger holds the jig steady, and the centering pin on each end mounts in any of the 3 holes (right).

■ When resetting a neck, how about doing it with the bridge and saddle at the bellied-up height of the top to eliminate guesswork? In the photo at right, a brace jack rests on a piece of wood spanning the braces and pushes the bridge area up to the dial-indicator measurement previously recorded when the strings were on (below).

■ We use the gauge to duplicate string tension for routing a saddle slot, so that the bottom of the saddle and the saddle slot match perfectly under string tension. It's especially useful when you're trying to get a flat-bottomed slot for a transducer pickup installation.

Practical Production Tip:
While you're at it, make enough of these bridge plate cauls to last awhile

Like many of us, Bryan Galloup is very fussy about how holes are drilled through a bridge plate—especially a brand-new bridge plate. A wood "backer-board" should be used on the inside to support the bridge plate as the drill bit plunges through, to eliminate tear-out. Hardwood backers are best, but the yellow pine shown here was hard enough. Here Bryan shows his setup for making a good supply of backer cauls, and a drill jig to hold them with the clamps well out of the way of the drill.

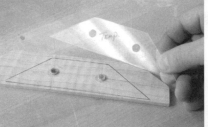

The acrylic template matches the area outlined on this maple clamping jig, which has two locating dowels glued into it. The dowels locate and hold temporary drilling backer boards.

Trace the patterns onto the wood, cut them to shape, drill the locating holes, and save them for future use.

The clamping caul holds the backer in position.

And the clamps are positioned well out on the bridge feet — clearing the drill body completely.

Practical Production Tip:

Hot-rodding your bridge clamps (?!) for speed and custom precision

Here's Bryan Galloup's adaptation of our Sloane bridge clamp and the Waverly bridge clamp caul. Actually the idea came from Dave Collins (photo, right), who works at Galloup Guitars. "Dave has been with me for three years," says Bryan, "first as a student, then as an apprentice, then as a repairman, then as a teacher, and now Dave is our senior luthier. He only builds guitars — about 45 or 50 of them each year."

"I was dry-clamping to check the fit of the Sloane bridge clamp, an interior caul, and the Waverly

bridge caul on some guitar," says Dave, "I don't remember what model, but it wasn't a Martin or anything like that. The braces were so tall that the Sloane clamp didn't have enough throat depth to allow the nylon cap to fit over the Waverly caul. So I backed out the clamp thread until the nylon pad popped off (center, above) — leav-

ing a ball end — and then it fit. The clamp wanted to walk around though, so I center-punched and drilled a countersink into the center of the Waverly caul with a 5/16"drill bit (above), just deep enough to form a dish for the ball. It worked so well that we started using it on a regular basis.

"Now we have six of the Waverly bridge clamps — all with countersinks (bottom photo) — and four Sloane clamps with nylon pads removed for that setup. Locating the caul and clamp on a bridge much is faster and more accurate now."

Dave Collins, Galloup Guitars

MIKE LINDSKOLD'S
GUITAR WIRING 101

Shielding: A *Real* Buzz Kill

With the big "retro" movement in guitars, amps and effects, more guitarists have had to deal with 60-cycle hum. That's the annoying buzz you hear when playing your favorite Strat,™ Tele™ or P-90 equipped Gibson, for example.

Lots of vintage instruments, and many new guitars, have single-coil pickups which are highly susceptible to 60-cycle hum. Gibson dealt with the problem in 1955 when Seth Lover patented the "humbucker." It "bucked the hum," as its name implies. However, a humbucking pickup just doesn't sound like a single-coil pickup, and many players want the tone and response of a true single-coil. It can have great brilliance, bite, clarity, grit, snap, twang, bottom, grind…the list of descriptions goes on and on.

One quick and easy method of eliminating much of that pesky noise is to apply shielding. You can shield your instrument with our #28 or #3798 copper foil tape, or with #29 conductive paint. My personal favorite for most of my shielding work is the conductive paint, but you may find that combining tape and paint is easier and more effective in many instruments.

In order to completely shield your guitar, you'll have to dismantle and desolder most of the guitar's components. It is highly recommended that you make detailed notes on how every component was originally wired. Mark specific wires and solder points with tape labels to help you rewire the instrument. Be very thorough—one mislabeled or unlabeled wire could cause a great deal of confusion when you rewire the system.

ALL of the shielding must be in contact with ground. There are several ways to apply a ground to a shielding network. When using copper shielding foil, the ground wire can be soldered directly to it. Another method is the use of a solder lug attached to the control cavity's sidewall (make the lug out of scrap brass attached with a small wood screw, or simply use a brass screw). Solder a wire from the volume pot casing to this lug for a good ground. If your volume pot housing is in contact with the foil, a ground jumper wire isn't necessary. Conductive paint is also very good for shielding control cavities, pickup routs, and drilled holes. The paint is easily applied to small, tight areas where foil isn't applicable.

It's easy to connect a ground from a shielded cavity to the pickguard foil in a Strat™ style guitar. Apply the control cavity paint or foil over the top of the body, in the area that would be under the pickguard and around the pickguard screw below the bottom tone pot. The foil on the pickguard should also surround this screw hole, so that when the pickguard is screwed into place, the grounded foil on the pickguard will come in contact with the cavity shielding.

MIKE LINDSKOLD Technical Advisor

Visit our Web site (http://www.stewmac.com) for previous issues of Guitar Wiring 101 by Technical Advisor Mike Lindskold.

Pots with a twist… or is it a click?

I'll continue my discussion of pots with a little powerhouse called a push/pull potentiometer. Our 250K ohm (#1215) and 500K ohm (#1216) push/pull pots (page 63) can be very versatile. Each combines a standard audio taper pot—sometimes referred to as a "log" or logarithmic taper pot—with a DPDT (double pole, double throw) on/on mini switch. The shaft of the pot controls both components, so you don't have to drill additional holes for a mini toggle switch.

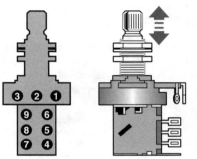

The pot and switch are electronically independent of each other, so hypothetically the pot could control the volume of one pickup, and the switch could do a coil-tap on another pickup. The variations on what you can do with a push/pull pot are limited only by the specific components you're trying to control with it, and by your imagination. Below are a new twist on wiring a tone control, and a volume and tone bypass switch arrangement. I hope you find them useful.

Wire a bass-cut instead of a treble-cut tone control: Using the electrical properties of a capacitor (it blocks lower frequencies, but allows higher frequencies to pass), we can vary the trebles and leave the bass—the opposite of a standard tone control. Use a 250K or 500K ohm pot and a 220 picofarad to a .0047 microfarad capacitor. Experiment with the values to find the best sound.

Lug 1 … "Input" of control (connect to output from volume pot or selector switch); also connect one leg of the cap to this lug
Lug 2 … Connect to Lug 1
Lug 3 … "Output" of control (connect to output jack); also connect to the other leg of the cap

Bypass the control pots: This simple switch-wiring arrangement allows you to bypass the control pots, as well as all of the resistance they add to the system, which tends to make the tone more brilliant.

Lug 6 … "Send" to volume and tone controls
Lug 5 … "Input"—connect to the output from the pickup (single pickup guitar) or selector switch (multi-pickup guitar)
Lug 4 … Jumper to Lug 7
Lug 9 … "Return" from control pots
Lug 8 … "Output"—connect to the hot lug on the output jack
Lug 7 … Jumper to Lug 4

MIKE LINDSKOLD Technical Advisor

Visit our Web site (http://www.stewmac.com) for previous issues of Guitar Wiring 101 by Technical Advisor Mike Lindskold.

Easy modifications for cool tone mutations

Guitarists are constantly changing—that's one of the beauties of the guitar industry. We're always changing gear, parts, pickups, electronics, and our minds. The killer sound of a year ago often isn't what we want or need now. "Here today, gone later today!"

Many players make changes to their sound and/or set-up without making radical changes to their pride and joy, that one special guitar that talks to them better than anything else on the planet. Sometimes they want a different voice, a wail, scream, thrash, or a tone that's warm, brown, etc. It's a lot to ask of a guitar.

Here begins the first installment to address this issue, covering many instruments and situations. Most of the simple modifications can make a big difference. Many require no external alterations to the instrument, yet give the player much more versatility.

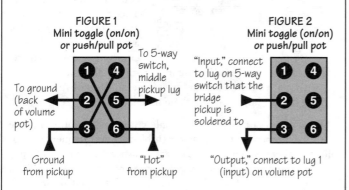

FIGURE 1
Mini toggle (on/on)
or push/pull pot

To 5-way switch, middle pickup lug

To ground (back of volume pot)

Ground from pickup

"Hot" from pickup

FIGURE 2
Mini toggle (on/on)
or push/pull pot

"Input," connect to lug on 5-way switch that the bridge pickup is soldered to

"Output," connect to lug 1 (input) on volume pot

Many Strat Cats out there are looking for some new tones without big changes. First, try a phase switch on the middle pickup (Figure 1). This lets the player throw the middle pickup in or out of phase with the neck or bridge pickups, in switch positions 2 and 4.

Another Strat mutation, which I find cool for country and blues, is to have all three pickups on, or the bridge and neck pickups, per a Tele's middle switch position. This can be accomplished with a push/pull pot or a mini toggle switch. Figure 2 is the diagram for this alteration. It lets you add the bridge pickup to any of the positions on the Strat's 5-way switch. Thus, in position 5 (neck pickup only), when you flip the mini toggle you'll have the bridge and neck pickups (Tele middle position). Click over to position 4 (neck and middle pickups) with the toggle engaged, and all three pickups will be on. Simple, eh?

Next time we'll look at some more Strat alterations, as well as a few for Teles and other 2-pickup guitars. Until then, keep messing around and trying, 'cause change is good…

MIKE LINDSKOLD Technical Advisor

Visit our Web site (http://www.stewmac.com) for previous issues of Guitar Wiring 101 by Technical Advisor Mike Lindskold.

New tricks for the New Year…

I'll continue with some simple but useful modifications for two- and/or three-pickup guitars. The first mod works well for a Strat™ or a custom 3-pickup Telecaster.™ It lets you go from wherever your pickup selector is set, to a preset single pickup or combination.

You can use an on/on mini toggle or a push-pull pot. This type of switch is usually set up to get the bridge pickup alone, but you can make it any one or two pickups you wish. This can be a good way to combine the bridge and neck pickups on a Strat, 3-pickup Tele or Les Paul Custom. See Figure 1 below:

FIGURE 1: Mini toggle (on/on) or push-pull pot

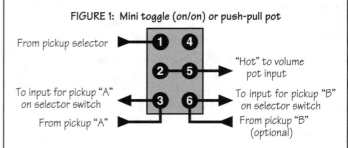

From pickup selector

"Hot" to volume pot input

To input for pickup "A" on selector switch

To input for pickup "B" on selector switch

From pickup "A"

From pickup "B" (optional)

The second trick is for Tele™ players. It changes the #2 position of your 3-way switch, so that the bridge and neck pickups are in series instead of parallel. This is not a hum-cancelling combination, but it gives the increased power of a series link. For this alteration to work correctly, isolate the metal cover of the neck pickup (if present) from its ground lead. Run a separate ground wire for the cover to the back of the volume control. Figure 2 shows our #114 and #3191 Tele-style switches. You may have to "mirror-image" the #3191 drawing if you use a Switchcraft or similar 3-way switch, to put the "common" lugs (#0, always in contact with the sweeper) in the proper locations.

FIGURE 2: 3-way Tele™-style switches #114 & #3191

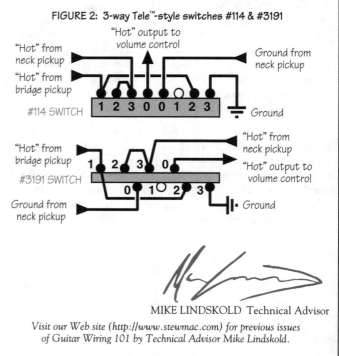

"Hot" output to volume control

"Hot" from neck pickup

"Hot" from bridge pickup

Ground from neck pickup

#114 SWITCH   1 2 3 0 0 1 2 3   Ground

"Hot" from bridge pickup

"Hot" from neck pickup

"Hot" output to volume control

#3191 SWITCH   1 2 3 0

0 1 2 3

Ground from neck pickup

Ground

MIKE LINDSKOLD Technical Advisor

Visit our Web site (http://www.stewmac.com) for previous issues of Guitar Wiring 101 by Technical Advisor Mike Lindskold.

New tricks with push-pull pots

Here are two push-pull control pot set-ups for those players and builders who wish to minimize the number of controls on the guitar. Figure 1 represents a volume/tone control. In the "down" switch position the pot is a volume control; in the "up" position it's a tone control.

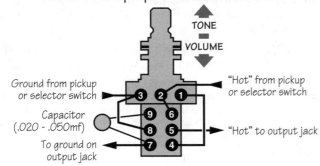

FIGURE 1: Push-pull pot as volume/tone control

The second modification (Figure 2) bypasses the volume control completely, giving you the pickup's full output. There is an optional resistor (use the same value as the volume pot) in this circuit. It emulates the resistance between hot and ground that is always present in a volume control. If you don't add this resistor, the guitar's tone will change when the volume pot is defeated—it will become brighter.

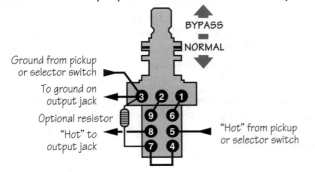

FIGURE 2: Push-pull pot as volume control / volume bypass

(Note: In either of these set-ups, instead of using a push-pull pot you could wire a regular potentiometer to an on/on toggle switch.)

More to come in the next installment!

MIKE LINDSKOLD Technical Advisor

Visit our Web site (http://www.stewmac.com) for previous issues of Guitar Wiring 101 by Technical Advisor Mike Lindskold.

Piezo Transducer Pickups For Acoustic Guitars

Modern stage performers require both electric and acoustic guitars that sound good, without feedback at high volume. The piezo pickup ("transducer") has become the most common method of amplifying acoustic guitars. ("Piezo" is from the Greek *piezein*, to squeeze or press; pronounce it with an Italian or Greek movie accent.)

A piezoelectric crystal generates an electric current (signal) when stresses are induced. The signal is sent to a preamp/buffer, and then to a guitar amp or PA. The use of a preamp, such as those from Fishman, Baggs and others, is highly recommended due to the piezo transducer's ultra-high impedance, and the capacitance effect as the signal travels down a guitar cable. For the best possible sound, the preamp "buffers" the signal down to high impedance, for which most amps and PAs are designed. The lowered signal impedance from the preamp is less susceptible to the cable's capacitance. The increased gain also reduces signal degradation caused by the cable.

A **soundboard-mounted transducer** "senses" vibrations at a specific location on the instrument; thus, positioning is critical to ensure a good sound. It should first be attached at various spots *outside* the guitar and near the bridge, to find the "hot spot." It can then be attached *inside* at the same location, depending on the guitar's bracing pattern.

Undersaddle transducers can have six independent piezo crystals, or they can be full sensors with one continuous piezo film. The two types vary in response and tone. Six-element transducers require much more care during installation. The fit of the transducers to the bottom of the saddle and the bottom of the saddle slot, while important with either design, is more critical with a six-element model. There must be no inconsistencies in pressure due to a warped slot or misshaped saddle.

I generally find full sensors more appealing; they have fewer dead spots, a more uniform tone, and a smoother response. This is not to say that six-element pickups sound bad; certain players prefer the sound of certain pickups. Just as General Motors offers Chevrolets, Buicks, and GMCs, Fishman, Baggs and other manufacturers offer full sensors, six-element models and soundboard transducers. Different strokes for different folks!

Next time I'll discuss other types of acoustic pickups, and hybrid (combination) systems.

MIKE LINDSKOLD Technical Advisor

Visit our Web site (http://www.stewmac.com) for previous issues of Guitar Wiring 101 by Technical Advisor Mike Lindskold.

Acoustic Pickups: Magnetics, Mics And Beyond...

Last time, I discussed the basics of piezoelectricity and transducers. Now, let's talk about some other methods of getting the sound you want from your acoustic guitar. As always, when dealing with different types of pickups, be aware of their impedance. This is important to get the best sound from a given pickup or custom pickup system.

Magnetic pickups and microphones are the other two primary methods of amplifying acoustic instruments. Soundhole or magnetic pickups have been around for many years and are still used by some of the world's top players. They sense the vibrations of metal strings, the same way an electric guitar pickup does, and can't be used with nylon strings. Soundhole pickups are also high impedance; unlike transducers and many microphones, they don't need to be buffered. The ease of installation and simple design of magnetic pickups make them ideal for players who just need to get louder, but don't need the ultimate acoustic amplified tone.

Microphones listen to the sounds that are coming off the soundboard and reflected within the instrument. They sense the natural ambiance of an acoustic instrument much better than a transducer or soundhole pickup, although they sometimes lack clarity and sharp response. There are two standard types of mics, *dynamic* and *condenser*. Condenser mics are generally preferred in acoustic instruments because of their flat response—they don't "color" the sound—and their size, output and impedance. Dynamic mics are often used to mic an instrument from the outside, but usually not internally.

The best sounds from an acoustic guitar are usually achieved with "hybrid" systems. These combine the outputs of two, or sometimes three, of the various types of pickups. There are many types of hybrid systems on the market. The Bourgeois and the Baggs Dual Source are two examples of hybrid systems offered in our catalog. Each includes a special preamp that will properly match/buffer the signals from the two sources, combine them, and then send them to the amp.

When searching for the right acoustic amplification set-up, try as many instruments and systems as possible, and always pay attention to what your favorite performers use.

In future features, I'll discuss how you can combine products to make your own hybrid systems, how to add passive controls to piezo pickup systems, and more. So until next time...keep on pluckin', plinkin' and noodlin' around!

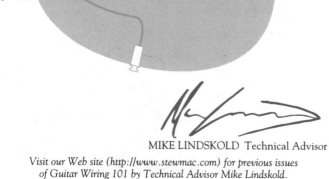

MIKE LINDSKOLD Technical Advisor

Visit our Web site (http://www.stewmac.com) for previous issues of Guitar Wiring 101 by Technical Advisor Mike Lindskold.

Combining Pickup Systems To Enlarge Your Musical Palette

Okay, so you want to use a magnetic soundhole pickup and add a transducer under the bridge saddle. Or maybe you want to install Mike Christian's saddle transducer pickups, or Fishman's Powerbridge—how do you do it?

As discussed here previously, impedance matching is the most critical aspect when combining pickup systems. In the situations outlined above, you must contend with the high impedance magnetic pickup, and the *ultra* high impedance of the saddle's piezoelectric transducer.

Here's a solution: try the Mike Christian "implant" onboard stereo preamp. It has one channel for high impedance, and the other is tailored for ultra high impedance. It's small (1" x 1" x 5/8"), and can be wired in many different ways. The diagram below shows how these signals can be directed, and where you can insert controls and other options:

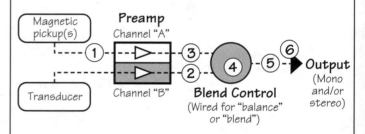

The diagram can be altered in several ways. You can insert *passive* volume and tone controls between the output of the magnetic pickup and the preamp (location #1 in the diagram). We don't recommend wiring a transducer through a volume and/or tone control *until* it has been buffered by the preamp (location #2). The magnetic pickup's output can also be manipulated *after* the preamp (location #3). Finally, both signals can be manipulated at location #5, *after* they have been combined.

Another consideration is how to blend the signals. A blend control (a "ganged-pot" consisting of two piggybacked potentiometers controlled by a single knob shaft) can be wired as a *balance* control, like the fader controls on your home stereo, or as a *blend* control. A balance control set-up uses a stereo output jack (location #6) and two independent amplifiers. The control determines how much of the signal goes to a specific amp from a specific pickup source. A blend control combines the two signals into a mono output. (Note: A 3-position on/on/on DPDT switch could be substituted for the blend pot.)

MIKE LINDSKOLD Technical Advisor

Visit our Web site (http://www.stewmac.com) for previous issues of Guitar Wiring 101 by Technical Advisor Mike Lindskold.

More Fun With Transducers...

Here are a couple of interesting set-ups that I've tried recently. They were for two musicians who knew exactly what they wanted, and how they wanted to control it—an ideal situation for me!

Instrument #1: This is a hybrid instrument that needs traditional *and* modern tones. It's basically a Tele (well, kinda sorta like a Tele). Imagine a bound, curly maple-faced Telecaster with a National-style resonator and biscuit bridge. It has a traditional National coverplate, and to finish things off, there's a Gibson P-90 single-coil pickup installed at the neck position.

This machine was made for one thing: blues slide playing. The resonator cone gives the guitar a great growl. The player wanted two sources for the amplified sound, a McIntyre pickup on the cone (our #4288), and the Gibson P-90 (our #3370). The controls are minimal—that's the way he wanted it. Here's the diagram:

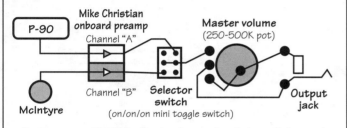

Instrument #2: This 4-string bass guitar is one of the coolest things I've seen in a while. It's essentially a solidbody Jazz Bass, with a pseudo archtop acoustic-style bridge strung through the tail end of the bass (like the custom Carl Thompson bass used by Les Claypool of Primus).

The design called for a transducer in the bridge (a rosewood base with bone saddle and a Fishman Matrix pickup), and a hybrid P-Bass/Jazz Bass set of magnetic pickups. The client wanted a Gibson-style pickup selector, a master volume control for the magnetic pickups, a master volume for the saddle pickup, a master tone control, and both mixed into a mono output. Here it is:

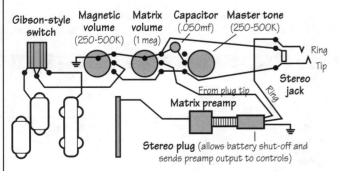

Since the Matrix has an onboard preamp designed for installation in an acoustic guitar tailblock, I had to use a stereo plug in the Matrix output. This allowed me to use a stereo output jack to turn the battery for the Matrix on and off.

Visit our Web site (http://www.stewmac.com) for previous issues of Guitar Wiring 101 by Technical Advisor Mike Lindskold.

A Switch Like No Other...

Yamaha's new 5-position lever switch replaces any standard 3-way or 5-way lever switch. It's now used by several guitar manufacturers because of its unparalleled flexibility and control. This 4-pole switch has 24 terminal lugs. Unlike traditional 3-way Tele or 5-way Strat switches, which are 2-pole switches with three positions

Yamaha 4-pole 5-way switch

(the 5-way Strat switch is the same electrically as a 3-way, with two more stops that are combinations of positions), Yamaha's "professional" switch offers complete control of all five positions, with four distinct poles or circuits.

How is this different from the Megaswitch? The original "E" model Megaswitch, and the "P" (Paul Reed Smith style) model give specific combinations with a set of pickups. The #3484 original Megaswitch can be used with a variety of pickup configurations (three singles, two humbuckers, humbucker and two singles, etc.), but only gives certain combinations depending on the pickups used. See its chart on page 62. The "P" model only works with two humbuckers, giving the same positions found on a Paul Reed Smith 5-position rotary switch. If either Megaswitch will accomplish your desired set-up, then we recommend using it. A Megaswitch is easier to wire than the Yamaha switch, and you won't have to use several connections and jumpers to get the same set-up.

So what can the Yamaha switch do for you? The limitation is not the switch, but your imagination! First, there doesn't have to be any specific order to when the pickups are active—many users like to jumble the order of the pickups on the switch. Since each pole has six lugs (one common, and one each for the five lever positions), you get a level of control not available in any other lever switch.

The chart and diagram below suggest how flexible and powerful this switch is. Lug "0" (the common lug of each pole), is connected to the lug representing the lever's position.

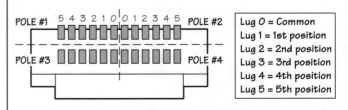

Lug 0 = Common	Lug 3 = 3rd position
Lug 1 = 1st position	Lug 4 = 4th position
Lug 2 = 2nd position	Lug 5 = 5th position

Why would you use this switch? I don't recommend it unless you're familiar with guitar electronics. It can cause unnecessary confusion to a budding repairman or builder. However, if you have requests from your clientele for out-of-the-ordinary or "impossible" wiring set-ups, you should familiarize yourself with this switch and its capabilities. We supply the Yamaha switch with sample diagrams for some cool wiring set-ups, but they're only a part of the switch's potential.

Visit our Web site (http://www.stewmac.com) for previous issues of Guitar Wiring 101 by Technical Advisor Mike Lindskold.

Mike Lindskold's GUITAR WIRING 101

Soldering Etiquette (Pass The Spaghetti Sauce!)

This photo illustrates the *wrong* way to wire a guitar!

Before you start soldering, you need to get a "feel" for it. It's 85% technique; 15% materials and equipment. You don't have to spend a bunch of money on soldering equipment for a successful job. High-

Thanks to Les Schatten for forwarding this amazing wiring disaster that came into his shop in Kitchener, Ontario, Canada.

priced soldering pencils are designed for professionals who use them daily. An inexpensive 40-watt soldering pencil will do just fine. The more experienced you are with your soldering pencil, the better your wiring project will turn out. Here are a few do's and don'ts:

■ Don't blow on a solder joint to make it harden faster. This can cause air pockets within the joint that can corrode or loosen it over time—a "cold solder joint."

■ Always use rosin-core solder! Standard 60/40 rosin-core is best, and we prefer smaller .032"-.062" diameters for guitar wiring.

■ Don't strip too much insulation from a wire, unless you want a potential troubleshooting nightmare. Just expose enough wire for soldering, usually 1/16" to 1/8". Too much exposed wire can contact ground wires, shielded pickup wires, or "hot" wires.

■ "Tin" the wire and the soldering points before soldering the joint. This doesn't mean applying a huge glob of solder; just a very thin pre-coating will do.

■ Always apply heat to the connection first, then apply the solder and let it flow over the joint. This also helps prevent cold solder joints.

■ When "breaking in" a new soldering iron or tip, tin the tip as soon as it gets hot enough to melt the solder for the first time. Flow the solder over the contact surfaces of the tip, and let it set for about ten seconds or so. Wipe the excess onto a damp sponge and apply more solder. Repeat this process several times during the first few minutes of its life, and your soldering tip will last longer and conduct heat better.

■ Use a soldering stand to hold your soldering iron, so you won't burn yourself or your guitar. A soldering stand usually has a sponge holder for cleaning the tip.

■ Plan the wiring ahead of time, to avoid soldering under an existing wire. Be sure the wires are long enough to allow removal of the pickguard or control plate for inspection without desoldering.

If you have more questions, read Donald Brosnac's *Guitar Electronics For Musicians*. It's a great source for learning the basics, with information about pickups, how volume and tone circuits work, and more advanced topics.

Visit our Web site (http://www.stewmac.com) for previous issues of Guitar Wiring 101 by Technical Advisor Mike Lindskold.

Lever Switch Voodoo

A wiring diagram for one version of a lever switch may not be correct for other versions. Below are diagrams of four common 3-way and 5-way lever-type pickup selector switches. This is my "cheat sheet" for transposing lug assignments. The "0" refers to the *common* or "sweeper" of a pole. The other three lugs for that pole are labeled "1" (the lever toward the bridge); "2" (the middle position) and "3" (toward the neck). Remember that a typical 5-way lever switch is the same as a 3-way. Two extra "stops" have been added to combine 1+2, and 2+3. *In each diagram, the guitar's neck is to the left.*

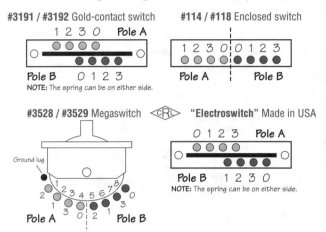

I'd also like to share two cool new wiring set-ups for Tele®:
Lever positions: **1**-bridge; **2**-bridge and neck in series; **3**-neck

LUG	POLE A	POLE B
0	Bridge Hot	Neck Ground
1	Neck Hot, and output to volume pot	Not used
2	Jumper to pole B, lug 2	Jumper to pole A, lug 2
3	Not used	Ground

For this set-up, and for the set-up below, the neck pickup's shielded cover must be isolated from the ground wire; run a separate wire for the cover to ground. Wire the bridge pickup's ground wire directly to ground as well.

Here's a 3-way mod with push/pull or mini-toggle switch. Lever positions: **1**-bridge; **2**-bridge and neck (with switchable series or parallel); **3**-neck

LUG	POLE A	POLE B
0	Bridge Hot	Neck Ground
1	Neck Hot, and output to volume pot	Not used
2	Send to mini-toggle or push/pull pot switch lug 2	Send to mini-toggle or push/pull pot switch lug 5
3	Not used	Ground

Wire the mini-toggle or push/pull switch as follows:

```
Pole B, lug 2 ┌─────────────┐ Pole B, lug 3
              ④    ⑤    ⑥
              ①    ②    ③
Pole A, lug 2 └─────────────┘ Pole A, lug 1
```

Visit our Web site (http://www.stewmac.com) for previous issues of Guitar Wiring 101 by Technical Advisor Mike Lindskold.

Put A Lid On It: Covers And Capacitance

Guitar pickup covers are an example of a small aspect that can make an appreciable difference. The metal covers on Gibson, Fender, DeArmond, Gretsch and other pickups have more than a visual effect. Metal covers, including Telecaster® bridge covers, are used as shielding against RF (radio frequency) interference, making the guitar quieter. A byproduct of having grounded conductive metal or shielding paint near a pickup's coil is a high-end attenuation (cut) caused by a capacitance effect. This is the same effect that will make your guitar set-up sound warmer—or duller, depending on your perception—when you use a longer cable between the guitar and the amp. A five-foot cable will give a slightly brighter sound than a twenty footer.

Pickup covers are typically made from nonferrous (iron-free) metals such as brass or nickel-silver, and are usually plated with nickel, chrome, gold, or black chrome finish. If a cover were to contain iron, it would alter the pickup's magnetic field, thus changing the pickup's tone and response significantly. A prime example is the copper-plated steel plate used under original '50s Tele® bridge pickups to focus the magnetic field up toward the strings. This helped give those old pickups their bite and presence.

Just for fun, take a piece of steel, about 1/2" x 2-1/2" x .060", and put it underneath your favorite single-coil pickup, as shown in the photo at left. The magnets will hold it in place. The pickup will have a new sizzle that may give you the "edge" you're looking for. This can also be useful for getting more of a Tele® sound from a Strat® bridge pickup. If you like it, you'll have to glue the steel in place with silicone or a glue that will isolate vibration. If you don't, she'll squeal like a pig!

Humbuckers without covers may look cool to some players, but they're defenseless against aggressive picks and playing styles that can penetrate the protective tape around the coils. A coil can be broken, leading to some serious repair work. The cover also warms the tone of the humbucker, which may or may not be to your liking. Much of the '60s and '70s craze to remove humbucker covers can be traced back to Jeff Beck, who was trying to get a slightly brighter tone from his Les Paul.

The moral of the story? Guitars are machines in which every component has a role in the overall tone and response. The right combination of stuff will sing! Remember too, that the amplifier is just as important. Use equipment that's suitable for the sound you want. Use the set-ups of your favorite players as guidelines for your own sonic impact. And don't forget about the little stuff, because even a simple pickup cover can affect your tone.

Visit our Web site (http://www.stewmac.com) for previous issues of Guitar Wiring 101 by Technical Advisor Mike Lindskold.

A Primer On Pickup Potting

A microphonic pickup can plague the player, builder and repairman. It produces an uncontrollable, unmusical high-pitched squeal that makes the instrument impossible to play at stage volume. The culprit is a loose component in the pickup. Either the coil windings were improperly potted (waxed), or age and abuse have loosened the windings or some other part of the pickup. For example, a common problem with Telecaster® bridge pickups arises when the metal base loosens and vibrates under the polepieces.

Before we jump into pickup potting, you should know that feedback may not be caused by the pickup, but by some other part of the guitar—and in some cases, the problem isn't in the guitar! If there's a loose ferrous metal component in close proximity to the pickup (a pickup height screw or spring, for example) it could resonate with string vibration when the sound pressure from the amp speakers reaches a high level. The pickup can "sense" this vibration and add to the feedback cycle. Microphonic feedback can also originate from a loose amplifier component, in the chassis or in one or more amp tubes. Therefore, it's a good idea to test with a different amplifier whenever possible, to help you determine if the problem's in the pickup.

The critical aspects of pickup potting are the temperature and the type of waxes used. You must have a heated pot that you can dip the pickup into. The pot must maintain a constant 140-150 degree Fahrenheit heat range (60-65 degrees Celsius). Our #668 electric glue pot is great for potting pickups. Other devices can be used, but *always* use a long probe-type cooking thermometer to monitor the heat. The wax should be a mixture of 80% paraffin and 20% beeswax. The beeswax helps lessen the expansion and contraction of the paraffin with temperature changes.

Hot paraffin, and paraffin vapors, can ignite! Wear safety glasses, and don't heat the wax on a stove or in a microwave oven!

It's possible to damage a pickup by potting it, so start with a junky pickup from your spare parts bin. The pickup should be suspended in the wax, without touching the sides or bottom of the pot. You can place a few marbles in the pot and let the pickup sit on them. Use the pickup's lead wires to suspend and remove the pickup from the wax, being careful not to put a strain on the connections. Immerse the pickup for ten to twenty minutes, or until the voids and air pockets in the pickup stop bubbling. The hot wax melts the original wax, allows air to escape, and replaces it with more wax. When done, gently remove the pickup and let it drip dry over the pot. It should be cool enough to handle in about ten minutes.

In the next Wiring 101, I'll cover a few other uses of potting. By the way, ace pickup winder and repairman Lindy Fralin contributed a detailed Trade Secrets section on pickup potting in our Spring 1996 catalog. Look for this article on page 43.

Visit our Web site (http://www.stewmac.com) for previous issues of Guitar Wiring 101 by Technical Advisor Mike Lindskold.

Installing Humbucking Pickup Covers

We'll conclude our discussion of pickup covers by noting a few things to consider when installing a cover on a humbucker.

First, the pickup will probably need to be wax-potted after you solder the new cover in place (for details on pickup potting see Wiring 101 in our previous catalog, or online at *www.stewmac.com*).

Your next concern is polepiece spacing, which can vary according to the pickup's age and manufacturer. Many modern pickups have different spacings for the bridge and neck positions. Gibson E-string polepieces were originally 1-15/16" apart, measured center-to-center. In the late 1980s, Gibson adopted a wider spacing of 2-1/16" for their bridge pickups (except the '57 Classic, which  retained the vintage specifications). This placed the polepieces directly under the strings for improved balance, output and response. Other manufacturers now offer extra-wide polepiece spacing for use with traditional Fender tremolo bridges and for Floyd Rose® units. The Schaller pickup covers offered in our catalog have 1-15/16" spacing for the neck position, as per vintage Gibson, but only a slightly wider 2" spacing for the bridge position, which works for pickups such as DiMarzio's "F-spacing" models. The bottom line: measure your polepiece spacings before you order your covers.

Now on to the installation process. Typically, the cover will slide right over the pickup's coils and baseplate. It should extend slightly below the baseplate and, as noted above, the polepieces must line up with the holes in the cover. If the cover won't slide on easily, you must carefully determine what's causing the hang-up. Don't force it—you could easily damage the pickup windings. You may need to carefully relocate or remove excess tape on the coils, but don't expose the coil windings completely. Be sure the tape doesn't cover the baseplate.

When everything fits well, it's time to solder the cover in place. I use a 45-watt soldering pencil with a medium chisel tip and rosin-core solder. I *don't* recommend using a soldering gun, which can alter a pickup's magnetic charge. Be sure the area is hot, and flow a bead of solder onto the cover and the baseplate, as pictured at right. Let the pickup cool, and it's ready for potting.

Visit our Web site (http://www.stewmac.com) for previous issues of Guitar Wiring 101 by Technical Advisor Mike Lindskold.

Trade Secrets